Front Cover:
1 – Victor Candlin
Dec. 14, 1898 – Oct. 17, 1918 (Courtesy of Dr. Elaine Joslyn)
2 – French medals: le fourragere and
Croix de Guerre with two oak bars – (Public domain)

ISBN – 978-0-9857603-1-1

Printed by Walsworth Publishing Company, Inc. Marceline MO.
Dennis Paalhar, Sales Representative

Dedicated to My Son,

John Ed Stovall, whose death at age 17,
taught me how deep is grief and how
long lasting it can be.

Sincerely,

Nancy Cramer

"The Lights are going out all over Europe; we shall not see them again in our lifetime." 3 August, 1914, said by Sir Edward Grey, British Foreign Secretary. The next day England declared war on Germany.

Certificate of Liberty
(Courtesy of Gail Long)

This certificate was awarded to Bryan Tedder with the words:
"… served with honor in the war and was wounded in action…"
(Courtesy of Gail Long, grand-daughter of Bryan Tedder)

CONTENTS

ROSTER OF VETERANS AND THEIR UNITS

3 rd Division . . . . John Lewis Barkley

26th Division . . . . .Charles McDaniel

35th Division Capt. Harry Truman – 129th Field

Artillery . . . . . . Rolla Runner – 129th Infantry
. . . . Roy Cardinell – 139th Infantry
. . . . Bryan Tedder – 137th Infantry
. . . . Clyde Miller – 140th Infantry
. . . . Corp. Oda Fuller – 140th Infantry

42nd Division . . . . Loren Goddard

**139th Company Ambulance
Corps** . . . . .Jesse Albert Dennis

78th Division . . . . . .Captain Wellstood White

82nd Division . . . . Dawson Clark

88th Division . . . . George Applegate
. . . . Walter E. Longhenry

89th Division . . . . .Charles McDaniel

90th Division . .Gordon Jester (315th Engineers)

1st Artillery Park, CAP . Howard Adolph Cook

61st Artillery, CAC . . . . Clyde Kirk

SOS . . . . . . Michael Charles Brunntraeger

Sanitary Corps . . . . . . Herman B. Engel

54th Pioneer Inf . . . . Cpl. Russell J. Wise

369th Regiment . . . . .Henry Johnson
. . . . Lt. Jim Europe

371st Infantry . . . . Freddie Stowers

French Air Corps . . Corp. Robert Gaston Charles

American Air Corps . . . . . .Lt. Ronald Knapp
. . . . Lt. Frederick Simonin
. . . . Frank Spurrier
Sgt. Harold Mensch

American Regulating Station B Sgt. Sylvan Gray

Veterinary Corps . . . . . . John Martin Miller

Base Hospital #5 . . . . Lt. William T. Fitzsimons

Base Hospital #120 . . . . .Nurse Bessie Hilton

Unknown Units . . . . . . .Hallie Oliver Young
. . . . Sam Benjamin
. . . . George Harrouf
. . . . George R. Oertel (German soldier)
. . . . Boban Zarkovich's Great-Grandfather
. . . . John Cardinell

U.S. Marine Corps Victor Candlin 6th Regiment

U. S. Navy . . . . Seaman Floyd Carlisle

Civilians . . . . .Evan Allen Hardy
. . . . Heinrich Uthof
. . . . Charles M. Tipton, Sr.
. . . . .Clara Candlin
. . . . .Marie Gaston
. . . . Sophie Shelley
. . . . Margaret Richardson

INTRODUCTION
to
"UNHEARD VOICES, UNTOLD STORIES"

Why did I choose to use interviews in addition to using documents? I knew no veterans still lived. I knew also that soldiers usually did not share the horrors and devastation they had experienced, as when a buddy next to them was literally blown to pieces; or when a soldier went berserk; or retreated into the lonely world of his own mind; or shrapnel tore off the soldier's arm. A wounded soldier could bleed to death until the overworked medic came to his rescue.

Therefore, I decided to interview families who had forebears in the war and had memories of what they had heard. Incomplete as those memories might be, they were important to the story. Much of the unpleasant information I would find in documents. But more revealing are the mementos of the deceased veterans that have been preserved by their families. The postcards, letters and mementos often revealed more about the veteran than the survivors may have realized.

If the families knew unpleasant details, they often chose to ignore them, and pretend that life would go on as usual. They had their husband, or father, or brother returned to them. He was one of the 4,300,000 Americans who were mobilized, one of the nearly two million who served in a combat zone. Only one or two persons out of those millions mattered to them, and that person or persons came home.

The few pages of each story, hopefully, are enough to reveal the soldier as the individual he was. Many stories tell about only personal matters and perhaps seem insignificant. A few stories relate moments of greatness.

Then there is memory. How accurate are these stories? Are they family legends or recollections? I don't know. I checked as many facts as I could. Indeed, I found information the family did not know and shared it with them to their grateful surprise.

Most of the keepers of these stories are in their 80's and 90's. The tales do not appeal to many of the second generation, whose interest might at best be marginal. Perhaps it is because that generation fought in subsequent wars: World War II, Korea, and Vietnam. They, therefore, have no information about World War I to pass on to third and fourth generations, the ones who may be curious about a relative who served his country in that long ago unfamiliar Great War. Sometimes it is the grandchildren or great nieces or great nephews who want to learn the stories. Now is the time to preserve what stories we can.

Here are some stories preserved for that generation and future generations to come.

YOU'RE IN THE ARMY NOW

How does a civilian, in a matter of a few days, become a soldier? This question was on the minds of more than four million young Americans as they signed their names to enlistment papers, and took the oath of allegiance to the Constitution of the United States. Shortly afterwards, they exchanged their civilian clothes for khaki uniforms.

These stories reveal some of the soldiers' reasons as to why they responded when Congress declared war on Germany on April 6, 1917. For some men their answer to becoming a soldier was simple. Their country had called them, and it was their duty to defend it. For other recruits, the answer was more complex. All World War I participants are now deceased and cannot personally tell us their answers. The last World War I survivor, Missouri's Frank Buckley, died in 2011. Therefore, we will never know many of the reasons why men volunteered to fight in a war that was thousands of miles away from their homeland.

These stories are my attempts to write the veteran's story as told to me by their relatives. My selection of veterans is random. I made no attempt to be scientifically selective or comprehensive. The sample includes neighbors, friends, or visitors I met in the National World War I Museum where I volunteer. Or sometimes at a social or business meeting, a person might mention, "My grandfather was…" and there I am, pad in hand, ready to ask for an interview. When these people I interview are gone, the veteran's stories likely will be gone also.

Stories of veterans from other geographical areas of the United States will necessarily differ in details. But common threads can be found in all soldiers' stories. These threads include patriotism, loyalty to family, courage, fear, pain, closeness to soldier buddies, and perhaps most important, keeping one's self-respect intact, despite witnessing the most unimaginable scenes. Many men would experience suffering and terror of such depth, that for some, their lives were never the same afterwards. This was true, regardless of whether they were serving on the front lines or in a support capacity behind the actual fighting.

Those who lost limbs or eye sight or received facial disfigurement suffered severely as a result. The crippled veteran could not have anticipated what hardships his disability would create. For those who lost their emotional stability, life became different, and forever difficult.

Most veterans, however, grew in stature. Raw farm lads became mature adult men. Small town boys became knowledgeable employees or business owners. America was growing. Soon it would assume a new and unsought position of power in a world full of turmoil. But, for some years after the Armistice, America allowed itself to retreat briefly from involvement in European affairs.

Within 20 years, Europe again became a scene of instability and conflict. Not until 1939-40 did the United States re-enter the arena to confront fascist forces in Europe and Asia. Finally, in 1941 America officially embarked on another world war. This time, she had to accept responsibility as the world's greatest industrial nation, a status which would eventually lead the United States to become the world's strongest military power.

World War I, which until 1939 was called "The Great War," had foreshadowed what would happen a generation later. Even though the United States fell into an isolationist mode in the interim between wars, it had learned important lessons in 1917-18. Lessons such as on how to mobilize, train, and move large armies overseas. This knowledge would serve her well when the time came. Like it or not, the United States had to step into bigger shoes.

The process of change in the course of world affairs started on June 28, 1914, when pistol shots were heard around the world. Across the ocean, America heard the shots, and in 1917, made its response loud and clear.

Map of Camps and Cantonment
(Courtesy Jan Lunn, WWVets.com,)

FINALLY — THE UNITED STATES HAD NO OTHER CHOICE

It was March, 1917. German torpedoes were sinking ships with American civilians on board. Our Allies were close to starvation. There were few men left in England and France physically able to take up arms. This meant that freedom and democracy were at stake. Now a telegram is revealed from the Germans to Mexico, our southern neighbor, offering help to Mexico in retrieving territories from the United States in the event we entered the war against Germany.

President Wilson had no more patience. The latest sub sinking of the *Illinois*, was preceded by the fatal attacks on the *City of Memphis*, the *Vigilancia*, and the *Algonquin*. These merchant ships carrying vital food stuffs and war materials, were all torpedoed within the month of March, 1917. Then the revelation of the dastardly insolence in the German telegram sent by Germany's foreign minister, Alfred Zimmerman, offering to finance the betrayal and cowardly action for Mexico to stab the United States in her underbelly.

President Wilson's cabinet, in a meeting taking place on March 20, had heard enough. Even the pacifists in their midst supported a vote for war. Still, it was not until April 4, 1917, that the president asked Congress to make a formal declaration of war.

The Pittsburg, PA Gazette ran a banner headline:

"U-BOAT CLIMAX MAY COME TODAY."

Later headlines also proclaimed in large type:

"U.S. Declares War on Germany!"   "Killing American Passengers Provocative"
"Laconia's Sinking"   "Wilson Withdraws Pledge to Keep America Out of War"

He had won the presidential election last fall on this pledge by only a narrow margin, but German belligerence could no longer be ignored. Although the Germans had taunted the United States in the past, the Central Powers believed America was still too isolationist to pick up a rifle. This was one more time that Germany erred. They had taken one step too far. There was now no turning back for either side. (Mead)

1912 — BEHIND THE SCENES IN GERMANY

On December 8, 1912, the German Kaiser Wilhelm called an informal meeting of the German Imperial War Council. Attending were a number of the leading admirals and army generals. Significantly, the political leader, Chancellor Bethmann-Hollweg, and the Prussian Minister of War, General von Heeringen, were not invited.

The recent Russian announcement of military reconstruction and certain British communications that had been intercepted were creating a worry for the Germans. The British Lord Chancellor Richard Haldane had recently met with France's Prince Karl Lichnowsky to issue an explicit warning that should Germany attack France, Britain would intervene in France's behalf.

German General Helmuth von Moltke was in favor of an immediate attack before Russia had time to complete reorganization and reconstruction. Russia was still suffering the effects of having lost the Russo-Japanese war of 1905. However, Admiral Alfred von Tirpitz asked for postponement for one and one-half years to allow for the completion of the widening of the crucial Kiel Canal off the North Sea. Also, he wanted construction of a submarine base at Heligoland. Both would be finished by the summer of 1914.

General Moltke objected to Admiral's Tirpitz's proposal. However, the Kaiser agreed with his admiral, but "only reluctantly," it was noted. Some historians say the meeting amounted to "nothing," as nothing was decided except the postponement. Other historians say that "nothing" meant the war would not start in 1912-13, but that 1914 would instead be the date to begin the war. A deadline had been set. It would be the summer of 1914.

General von Moltke then demanded an armament race to match the Russians. However, the financial structure of the German state gave the central government limited power to levy taxes. The giant expenditures of the race might therefore bankrupt the government. Raising taxes was generally the obligation of the States in the Reich, and they typically responded dutifully to the demands of the Reichstag, the governing body.

There was always the threat of holding elections if the Kaiser did not obtain his request. If that did not compel the States to bring in more monies, rumors of a takeover or *coup d'e`tat* would frighten the Reichstag. This threat was used repeatedly by the Kaiser, and always proved to be powerful. He would use it, if necessary.

General von Moltke afterwards became a leading advocate for more arms and was reported to have told the German Foreign Secretary Gottlieb von Jagow during May, 1914, that the latter needed to conduct a policy of provoking a war in the near future. The new French president, Raymond Poincare, elected in 1913, was in favor of improving relations with Germany. He was more interested in developing interests in the Middle East, than in taking revenge for France's loss of the Alsace-Lorraine Province to the Germans in 1871.

Europe experienced a depression in 1873, several years after the Franco-Prussian war, but within a few years, most of Europe had recovered. Only England suffered financially for 20 more years until the 1890's, after the rest of Europe had survived their financial difficulties. All the leading nations belatedly realized they needed to find new sources of resources, as well as new markets for their exports. England's eventual recovery was based on the discovery in 1871 of vast quantities of diamonds in South Africa by Cecil Rhodes. Once again England could assume the role of the power house of Europe.

Nonetheless, Germany was not interested in Poincare's ideas, but preferred its own agenda of destroying France by means of a war. Germany's population was twenty million more than the French population, and German industrial power and economy were much larger also.

Meanwhile, in Serbia two factions in the government were at opposition to each other. The factions were led by Prime Minister Pasic on the one hand, and his chief opponent, the radical nationalist chief of Military Intelligence, Colonel Dimitrijevgic, on the other hand, The colonel was known by the code name of "Apis." In May, 1914, Serbia's King Peter dismissed the Prime Minister on the recommendation of the Colonel. This action with the Prime Minister was taken despite the Prime Minister's leadership of Serbia's victory in 1912 over the despised Ottoman Empire. This led to the overthrow of the centuries' rule by the Ottomans. The second war in 1913 was a territorial dispute with Serbia's long time enemy, Bulgaria, of which Serbia was the victor again.

This alarmed Russia, Serbia's ally, which intervened to have Pasic restored to power. Pasic knew that Serbia was near bankruptcy because of the 1912 and 1913 Balkan Wars and the recent suppression of a revolt in Kosovo. Russia, on the other hand, preferred peace in the Balkans and acted to insure this would happen.

In the meantime, certain politically powerful members of the Serbian military induced some Bosnian student dissenters to be trained as assassins. The students were sent into Sarajevo, Bosnia-Herzegovina, with various small weapons at the time the heir to the Austria-Hungarian Empire was to pay an official visit.

Their actions, as members of the terrorist group known as the Black Hand, provided the reason, or some say "the excuse," that threw Europe into turmoil that lasted more than four and one-half years. The third assassin, Gavrilo Princip, was the student who successfully shot and killed Franz Ferdinand, Archduke of Austria-Hungary. (Perisco) (Meyer)

Enlistment record for James Albert Dennis
(Courtesy of Denise Omstead)

VOLUNTEER OR DRAFTEE ? — A BIG DECISION

How to Build an Army of Two Million Men in One Year

The problems of building a huge army arose soon after President Wilson declared war on Germany. The United States Army had scarcely 130,000 professional soldiers, and the National Guard Units consisted of about 180,000 men.

A small number of Americans had joined the British and French forces in 1915 as volunteers. Most were attracted to the French Air Corps and formed what was known as the Lafayette Escadrille. The pilots were American volunteers, trained and commanded by French officers. Americans who joined the British Royal Flying Corps were under the training and leadership of British pilots and officers.

After the United States declared war, many young men volunteered as a way they thought would show their patriotism and courage. But these early volunteers did not make up the numbers needed. Many potential volunteers hesitated, having read newspaper accounts over the past three years about the huge losses of the British and French forces. Consequently, daily recruiting efforts failed to entice enough volunteers. Of those who did sign up, about half were rejected for physical and or mental reasons. (Sasse.)

It became evident to the government that a system of national conscription was required. The United States had never before resorted to this, although it had been a long time practice among most European nations. Only Britain had abstained from the draft in 1914. Congress hotly debated the issue, but quickly realized the necessity and passed legislation calling for two million men to be drafted during 1917. (Ellis.) The army was to be called the American Expeditionary Force (AEF).

Secretary of War Newton Baker and others worked out a plan of setting up local draft boards and levels of acceptance or rejection of a draftee. Posters in many foreign languages were printed for various immigrant groups to read in their own language. The law provided that citizenship in the United States would be more easily available to immigrants who signed up and were accepted. Consequently, about one-third of the total four million recruits in the service by the end of the war in 1918 were immigrants.

Registration cards were sent to all eligible men, and the first sign up date was June 5, 1917. (See sample card) Nearly ten million men between 21 and 30 registered. They were required to furnish their name, age, address, physical features, occupation, and reason for being exempted, if such reason existed. Results were that only about one in every five males qualified for duty.

From the pool of qualified men, the names of 687,000 were drawn by lottery. Great ceremony and publicity accompanied the first drawing by Secretary of War Baker. He was blindfolded and drew a capsule from a bowl of 10,500 capsules. The number he drew was "258." This was an historic moment. In all the 4500 participating precincts and villages each man who had the number "258" was the first male to be drafted. This procedure continued until all 10,500 capsules had been drawn. The numbers not drawn were saved until the next lottery. (Sullivan)

Within a few days the men whose numbers had been drawn were required to report for physical examinations or to appeal their selection. Two results became evident: 1) Physical exams showed that about 70% of the men qualified physically. 2) There were a minimum number of protests, much fewer than expected. Disqualifications were made for such physical conditions as flat feet, tuberculosis (common in those days), deafness, blindness in one eye, heart defects, missing digits or limbs, lameness, other deformities, epilepsy, neuroses, mental deficiency, and similar incurable disabilities. An interesting and extensive report on physical status of men by states, nationality, and occupation can be found in the War Department's 1920 report, "Defects Found in Drafted Men." Medical practice was beginning to recognize the importance of knowing the health of the nation's population, and as a result, began to create public health services.

Of the one million names drawn, about 600,000 were selected to begin military training by December 15. This resulted in the incredible task of organizing men, material, and housing. It called for rapid construction in the South of 16 camps, with the buildings consisting of canvas tents. Each camp was designed to hold 40,000 to 50,000 men. In the North, because of the colder weather, "cantonments" were built of a semi-permanent nature with wooden barracks and dining halls. (Sasse)

A typical camp or cantonment might have 1200 buildings on a site occupying 5,000 to 11,000 acres. This provided space for drill grounds and rifle ranges. In addition, sewer lines had to be laid, sources of water located, and pipes installed to bring water to the camp. Usually about 25 miles of paved road were needed for each site. (Sasse)

The construction industry rapidly rose to the challenge of one of the largest building jobs in United States history. American construction companies responded to the urgency by completing the first cantonment on September 8, 1917, at Camp Taylor, Kentucky. Cost per cantonment was $8,000,000 and for each camp, $1,900,000. Contractors were allowed only a 3% profit. (Note: No information was found on how this was enforced and the penalties for overruns or graft.) (Ellis)

The enormity of the job has been ranked as second only in difficulty to the construction of the Panama Canal, which took ten years to complete at a much lower cost. The Canal was finished in 1905, and labor and material costs likely were also lower then.(Ellis)

However, later, the Allies determined that the Germans would make one more "all out" offensive in the spring of 1918. Therefore, the draft went into operation again and age limits were extended to include men up to 45 years of age. One of the nation's biggest publicity campaigns succeeded when more than 13 million men appeared at the draft boards. This meant a total of 23 million men or 44% of the total male population showed up. America's population had grown much larger than the latest census of 1910 had counted. From this second draft, 2,702,687 men were accepted. (1920 census.) (Ellis.)

Many recruits were jobless men, drifters, farm hands, cowboys, and idealistic younger men whose brothers were already in the armed forces. Britain, and especially France, enlisted men from their last ranks of reserve troops. It would be difficult for them to make a defense against a massive last charge by the Germans. The Allies were desperate for new soldiers, and the Americans supplied those troops by transporting hundreds of thousands each month to France.

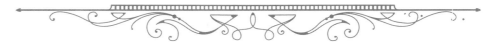

DO YOU HAVE WHAT IT TAKES?
Passing Physical and Mental Exams

For the first time in military history, being young and strong wasn't enough to become a recruit. Draftees had to pass a number of physical, mental, and educational tests before they were assigned to a unit. Sometimes the standards were relaxed when troops were in short supply for a particular assignment. However, the time had come when the army needed to learn which jobs a man could best perform, and if possible, assign him to one of them.

In order to do this, vocational testing was done for the first time. Several days were spent interviewing men about their interests, skills, aptitudes, and previous work experiences. This was necessary because many army jobs in 1917 were complex and required a higher level of ability and education. Jobs such as radio operator, electrical repairman, and artillery range finder needed previous experience or, more likely, some advanced training. The potential for a man to learn these skills had to be assessed.

Industry had set standards for 40 industrial trades, and the military utilized these trade standards. The assessment of a soldier's talents and interests resulted in assigning him to a job that nearly always requiring more training. This proved to be an advantage for many soldiers. When they left the service, they had skills and knowledge making them more employable.

Officers had to possess certain qualifications. These included physical qualities, intelligence, leadership, personal qualities, and general value to the army. Because these terms were vague, each was defined by specific characteristics. This was when the first IQ (intelligence quotient or measurement of intelligence) tests were administered. (Sasse)

The military used an adaptation of an intelligence test, the Stanford-Binet, developed by two French psychologists. No longer did the army resort to assigning a man to an important job because he looked like he could do it. In that former system, if he didn't succeed reasonably, the system required him to be "fired and replaced," resulting in disgrace or humiliation. In the new system the appointee was believed to have the necessary skills and the ability to succeed. This was not always the case, of course, but it was more reliable than the former random selection of candidates. For some positions such as pilots, reputable recommendations were required and judged as part of the selection process. (History Matters)

With immigrants, as well as many Americans, their lack of education became evident in the evaluation process. Many had left grade school early for numerous reasons. Now their educational limitations were evaluated. Many had an opportunity to learn important skills of reading, writing and math they otherwise might never had learned. The army provided some classes, as did numerous volunteer groups including the YMCA and the Salvation Army.

The popular war song, "You're in the Army Now, You're Not Behind a Plow," was true for millions of Americans who enlisted in 1917-1918. When the war ended, many did return to the plow. Others, however, returned with new skills and knowledge. For the vast majority of veterans, the military training and education began to provide long overdue skills required by the booming industrial age of America.

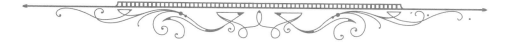

THE YANKS ARE COMING

At last. Basic training is over, and how brief and incomplete their training was, they would soon learn on the battlefield. The jitters and sadness of saying goodbye to family and friends was final. Now the soldiers had to contend with the trip over the Atlantic. Due to its occasional rough waters the soldiers were often beset with the accompanying stomach reactions. Finally they arrived in France, where the people excitedly welcomed, "Les Americains!" All other words the soldiers heard were just so many unfamiliar sounds.

The Allies and English and French civilians cheerfully welcomed the 300,000 Yanks that disembarked at their ports each month. The French and English, despite the thousands of troops conscripted from their many dominions, had depleted their supply of manpower. They were requiring young boys and older men to join the army to do whatever jobs their strength and training allowed.

By now, the British and French had sustained unimaginable causalities. Worse yet was the diminished morale of those left in the ranks. For example, the British had had what amounted to a massacre at the First Battle of the Somme in 1915. There were 60,000 British casualties on the first day. More than one million men, counting both sides were dead or wounded in the four to five month campaign at this historic battle zone.

The French, in turn, lost almost 350,000 men in the nine month battle at Verdun while Germany's losses, likewise, were huge and amounted to 337,000 causalities. For the Allies, victory seemed out of their hands. The famous phrase, "on ne passé pas," (no one shall pass) which the French declared earlier at Verdun, described the continuing stalemate. The Italians, another Ally, had their periods of disaster including the Battle of Caporetto River, where 600,000 men were taken prisoner or deserted. The Allied troops were exhausted, and many were demoralized as well.

French units began to mutiny in small units in 1917 until about 40,000 troops from 68 divisions were involved. They did not refuse to fight, but they announced they would defend France on their own terms. These terms included having more leave time, better food, replacing the ineffective officers, and improving the "poor conditions of service." (Strachan)

The disasters at Verdun, followed by the Allies defeat at Chemin des Dames, were imitated on the home front by textile workers strikes. Even munitions workers refused to work. Cost of living had increased drastically, while wages had fallen in purchasing value. (Strachan)

President Wilson's speech on April 4, 1917, spurred Congress two days later to declare the long awaited news: America had officially joined the Allies, and "the Yanks were coming."

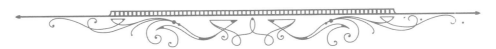

BASIC TRAINING PREPARES SOLDIERS FOR WAR:
Hup, Two, Three, Four - Drill, Drill, Drill

Basic training was just that – training in the basics of how to become an effective soldier on the battlefield. Most importantly, it was how to survive whatever the enemy throws at you. For many soldiers, the hours spent marching, doing calisthenics to build a tough, muscular, mobile body, and practicing saluting, were, well, just boring. They much preferred the rifle range, bayonet practice, and man – to – man fighting.

Unfortunately for the first draftees, there were not enough qualified trainers in the mold of "I'm tough, don't mess with me" sergeants to train all the men who had arrived at the camps. To remedy this shortage of trained personnel, England and France sent about 250 each of their best non-coms to provide the expertise and knowledge the Americans needed.

On the rifle range, the man learned how to shoot from four positions; lying flat on the ground, sitting, kneeling, and standing. He learned the rapid way of firing the rifle spraying the advancing troops; and "slow fire," and taking the time to aim accurately. They also practiced shooting at targets of varying distances. To the rural lad, all this was probably second nature. To the city boy, who may never have held a gun, it was new and awe inspiring.

Marching in order and in a proper sequence could mean the difference between winning or losing an attack or even a battle. Men learned the proper pace of walking and spacing so they

Basic Training included the proper way to carry a wounded or dead soldier from the battlefield.
(Public Domain, Sasse)

could safely advance under a "creeping barrage," a new tactic Pershing used. They learned how to carry their rifles safely so they would not accidentally put a bullet in the fellow in front or behind them. The pace might be set at marching 2 ½ miles per hour, or 12 to 15 miles per day. A certain speed and length of stride were required when units were being moved from site to site during war. Add the 70 pound pack to be carried on their backs, and it meant tired Rookies that night.(Note: The term "Rookie" was given to a new recruit.)

More basic training consisted of mounting and riding a horse, a saw horse that is, because the real horses often were not available. Other substitutes included bayoneting a straw dummy hung from a beam; setting the sights and loading shells into artillery guns, well, not real shells because they, too, were in France. Still, the crew needed to know how to handle the shells (or their substitutes) in a routine pattern. "Lift, carry, hand off, load, and fire." Over and over again, so a trained crew could fire the 19 pound shells at a rate of 20 per three minutes.

Even the rifle might just be a piece of carved wood to place over your shoulder or hold in the various required positions. Sometimes a Rookie might not handle or take apart an actual rifle until he reached France as a real shortage existed from time to time. How to carry a wounded buddy, or engage in hand to hand fighting could be learned in the camps in Oklahoma, Kansas, Arizona, a New England state, or elsewhere in the United States. It was valuable practice the Rookies, as the new recruits were called, had to learn.

By now many AEF sergeants were experienced enough to take over the job of the foreign trainer. The sergeant emphasized the proper way and speed required to put on a gas mask. Drill, drill, drill. "Your life does depend upon it," they emphasized. So did learning how to fight from a trench line. This was done in France in an area usually away from enemy presence, often the Vosges Mountains in southern France. Such techniques as sniping, crawling through barbed wire, and throwing hand grenades may have been delayed for training on French soil also.

When time and availability of equipment permitted, instruction included how to use the machine guns and the bayonet and how to fire trench mortars. During the last months of the war, however, soldiers often had to be sent to the fighting line without this important last stage of training. Hence, the casualties were horrendous. Average training time was shortened from seven months in 1917 to less than four months in late 1918.

Then there were the rules of behavior for the Rookie to learn: How to keep the barracks and your pack neat. Doing KP, that means the kitchen work Mom always did at home, was now yours to do. Also, policing the grounds, carrying wood for the stoves, washing your own laundry, that is, once you were issued your own uniforms. Sometimes men had to wear their civilian clothes for several weeks until enough uniforms arrived to clothe all of them.

Basic training may have been tedious, exhausting and frustrating, but it was the Army. The sooner you learned all this, the more pleasant your life as a Rookie was. And your chances of survival on the battlefield increased immensely. (Sasse)

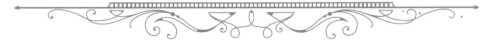

UNCLE SAM'S BOYS GO BACK TO SCHOOL

Sweeney School
(Courtesy Missouri Valley Special Collections,
Kansas City Public Library, Kansas City, Missouri)

For thousands of young draftees and enlisted men, school days began again once they entered the service. There was no time to build proper buildings, so the government requisitioned all types of appropriate private buildings to serve as schools. Such a building was "Sweeney Automobile School" in Kansas City. Missouri. Popularity of automobiles had made it necessary to provide training for new mechanical repair jobs.

During the war, 5,400 soldiers learned some of the 14 trades taught there. The flu epidemic of late 1918 -1919 caused the death of 15 students from the disease, but after the war ended, the school continued to be in existence a few more years. In its total years of operation, the school had trained about 80,000 students in various mechanical trades. Automobile and truck repair mechanics became good jobs to have.

So, move over, Mr. Mule. Here comes a Sweeney graduate!

SUNK BY A SUB

Seaman Floyd W. Carlisle spent four miserable hours in the cold waters off Fire Island, New York, on July 19, 1918. Miraculously only six lives were lost when the German submarine, U-156, torpedoed the *USS SAN DIEGO*, a highly valued armored cruiser, which sank in only 28 minutes. Quick action was required by the more than 1,100 American sailors who escaped the rapidly disappearing ship. (The following account of the sinking was found in an internet article, "USS California/San Diego, ACR-6, WWI)

Drama intensified as the violent explosion hit the ship which had been in a zigzag pattern sailing at 15 knots. It had been only an hour earlier at 10 A. M. when lookouts spotted what seemed to be a barrel coming quickly toward the ship. The gunners, firing for the first time in the war at what they thought was an enemy's object, shot the barrel which disappeared. The ship sailed toward Fire Island when at 11:18 A. M. a torpedo hit the ship, opening a hole on the port side, allowing water to pour into the engine rooms. The gunners, following orders, kept firing in the path the torpedo had taken until water reached the guns and they jumped overboard.

Floyd W. Carlisle, left, on his wedding day to Marjorie Filmer on Feb 1, 1938, with his brother.
(Family photo)

Meanwhile, in the engine rooms, firerooms, and other rooms below deck, officers and seamen were taking heroic actions that most likely accounted for the escape of so many sailors and the minimum loss of lives.

Lt. Commander Robert Webster Cary, Kansas City, Missouri, was awarded the Congressional Medal of Honor for his actions in the firerooms. Five boilers around him had exploded and two more were potentially likely to explode. He was commended on his "examples of coolness and (being) collected and showed an abundance of nerve under the most trying circumstances. His action on this occasion was above and beyond the call of duty."

Two brothers, Louis Patrick Haack and Bill Haack, both were rescued by ships alerted by a Navy pilot who reported the incident when he flew to shore. (Two way radios were not invented yet, and few pilots even had a one way radio.) His report caused rescue ships to be sent to provide assistance. Also three merchant ships heard the brief SOS signals and quickly arrived at the scene. All this help was needed to rescue the 1,156 survivors. Six of the rescued were injured.

The dead included a sailor crushed by a smoke stack falling in the water on him; another was killed when a life raft fell on his head; and one sailor drowned when he was trapped in the crow's nest. Three had been killed initially by the explosion. All sailors somehow remained true to their duty to wait for the "Abandon Ship" command, possibly dramatically reminded when an officer shouted, "If anyone jumps before abandon ship is given, I'll shoot him." This is a recollection attributed to C.E. Sims that may not be in the official records.

Fire Island is the large central barrier island not far off the south shore of Long Island, New York. While numerous reports of sightings of German submarines were announced once war with Germany was declared in April 1917, this is believed to be the only incident in which a United States ship was sunk close to the mainland, and was the only United States "major warship" lost in the war.

According to official Navy records, the parents of Floyd Carlisle were notified the next day after the sinking that Floyd was rescued and landed at New York. The parents were instructed to address future letters to him in care of the *USS SAN DIEGO* in care of Postmaster, New York. He later was attached to San Diego Barracks, Pelham Bay Park in New York, where he remained until assignment to the *USS TACOMA* on August 16, 1918.

Meanwhile, Floyd filed a "Claim for Reimbursement for Personal Property Lost in a Marine Disaster." on a form entitled "Such loss was due to the operations of war" "in the disaster to the U. S. S. SAN DIEGO." Using the official list of articles, he filed for loss of: "2 blankets, woolen; 1 boots, rubber; 1 brush, shoe; 1 cap, cloth; 2 caps, watch; 3 drawers, heavy; 3 gloves, woolen; 3 jerseys; 4 jumpers, white, dress; 1 jumper, undress; 1 leggins (sic); 1 overcoats; 2 shoes, gymnasium; 4 shoes, low; 2 socks, woolen; 4 towels; 4 Trousers, dungaree, 2 Trousers, white; 3 undershirts, heavy; 1 bathing trunks; 1 brooms, whisk; 1 brushes, hair; 2 clothes stops pkgs.; 1 combs; and 6 handkerchiefs." (Note: This is the exact wording on the form. Other items Floyd could have included but curiously omitted, were soap, buttons, and needles and thread.)

The listing of heavy clothing and woolen gloves, instead of cotton undershirts and drawers likely reflected his recent sailing in the colder waters of the Atlantic, where the *USS SAN DIEGO* had been escorting ship convoys to Europe for seven months. She had just completed 16 days of being dry-docked in Portsmouth, New Hampshire for repairs when she was torpedoed.

Shortly before the sinking, Floyd had been promoted from his enlistment rank of Apprentice Seaman to Seaman, and at the time of his discharge he had risen in rank to Seaman 1C. (Now the rank is called Petty Officer, Second Class.) His gunnery scores were good, but it is not known if this was his duty station at the time of the sinking.

The cause of the sinking is still debated by naval authorities. Some think it was caused by mines that had recently been laid, because the day after the sinking, patrolling Navy ships found six mines in the area. This was the conclusion of the official Navy Court of Inquiry that "an external explosion of a mine" was the cause.

However, a British Admiralty report, released after the war ended, concluded that a torpedo from the U-boat 156 was the cause of the explosion. The U-boat 156 had 56 kills credited to her, including war ships, until she was lost September 25, 1918, by hitting a mine in the Northern Passage, which were the waters between Scotland and Norway.

For Seaman C-1 Carlisle, his days on the *USS TACOMA* were less perilous, although the ship made five round trips to Europe during the war, guarding troopships and supply convoys. Carlisle, while aboard the *USS TACOMA*, later sailed the Caribbean and Latin American waters, protecting American interests in those areas until his discharge August 26, 1919, after two and one-half years in the navy. His pay then per month was $38.50, having increased from $17.50 at his enlistment.

As for his reimbursement for lost items —official records are not available to show that Carlisle received payment unless the unexplained amount of $116.78 paid upon discharge included the delinquent payment. Correspondence dated January 9, 1919, and titled "3rd Endorsement" for his claim, was forwarded, indicating he was still pursuing payment.

Another mystery surfaces in correspondence from his father dated July 4, 1919, to the Navy requesting Floyd's discharge. The reply from E. S. Jackson, Captain, informs Mr. Jesse Carlisle that within three or four days, Floyd Carlisle will be sent to the Recruiting Station in Denver, Colorado, for demobilization. Was Floyd needed on the farm? Was there a family emergency? Mostly likely he was desperately needed on the farm. Farm hands were scarce, many having joined the service, and his father was elderly then.

Floyd had fulfilled his duty as a seaman, rose in the ranks, scored well on various gunmanship tests, survived a torpedo from a sub, and crisscrossed the Atlantic numerous times. He had sailed in the icy waters of the north and the mild waters of the Caribbean. Now it was time to return home to Nebraska where there are some farm ponds and a few streams. The son of Jesse A. and Margaret (Grace) Carlisle, Floyd married Marjorie Filmer on February 1, 1938, having made Tilden, Nebraska, his home. He died October 9, 1971 and is buried in Tilden.

Seaman Carlisle was the grandfather of Patrick Donnelly, Omaha, Nebraska, who sent this story. Carlisle, the son of Jesse A. and Margaret (Grace) Carlisle, was born August 14, 1889, in Avoca, Iowa. Records show the dates of both July 14 and August 14, but enlistment papers show the August date. Carlisle was one of the first men to volunteer for the services and signed up on April 12, 1917, less than a week after the United States declared war on Germany on April 6, 1917. He enlisted at the U.S.S. Navy Recruiting Station in Omaha, Nebraska, having traveled from his home in Tilden, Nebraska, to volunteer for military service to his country.

Other US Ships Sunk by German Submarines

Earlier that month, German submarines struck another United States ship, the *USS Covington*, when it was westward bound from Brest, France about 150 miles from port. Six of the crew were killed when the torpedo struck, but the rest were rescued by the convoy of 13 ships including destroyers that accompanied her as she was towed back into Brest for repairs, however over a span of 24 hours, the ship slowly sank in the afternoon of July 2. There were no military personnel aboard the ship. The *Covington*, unlike the *San Diego*, was formerly a German passenger ship, which the United States "interned in Boston with other German ships until March, 1916". (freepages.military.) After the United States declared war on Germany in April 6, 1917, the naval officials seized the ships and put them under the custody of the United States Shipping Board.

TRANSPORTING THE TROOPS

AEF soldiers traveled by all the modes of transportation available in the early 1900's. These included wagons pulled by mules, British lorries, steamships, freighters, fishing boats, and the famous French "40 & 8" railroad boxcars. Soldiers marched hundreds of miles over roads that were well paved, or trod roads almost erased by constant rains; crossed fields and meadows; wound their way through dense forests; or climbed up steep mountain paths made by farm animals. A few men even flew to their destinations with short hops in the flimsy light weight airplanes constructed of plywood and cable wire.

Whatever their means of transportation, bumping along in English lorries, riding a motorcycle or mounted on a galloping horse, the journey was usually rough and uncomfortable. This was especially true of the ships that carried soldiers back and forth across the Atlantic. A few accidents occurred on the Atlantic, although it is recorded that few American troopships were damaged by subs due to the protection provided by the newly developed convoy system. One story tells of two ships which collided while crossing in October, 1917. The only damage fortunately, was the displacement of guns and destruction of some life boats. Needless to say, the crew and the Marines on board wore life belts the last six days of the trip. (http://www.vets.com/Marines)

Early in 1917 after the United States declared war on the Central Powers, ships of all kinds were commandeered. Some captured German ships including the liner *Leviathan*, which had been interned on its arrival in New York in 1914, were loaded with the AEF. English pleasure steamers, including the *Golden Eagle*, the *King Edward*, and *Duchess of Argyll*, were already comfortably outfitted, and for those lucky troops, the journey was almost luxurious.

Small steamers were ideal for carrying horses, munitions, artillery, and supplies of all kinds across the English Channel to France. At first, all crossings were dangerous due to lurking German submarines, but by 1917 the United States Navy had that threat subdued. Losses to sub attack then were few. In fact, the White Star liner *Olympic* was the only troopship believed to have sunk a German submarine by ramming the sub after the torpedo fired but missed the liner.

One of the worst atrocities of the war was the German sinking of the *Llandovery Castle* on June 28, 1918. Despite her display of large Red Cross symbols indicating she was a hospital ship and her cross lights showing, the Germans, without warning, torpedoed the helpless unarmed ship. Of the 258 people on board, only about 10% or 24 survived. Twelve who drowned were Canadian nurses returning from Canada where they had taken injured soldiers.

The sinking took place about 40-50 miles from the Irish coastline. The sub repeatedly rammed the life boats and machine gunned most of the survivors, rather than rescuing them. The Germans explanation for torpedoing was that there were some American soldiers aboard, a sinking claim later that was disproved in the court trial afterwards of the German officers. (http://www.gwpda.org/naval/lcastl11.htm)

An unusual conversion was made of the *Campania*, a Cunard line ship sold to the British Admiralty. The ship was remodeled to carry ten specially built airplanes on the deck. There were only a few aircraft carriers, but the usefulness of such ships was another first event for the War.

The United States also used ships owned by the French and Italians to deliver troops to France. Then in return trips, those ships were used to bring troops home after the war's end.

Nearly seven months were required for all the troops not assigned to the Army of Occupation of Germany (AOG) to return to the States. Even then, a few thousand soldiers assigned to the AOG did not return until summer of 1923.

The huge numbers illustrate the enormous problems providing and scheduling enough transports to carry soldiers and minimal amounts of equipment across the Atlantic, both to the war and afterwards, from France back to the United States. To take the 2,079,880 soldiers to their destination in France required a total of 1813 ships. The newly developed convoy system in 1917 had protected the vast majority of ships from being targets for dangerous submarines. The convoy included small speedy boats, called "submarine chasers," and destroyers curtailing the menacing power of the submarine as a weapon. (U. S. Troops Transported...)

However, one other horrific torpedoing took place September, 1918, when the *Mount Vernon* was leaving Brest, France, for the States. The 350 troops aboard heard a terrific blast when they were about 250 miles from the port. A sub had slipped in between the *Mount Vernon* and the next ship, the *Agamenon*. After the *Mount Vernon* had a hole 19 feet wide blown in its side, the *Agamenon*, pursued the sub. Six destroyers, part of the convoy, dropped depth charges on the submarine and put out a smoke screen to protect the *Mount Vernon*, which by then was rapidly filling with water.

All the coal stokers rushed to their stations even though there were only eight boilers left. The stokers loaded coal fast and furiously as they could. Their lives and the lives of everyone on board were at stake. The soldiers began bailing, singing all the time. Finally at 2:30 A. M. the badly damaged *Mount Vernon* made it back to Brest harbor.

There are a few other stories of ships that almost didn't make it safely, or were even destroyed, but the total record is remarkable. In addition to troops, each ship carried up to four tons of supplies and equipment. The end result was the safe passage of over two million soldiers carried by 1,142 ships. The British Navy provided 70% of the escort ships which offered the unusual protection. (Freidel)

Small anti-submarine chasers were ordered to be built as soon as possible by Franklin D. Roosevelt, then the Assistant Secretary of the Navy. (http://www.splinterfleet.org/sfww1.php) The result was a 100 foot wooden boat with three gasoline engines. The boat emphasized seaworthiness rather than speed. By using wood, these chasers could be built quickly. (Delaware Military History) On some ships the riveting process was a big concern. Riveting held two sheets of steel together making the ship watertight. However, thousands of rivets were required of each ship. A process of reshaping a plate saved one rivet. Many plates meant many rivets saved, and the worker's time was reduced as well as the cost of the rivet. Thousands of rivets per ship became unnecessary, thus a big saving from a tiny item.

Not only was transportation for the soldier required on the oceans, but also on many miles of land in the United States. America's railroad system was challenged and met the challenge admirably. Almost 70% of the troops were, at one time or another, passengers through one single railroad train station, Union Station, in Kansas City, Missouri. To get the troops to the different camp locations required a fleet of trucks to carry troops, who sat hunched over on wooden benches, 20 or more men per truck, bouncing over the rough rural roads. (Heiman)

No one ever said "going to war would be easy." They should have added, "getting to the war was a rough bumpy ride."

THE "FIRSTS" OF THE FIRST WORLD WAR

1. First war to be fought on three continents
2. First industrialized conflict
3. First use of "flame thrower," (although ancient Greeks used a fiery weapon they threw)
4. First battle of tanks
5. First use of masses of airplanes
6. First use of x-ray for military medicine
7. First use of a blood bank and transfusions
8. First use of guide dogs by blinded soldiers (in Germany in 1916)
9. First use of "trillion" in estimating war costs
10. First commissioning of art for wartime propaganda
11. First use of IQ tests to determine military assignments
12. First president (Woodrow Wilson) to visit Europe while in office
13. First massive use of machine guns
14. First use of large artillery guns
15. First widescale use of trenches, perhaps as much as 25,000 miles of them

(World War I Facts)

SEVEN LETTERS TELL HIS ARMY STORY

Clyde Miller, center, with sister, Marie, on his right; and Mary, who later became his wife, at his left
(Courtesy of Frances Miller)

In one of the seven letters preserved and now in the care of his daughter-in-law, Frances Miller, Raymore, Missouri, Private Clyde Miller discussed his reasons for remaining a loyal soldier assigned to the 140th Infantry, 35th Division.

Dec. 17, 1918 – Hospital in France – Private Miller explained in a letter to his parents his decision to enlist in the army the year before. Written from a hospital bed, he said he signed up, "in the interest of humanity… and duty." Expressing no regret that he was sick, possibly exposed to the "Spanish flu" as were hundreds of other troops, he was his usual positive self. His illness may have been influenza or a previous wound that refused to heal. The hospital was one of many French hotels converted to hospitals.

Military service had changed many things about the young lad who had worked in a hardware store in Kansas a year ago, but his values were still the same. He wrote he "had traveled much (from home in Kansas to England, then France)…had observed much and undergone temptations as well as hardships." He closed the letter with, "Our work in France is nearly done…people at home have {helped} finish the cause and make victory possible."

After six months fighting on the frontlines, the 20 year old soldier was still patriotic and idealistic. Possibly in an effort to convince himself, he was quoting the official Army reasons for being in Europe. (Note: More of this letter later.)

Back to the first letter preserved in the packet:

April 19, 1918 – Camp Mills, Long Island, New York – This is the earliest letter in the collection owned by Frances Miller. It appears that Clyde had written more frequently, but these seven letters are all that Frances has. The letter described the trip from training camp, probably Camp Doniphan, Oklahoma, to New York, where Clyde embarked for Europe.

Born and raised in the small village of Hillsdale, Kansas, Clyde was greatly impressed by the even slightly larger towns where the soldiers got off the train en route and staged occasional parades. Small towns such as Brookfield, Missouri; Elrene (sic) (El Reno), Oklahoma; and finally, the big Pennsylvania capital, Harrisburgh, left Clyde in awe. (Spellings are his.) Once he reached New York, he had few words left to describe it. "N.Y. is some town all noise and large buildings and everything imaginable (sic)." He probably did not even try to envision larger and more magnificent cities such as London or Paris.

He wrote that Camp Mills was a "fine camp," but wet because it was near the coast. Was he thinking about the ocean he soon would cross? Sometimes his thoughts are difficult to determine, because Clyde never expressed a negative thought in any of his letters. The letters follow a pattern: Inquiries about the health of his parents; the grades his sister, Daisy, was making in school as she prepared to be a teacher; and his reassurances that he "will be fine" throughout his tour. He also asks, almost pleads, for a letter from home.

The family had moved from Hillsdale to Carrollton, Arkansas, before he enlisted. He stayed in Kansas City, Missouri, with a brother. There he met Mary, "entirely a lady," as he described her to his mother. She "has a Sunday School Class that she takes the greatest interest in and she reminds me of Daisy in her enthusiasm for Christ's work." Curiously, nowhere else in these seven letters did he mention religion or a belief in God or Christ. He asked his mother to write Mary. (Note: We don't know if his mother complied with his request.)

May 18, 1918 – "Somewhere in France" – Clyde said he enjoyed the trip over the Atlantic "hugely," although in a later letter he confessed to having been seasick. This short letter, announcing his arrival in France, ended by his regretting he knows only a few phrases in French, which are "seldom of any use." Also, the money was different, but he "soon will learn the value of it." He said he would write every week. Was he hoping that his family would also write more often? He bade them "adieu," but this was marked over by the censoring officer, a 1st Lt. N.G. 140 Inf. (sic), almost obliterating the word.

June 23, 1918 – France – It was Sunday and he was writing home again. "I haven't heard from you since arriving overseas"(over a month). He boasted the Americans have "Fritz on the jump" and "Americans are eager to do their bit... I look for a letter from you soon." (Note: Army mail service delivery was considered good, but for the first month or so, the units were moved around often. So it is possible mail was delayed.)" As ever, your son, Clyde." Censored by a Lt. Thomas and marked "OK."

October 17, 1918 – Hospital in France – Military records show he was "injured"on September 30, just before the last big offensive of Meuse-Argonne. However, his letter said he "left the field the 26th of September." Sometimes official records do not show the actual date of injury or wounding. His unit, the 140th Infantry, 35th Division, saw action at the battles at Gerardmer and Compte le Court in the Argonne area. The Americans had been transported by more than 200 French trucks from their reserve area at St. Mihiel to Grange-le-Compte. On the morning of September 26 began what has been described as "the greatest battle in American military history," up to 1918. That was the battle of the Meuse-Argonne (Delos-Pipes)

It was here Clyde collected souvenirs which he later had to abandon when his company was quickly ordered into quarantine in December. Because Clyde obeyed censorship regulations, details are scarce in his letters. The company commander was required to read and sign each letter his men wrote. However, one letter ended with a puzzling comment written in a different and more precise handwriting than that of the censoring officer. It said, "May God bless him protect him and guide him by his good council is my earnest prayer. Follow his letters with prayer. Matt. 7:17; 9." (Note: Punctuated as printed.) No name or rank explains who gave this advice. A chaplain? Or a new company commander?

Clyde told his family he was getting "good treatment at the hospitals." He may have been moved for additional treatment to a hospital farther from the front. (See "U.S. Medical Care p???.) Note: The war's two final battles at St. Mihiel and the Meuse-Argonne.) (Sullivan) As usual, he signed the letter, "Your son, Clyde."

December 17, 1918 – (Same day, different location) – Convalescent Camp – This is the briefest letter, saying only "we have seven squads under quarantine (about 140-150 men) and several more in the base hospital…" This time he wrote on Red Cross stationery instead of the YMCA paper. His tone was more somber. He said he expected to be shipped home in the spring.

Gone were his enthusiasm, patriotic remarks, and boasting of victory. He had become wiser and more mature because of his experiences on the battlefield. The fighting, bombardments, being wounded, and sick with flu certainly must have affected what he had endured. He had changed. He was no longer the Clyde Miller who left Hillsdale, Kansas, a year ago.

May 13, 1919 – (Note: Written on his discharge papers.) The officer marked his character as "Excellent." Clyde married Mary and they raised four children, two girls and two boys. He settled down to an otherwise unremarkable life. He had seen Paris and London, had fought on scarred battlefields, and witnessed the death and total devastation of war. He observed all this and more.

For Clyde Miller, a small town in Missouri was where he wanted to spend the rest of his life.

"All along the line, Englishmen could be seen throwing their arms in the air and collapsing, never to move again."
A German soldier describes the First Somme attack in July, 1915
(World War One – A Very Peculiar History.)

CALLING CHARLES MCDANIEL

Charles J. McDaniel
(Courtesy of Dorothy and Al Morse)

The name, Charles McDaniel, was a favorite name in the long line of McDaniels of Miller County, Missouri. However, several times it brought sorrow to the family, as was true in the case of Charles J. McDaniel.

He was born March 10, 1893, the fifth child of George Washington McDaniel and Ann Liza Colvin McDaniel, in Bagnell, Miller County, Missouri. Their first three children had died. A fourth child, James F. McDaniel, born October 8, 1891, survived to see his little brother, Charles J. McDaniel, arrive a few years later. The two boys grew up as playmates.

Like his father and neighbors, Charles grew up farming in the Ozarks area of Missouri. The soil was poor and making a living was difficult. Charles probably had little schooling because he was needed to work on the farm. However, when the United States entered World War 1, he did not hesitate to join the army. On September 20, 1917, at age 23, he signed the enlistment papers.

He trained at Camp Funston, Kansas, probably as a member of the 356th Battalion of the 89th Division. Then in March, 1918, he was transferred to the 4th Infantry and finally to the 103rd Infantry of the 26th Division. It was nicknamed the "Yankee Division," because most of its members were New Englanders. This was a time of building large groups to form divisions which required up to 28,000 soldiers and support troops, and that is probably why Charles was transferred so many times. It was at Camp Merritt, New Jersey, where on March 15, 1918, he shipped out to France.

There he was assigned to Company C, 103 Infantry Battalion, which was engaged in the heavy fighting near Belleau Woods and the Second Marne. The 26th Division marched from July 5 through 18th to support positions northwest of Chateau-Thierry.

It was during this time that Charles was killed in action on July 14. Although it is not known exactly where he was killed, it was possibly near Chateau-Thierry because his battalion fought there during that period. As this area was constantly being attacked and counter attacked, the French words, *Pas Fini,*" meaning, "Not Finished" or "not the end" designated the battleground. His body eventually was brought back to Missouri, where he is buried in the family cemetery, the Colvin Cemetery in Miller County.

Finally, the 26th were victors in the *"Pas Fini"* sector. The next battle, retaking the Second Marne River, gave fame to the 26th Division and the Second Army, later known as "Rock of the Marne" for its tenacity and bravery in routing the Germans. At that time there were some 85,000 AEF soldiers assigned to the French army for this action.

The Marne River sector had important transportation hubs making it a strategic location, one the Germans wanted to keep. A costly battle had been fought there in September, 1914, with the Allies finally victorious. If the Germans had won, the road to Paris was only some 20 plus miles away. The Germans could easily have captured it and the war probably would have been over. The promise of "All will be home by Christmas" would have been fulfilled. The total number of dead and wounded exceeded 512,000 for both sides in this second conflict. This was the battle ground where the French general commandeered 600 Parisian taxis to take 6,000 troops to the front lines as quickly as possible.

The 26th Division distinguished itself by being awarded 229 Distinguished Service Crosses (the second highest United States medal); while experiencing a total of combat deaths of 2,168 with more than 13,000 wounded. McDaniel would have been proud of his comrades.

A namesake nephew, Charles H. McDaniel, was born a few months after Charles J. McDaniel's death. The, nephew, also named Charles, would suffer a similar fate a generation later, after serving in World War II as a medic. He and his wife, Gladys Watts, had a son born April 17, 1947, named "Charles," again following the custom of keeping a "Charles" in the family. The baby's name was Charles H. McDaniel, Jr. Shortly after the baby's birth, his father rejoined the army and was sent to Korea where on November 2, 1950, he was declared missing in action. His status was later changed to being declared dead. The family never knew if he was killed in action or died in captivity. They still seek the details of his death.

The son, Charles, Jr., has honored his father by serving also with the military, in a different capacity. He is a chaplain in the Army Reserve. In the 1990's Charles, Jr. served in Bosnia during the Serbian conflict. He lives in Indiana where he pastors several small churches.

The family is trying to learn the fate of Charles, Sr. and has participated in some DNA testing of bones which may be proven to be those of Charles, Sr. A relative, Dorothy Morse, has provided the DNA material for the tests. At the time of this writing, the family is still awaiting the outcome of the tests. Dorothy and her husband, Al Morse, Raymore, Missouri, provided the information for this story.

To many in the McDaniel family, the name, "Charles McDaniel," denotes a patriot, one who is brave and courageous. It is a proud family name, the name of a man willing to risk his life for his country, despite the possibility of a fateful ending.

FROM MULE SKINNER TO LORRY DRIVER

Clyde M. Kirk, 29 years old and single, was a rural Missouri farmer who used only mule power to pull his plows and wagons in 1917. His ideas about animal power and mechanical power changed drastically after he enlisted in the American Expeditionary Forces (AEF) on December 14, 1917. As a former "mule skinner" (driver), he was well qualified to handle mules in France. With his new rank of "Waggoner," he was assigned to drive the mules used to haul artillery from one gun emplacement to another.

Poster urging men to sign up for CAC.
(Public Domain))

He grew up on a farm near the small Missouri town of Lathrop, the area known as "Mule Capital of the World." In France, after driving mules for a short time, he soon found himself behind the wheel of a "lorry," the English name for a truck. Driving a mule team was one thing. Driving a big British lorry was an unexpected challenge. This story is shared by his only child, Betty Dell Kirk Waite, Raymore, Missouri, daughter of Clyde and Ruth Kirk.

Kirk trained in the 7th Company, CAC, at Ft. Moultrie, South Carolina. In France he was assigned to Battery B, 61st Artillery, CAC, which is the abbreviation for Coastal Artillery Corps. These units are responsible for handling the heaviest guns which were naval guns that had been stripped from ships. They were usually stationed on coastlines. The shells contain eight pounds or more of ammunition. Moving and installing these guns required special equipment and skills. The smaller guns, firing shells containing 4 to 6 lbs. of powder, were called "light field guns" and could be easily moved by animals or even men, if necessary. They were the most commonly used guns at the beginning of the war.

A heavier gun was the French 75 mm artillery gun used by the teams commanded by Captain Harry Truman of Battery B, 129th Field Artillery, who later became the 33rd president of the United States. When the Allies needed bigger guns, the Americans removed heavy ones from battleships. They were mounted in concrete bases and used to provide the heavy shelling power needed. Again, the CAC would be called in to do the installations.

Large artillery guns now played a more important part in warfare. Because of their size, they usually were mounted and stationary. The CAC was needed to move both guns and ammunition. As the war progressed, guns became larger and more powerful. The war had changed from an infantry battle to a battle between the big guns. The largest and most powerful gun of all, Germany's "Paris Gun," had a range of 91 miles. It was fired from a railroad car and hit Paris several times. The damage was minor but the psychological effect upon Parisians was terrifying.

Heavy artillery were used by both sides and caused many casualties. It is estimated that 80% of battlefield deaths were caused by artillery fire. (WW1 Vets.com /CoastalArtilleryCorps.html) It is not known whether Kirk was a gunner also, but it has been confirmed he drove the big bulky British lorries that towed the guns. By war's end the AEF had more than 100 such guns ready to be shipped to France.

After the war ended, Kirk returned to the family farm and his mules. Upon the early death of his father, he helped his widowed mother raise two younger brothers and two sisters. Kirk became a successful cattle feeder and grew blue grass seed for the commercial market. But mules were still on his farm. That was because the hired hands did not want to learn how to operate and maintain a modern tractor and other mechanical equipment. They may have said, "Give me a mule any day over that 'new fangled,' noisy, smoky hunk of metal." Perhaps Kirk would have smiled at their remarks while remembering his army days with mixed feelings.

Those memories would be of the days and nights he drove men and supplies many hazardous miles over muddy pools of water that used to be roads. When the lorry got stuck up to the wheel caps in mud, it became a helpless target for German artillery or snipers, and had to be hauled out by a team of mules, if available, or another truck. Those were not such pleasant memories.

He might have then concluded, "Maybe the stubborn Missouri mule wasn't such a bad fellow after all."

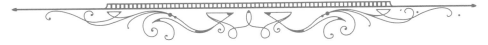

Red Cross Volunteers provide refreshments to troops on train, probably on their way to France.
(Our Times. Public Domain))

THE FLYING MACHINE AS A WEAPON

In 1910 the United States Air Corps consisted of only one pilot and one plane. The pilot was First Lieutenant Benjamin Foulois, of San Antonio, Texas, and the plane was his Wright Flyer. He was successful in leading the first experimental maneuvers with ground troops at Fort Sam Houston, Texas. This was the birth of the United States military aviation.

Although pilots in other countries were dramatically attacking their enemy in the air, Americans lagged behind their European counterparts in grasping the potential usefulness of an air corps as a combat unit. The world's first bombing raid had taken place as early as

November 1, 1911. Italy's Giulio Gavotti dropped four bombs by hand over the side of his plane onto Turkish soldiers hidden in two oases in Libya. The next year Lieutenant Gavotti became the first pilot to take aerial photographs.

Meanwhile, impatient American flyers crossed the Atlantic to join aero squadrons in France and Great Britain. These were mostly men from prominent United States universities. Some formed the ranks of the famous Lafayette Escadrille which fought under the command of the French.

It was not until 1916 that Congress belatedly awarded $13.3 million to build and improve the aviation section, which was assigned to the Signal Corps. Congress had been disappointed in the one and only air attack by the Air Service's first Aero Squadron during the punitive ventures against Mexico's Pancho Villa that year. This unsuccessful effort to capture the bandit used some airplanes as well as cavalry.

The Americans' effort in Mexico was an embarrassing failure, in contrast to the daring and brilliant actions of European planes during the early war years. This contrast challenged Congress to catch up with Europeans in this newest of fighting methods. Attracting potential pilots was no problem despite the dreadful attrition rate of foreign pilots. Loss of life was estimated to be about 75% due either to combat activities, mechanical failures, lack of flying experience or training, and fatigue. The lure of conquering the skies brought thousands of recruits, once the United States declared war on Germany on April 6, 1917. It happened that the day before, four JN-4 Jennies landed at the new Kelly Field in Texas.

The new flying field, Kelly Field, was named to honor the first American pilot to die while piloting a military aircraft. It soon became obvious that one field could not accommodate all the new recruits and cadets. So another field nearby was opened. By the end of the war Kelly Field had organized 250,000 men into aero squadrons, as they were called. An average of 2,000 mechanics and chauffeurs completed training each month resulting from the work of the Enlisted Mechanics Training Department. (History of Kelly Field.)

In the years leading up to 1914, Great Britain, which had always relied upon the strength of her Navy, also was slow to develop air power capability. In 1914 she had only about 30 planes from a fleet of 184 that were serviceable. This quickly changed, and by the end of the war, British planes numbered over 21,000, including 1,300 seaplanes and 103 airships. Meanwhile, AEF pilots flew either British or French airplanes, although by November, 1918, U.S. factories were producing a number of planes fitted for combat.

France led the Allies with an air force of 33,350 officers and enlisted men in all branches of aviation. Britain was close behind with 30,570, while the number of American aviation personnel had increased to 13,000. (Sasse). Also, to France's credit, the SPAD.XIII was considered the finest French aircraft flying and was superior to those of the British and American aerial forces.

Although many American military and governmental leaders were highly skeptical of using aircraft in war, the results spoke for themselves. The Germans successfully used 180 huge 500 foot long Zeppelins in bombing both London and Paris. The bombs created terror and panic mostly, as well as loss of life and property as well. In 1915 there were 127 civilians killed and 352 injured in the raids on London from May to December. Other sites were bombed, including Paris, but London was the chief target. (Gilbert)

At first aeroplanes (the European spelling) were used to provide only ground intelligence. This was an important advance over the former method of sending cavalry scouts to supply information about the size and location of the enemy to artillery spotters and ground commanders. However, at first, planes were not equipped with radio communication, and the pilots had to drop various color flags signaling direction and size of ground troops. As can be imagined, this was not a successful way to send information to ground troops or artillery batteries. Pilots also used carrier pigeons to transmit the coordinates by attaching messages to tiny capsules fastened to the pigeon's feet. These clumsy and inaccurate methods were far from satisfactory, and occasionally the unfortunate pigeons were shot down by the enemy.

Soon planes and engines were enlarged to accommodate a second passenger, an observer, who sat behind the pilot. The plane carried a simple radio transmitter with the Morse code. But having no receiver, the transmission was only one way. For a while the flyers resorted to simple means of displaying various strips of white cloth in pre-arranged patterns. Other observation men rode in the baskets of observation balloons, called "captive balloons" because they were anchored to cables in the ground.

Because the balloons were stationary, their observers could not see as far as a plane could. Sometimes messages were dropped from the planes to ground patrols, but again the primitive method did not provide accurate or timely information that would reach the proper person.

This type of early flying was hazardous, as was all future flying performed by pilots. In the month of April, 1917, the worst month in the war for the British Royal Flying Corps on record, the average flying life of British pilots was only 93 flying hours. This was partially because the pilots were exhausted from making many flights per day for reconnaissance. In all the services, the highest percentages of loss of life occurred in the air squadrons. (www. westernfrontassociation.com..../59...)

Engineers and inventors continued to make rapid improvements in the engines, the body, wing span, and added simple instruments to the planes. As a result, more advancement appears to have been achieved for the airplane than any other weapon of the war.

Another useful communication tool was the invention of wireless telegraphy, developed by the British Royal Flying Corps. In 1914 telegraphy could communicate from a distance up to 2,000 miles. Carrying a wireless set and a map, the observer could locate the enemy's position and send messages back to his own army's artillery commander. This proved a more efficient method. The observer also learned to locate bombers or planes miles away by using the wireless set. This improvement helped to protect London and other English cities from the terrifying German Zeppelins which could fly at great heights, some at 20,000 feet for a short time. Also the development of the rapid ground – to – air capability of the Sopwith Camel airplane brought the elimination of most airship raids. The Camel was a swift attack plane and destroyed a number of the German airships.

Other valuable additions to aerial fighting were provided by the Russians under the leadership of Maj. Gen. M. V. Shidlovski. The Russians were the first to design a self-contained aircraft force in 1915. In the next two years they made more than 400 raids over Germany and the Baltic States. The Russians also made other helpful improvements but unfortunately for the Allies, they signed a peace treaty with the Germans in late 1917. Their ideas and skills were no longer available to either side.

By 1918, at the urging of influential generals in the air service, Congress activated The Air Service of the First Army, under the eventual leadership of Gen. Billy Mitchell. He became chief of the Army Group Air Service, First Army. The Air Service, Second Army, was formed in 1918 also, but was not ready to take part in the fighting before the Armistice was signed. The Air Service, Third Army, was created immediately after the Armistice and provided aviation support for the Army of Occupation of Germany which lasted until 1923.

During the war, American pilots flew either French or British made airplanes while American factories were being built. By the end of the war, however, these factories began producing hundreds of planes, which no longer were needed for the war.

It was almost 30 years later, after the end of World War II, during which aircraft proved to be invaluable, that the first Department of the Air Force was finally elevated to equal status with the Army and Navy departments. It was re-designated the United States Air Force because of the valuable, extensive use of fighter planes, long-distance bombers, and aerial transports in fighting the enemy. The first Secretary was Senator Stuart Symington of Missouri.

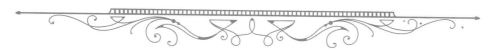

HAZARDS OF THE PILOTS

In April, 1917, the worst month for British pilots, the Germans shot down 245 planes.

KNIGHTS OF THE AIR – THE TOP ACES BY NATION

Manfred von Richthofen – 80 kills – Germany *** Rene' Fonck – 75 kills – France*** William Bishop – 72 kills – Canada *** Edward Mannock –61 kills – Britain*** Robert Little – 47 kills – Australia *** Andrew Beauchamp-Proctor – 47 kills – South Africa*** Godwin Brumowski – 35 kills –Austria-Hungary*** Eddie Rickenbacker—26 kills – USA

Other aces included: Albert Ball, England, 44, who died in combat; Vernon Voss, Germany, 48; George Guynemer, France, 54 (he once waved off a German who was struggling to fix his jammed machine gun); Francesso Baracca, Italy, 34, his symbol of a rearing stallion is the logo for an expensive sports car; and Petar Marinovich, Serbia, 21, who flew for the French.

Pilots began combat in the air by throwing bricks, rocks, long steel darts, and grenades aiming at the plane's fragile wings. If they broke the canvas coverings, the plane would lose altitude and crash. Sometimes they threw pieces of rope trying to tangle the single blade propeller.

The first kill came early in the war on October 4, 1914 when the French airman, Louis Quenault, used a machine gun at a German plane. The French and English declared a pilot to be an "ace" when he downed five planes that could be verified. The Germans raised that number to eight for their pilots.

A MAN OF ACTION

Harold Mensch, "Man of Action," in front of his camouflaged French plane
(Courtesy of Adrienne Landry)

Harold E. Mensch wanted action when he enlisted as a sergeant in the Aviation Section, Signal Enlisted Reserve Corps. At the war's beginning, aviation was placed under the supervision of the Signal Corps. The purpose of flying was to observe enemy movements, and by use of various signals, provide the infantry or field artillery with information about enemy activities.

Airplanes at this time did not have access to radios, only to a Morse code transmitter. A radio set would have been too heavy for the fragile planes. The pilots and ground observers had previously agreed upon signals which included hanging different colors of cloth over the side of the plane indicating certain directions.

Mensch's story is told by Adrienne Landry, a great-granddaughter, of Lawrence, Kansas. She has an old envelope addressed to Harold Mensch, c/o J.E. Mensch, in Rupert, Pennsylvania. It was from the Adjutant General's Office and is marked "Official Business." The cancellation postmark is intriguing. It says: May 7, 9 a.m., 1917, Washington, D.C. TWENTY-SEVENTH REUNION UNITED CONFEDERATE VETERANS, Washington, D.C. June 4—8, 1917. In those days when Confederate Veterans were still alive, they met annually for a reunion. Union Veterans also held annual reunions.

The envelope contained a certificate of enlistment for Mensch with the rank of sergeant in the Aviation Section, Signal Corps and was dated Feb. 27, 1917. Adrienne has one letter from her great grandfather to his parents in which he wrote briefly, "I've been flying a lot lately."

Later, as the Allied airplanes proved to be capable of performing other jobs, the Aviation Section of the Signal Corps was officially legislated by Congress on June 3, 1916. This was still before the United States had declared war. Harold, known as "Gus", enlisted on February 22, 1917, almost two months before America entered the war. He wanted to be one of the 2,000 men to join the Corps, which recent legislation had authorized. After some preliminary training in the States, he was assigned to an aerial training school "somewhere in France." He flew missions and also taught new pilots, possibly Americans, who were eager to get into the adventurous, developing field of air warfare.

He survived many crashes. The family has multiple pictures of him standing by different airplanes in various stages of destruction. But he suffered no serious injuries. Plane crashes could also have been caused by improper mixing of fuel or to mechanical failure. Many other reasons made the life of a pilot the most hazardous of all the men in the armed services. His action of enlisting early may have been characteristic of his personality which sought excitement and action.

The Army knew little about how to train its pilots, who acquired much of their knowledge after learning the basics by flying solo. Pilots were needed as quickly as possible. Learning also came from experiences of other pilots. They were limited by lack of weather forecasts, as the weather instruments on the ground were primitive, and non – existent on the dash board of the plane. A sudden thunderstorm or powerful winds made life unpleasant if not deadly for the pilot. Also the study of meteorology was in its infancy.

"Mechanic Mike," his nickname, was tall for a pilot, standing 5 feet, 11 ½ inches. But evidently he could climb into a cockpit at a moment's notice. He also was the correct age, 22 years and 6/12 months, as the Army recorded it. The age range was 18-25 years old.

When the war ended in 1918, "Mechanic Mike's" exciting and dangerous life ended also. He lived in Detroit, Michigan, where he was successful in selling heavy equipment. Then came the years of the Depression when this equipment was not needed, and his sales and income plummeted. As he reached middle age, he became deeply depressed. When World War II came in December, 1941, he was too old to join the air corps, but he continued to fly private planes at every opportunity. He would go to his office every day and drink as a form of self-medication for his depression. It became a source of self-destruction, and he died of alcoholism in 1949 at age 51.

Gus left a wife and five children behind in Detroit. Adrienne says her father, Hal (son of Gus), used to tell this story: "Gus continued to fly, and at age 5, I would call my friends and say: 'Look, there's my father in that plane flying over us.' " His friends would scoff at him. Adrienne says what little Hal said was probably true. Gus was famous for flying under a bridge as a result of a bet he made with some of his buddies.

Gus had lived his early years as a man of action, seeking thrills and adventures. He found these as he flew the small, fragile World War I airplanes. This was a time in his life when he could satisfy this aspect of his personality in a respectable way.

Gus risking his life every time he climbed into the cockpit, fulfilling a mission that served his country and trained other pilots.

TWO FRENCH HEROES — A HUSBAND AND WIFE

Robert Gaston Charles

Robert Gaston Charles, a French citizen aged 17, rebelled at his mother's response soon after war was declared in 1914. He announced he intended to fight, and even threatened to join the French Foreign Legion if she did not approve of his enlisting. Finally, he signed up in the Armee de L'Aire, the French Air Force. It had been formed in 1909 as more efficient airplanes were rapidly being designed. By mid-1912 France had 132 planes and when war was declared two years later France had the first group of World War I pilots. Young Robert, despite his mother's protests, was determined to be a part of this exciting group. This story is told by Dr. Kathy Brumagin Scott, Raymore, Missouri, about the lives of her French grandparents in World War I and World War II.

The first planes bought by the government were usually the Farman MF2 which pilots flew for reconnaissance work. Robert served as an observer in the back seat as part of his training. When planes were later armed with machine guns, Robert became the back seat gunner instead. The pilot also had a machine gun (this was after the interrupter gear had been invented by the Germans) so both men could attack planes in every direction. Previously before the coming of the gear, the pilot had to risk damaging his propeller when firing. Robert wore his white scarf which he said he used to wipe the oil from the engine off his face. His uniform included goggles, a leather hat with fur around the eye openings, and a leather jacket. Underneath the jacket he wore a heavy coverall. The men were exposed to extremely cold temperatures when planes flew at 10,000 or higher.

The first bombing raids had one of the flyers manually dropping bombs over the side of the plane or throwing at a specific ground target. The planes were extremely light, and the engine had limited horse power, so they could only carry two bombs on each flight. Although the bombs created some damage and even deaths or injury, most of the damage was the fear engendered by the individuals below. Accuracy was almost impossible.(See story about Lt. Fitzsimons for an unfortunate bombing raid.)

Later after being promoted to pilot, he flew throughout the entire war. This was unusual, as the mortality rate of pilots was as high as 75%. Other flying corps had fewer casualties, but the percentage of risk was still higher in the flying corps than in the infantry. Robert was promoted to corporal, and received a citation for "Courage and Fearlessness" from General Daugan of the Moroccan (Morocaine) Division on August 19, 1918. When the war was over, Robert married Maria Villequenault in 1919, and became a successful businessman. He and Maria raised four daughters. He never flew again, but he never lost his fearless spirit.

This became evident when World War II started, and the Germans quickly occupied France. Robert joined the partisan underground. He owned the largest meat packing company and fish cannery in France and had become wealthy. Because of his partisan activities, he had to constantly evade Nazi attempts to capture him. On more than one occasion, he narrowly escaped capture. However, one time he was caught and detained by the Nazis, but he escaped and fled to safety in Switzerland for six months.

His wife was not so fortunate. The Nazis imprisoned her, hoping to draw Robert from hiding so they could capture him. She was several months pregnant at the time and the prison food was insufficient for all the prisoners, but especially for one who was pregnant.

Despite her pregnancy, she still had to endure the great hardships imposed by the prison conditions. No exceptions were made for her, but Maria was able to survive because of the food her sisters brought. Maria occasionally hung a scarf outside her prison window to let her sisters know she was still alive. Then they rode their bicycles more than 10 miles to the prison, passing by the guards and bribing them with cigarettes. The sisters were 18 and 16 years old, old enough to know the consequences if their plot had been discovered.

As the Allies advanced, they bombed the railroad tracks that ran near the prison where Maria was held, causing injuries to some prisoners. When the Allies closed in, the Nazi guards unlocked Maria's cell and left her behind. There had been several hundred French partisans imprisoned there, but most were loaded onto trains and taken to Germany as the Nazis withdrew.

After the war it was revealed that Maria, before she was imprisoned, also helped to hide Jewish families from the Nazis. In 1966 she received a special commendation from the French government for resisting the Nazis and for hiding Jewish French citizens during the war.

But tragedy still stalked the family because of the unknown wartime status of her brother, Maurice Villequenault, a French soldier in World War I, but who never had returned home. For years the family did not know his fate. Then in 1966, Maria and her grandson, another Robert, happened to visit a French cemetery in Alsace-Lorraine. Wandering among the graves, young Robert came upon the grave of the missing uncle. The marker said the soldier died when he was 19 years old. After 50 years of not knowing, Maria finally had the answer as to when and where her brother had died.

At some time in his life, her husband, Robert, lost his leg in an accident. He had developed a blood clot which turned gangrenous, and the leg had to be amputated. Kathy remembers visiting her grandparents in Paris in 1968 and seeing her grandfather's artificial leg for the first time. It shocked her, but her grandfather just laughed.

She has a picture of him taken after World War I. He was tall and handsome, and an avid hunter. The amputated leg did not interfere with Robert and Maria traveling around the world after World War II nor interrupt his hunting. The American grandchildren, including Kathy, visited Robert and Maria in France several other times. During those times, Kathy learned the French language. More importantly, she learned firsthand from her grandparents' actions, many personal examples of courage and patriotism.

Proud of them as she is, there remains one regret for Kathy. She saw the hat and scarf of "Papy Charles" when she was a child, and wonders where they are today. She hopes they are being well cared for, or better yet, she could take care of them. They would be lovingly treasured, along with the stories of her adventurous and daring grandparents.

Moroccan Division
General Daugan
Citation under the command of the Division
General Order 164 - August 19, 1918
Aviation Squadron Bar.104

TRANSLATION OF CITATION:

Robert Charles, corporal, machine gunner, 2nd aviation group
A young machine gunner, full of courage and fearless, called upon to fly into a rough sector, had a superb attitude. In the course of the attacks of July, 1918, by his skill and shooting accuracy, he escaped an enemy patrol far superior in number.

Certificate awarded Corp. Robert Gaston on July, 1918, for actions taken against enemy that month
(Courtesy of Kathy Scott)

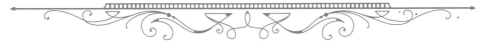

STOPPED BY THE CLOCK

Lt. Ronald G. Knapp arrived in France too late to fly in the war.
(Photo courtesy of Ruth Knapp Gieschen)

Only a few hours earlier, and Ronald Glenn Knapp might have fulfilled his desire to fly a combat airplane as a Second Lieutenant in the American Army Air Corps. He even had his orders in his hands waiting for a specific assignment. But that dream ended when an important paper was signed at 11 A.M. on November 11, 1918. It contained the terms of the Armistice, which was mainly a cessation of fighting, between the Allies and the Central Powers. Germany was the significant signatory, as Austria and Bulgaria had already surrendered. All combat actions stopped then.

He had arrived in France only a few days before, ready for action. Mixed feelings of disappointment, and perhaps, relief, filled him at this last minute cancellation of his ambitions. For the two sides, four terrible years had passed with more than 9,000,000 combatants killed when the fighting finally stopped. There were more than 37,000,000 casualties including killed, wounded and missing in action. This is 57% of the 65,000,000 men mobilized by both the Allies and Central Powers (www.historylearningsite.uk) Lieutenant Knapp enlisted August 8, 1918, in the Cadet Air Service at Ellington Field, Texas, with the rank of Second Lieutenant. Important requirements included character references and scholarship, and he had a handful of them, testifying to his worthiness as a potential pilot. He was a 24 year old junior at Cornell University when he enlisted at Garden City, New York, near Port Byron, Cayuga County, N. Y. This also was the place of his birth on June 14, 1893.

His training at Ellington Field, Texas, an advanced flight training base, consisted of practicing aerial gunnery and becoming familiar with a bombing range. Both sites were located on a small peninsula in the Gulf of Mexico near San Leon, Texas. His opinion of France, once he arrived, was that it was "one muddy h--- – hole." No doubt other Americans shared his reaction.

The United States had no air corps before the beginning of World War 1, just a few planes and pilots. Some planes had been used in the punitive action against the Mexican guerilla, Pancho Villa. From these few experiences, Congress realized how far behind the United States had fallen with respect to what the European powers possessed in terms of aircraft. At that time, an American who wanted to fly a military airplane, had to go to France or England to train and then fly. After enough Americans had been trained and were flying under French command, they formed the famed "Lafayette Escadrille." Other Americans enlisted in the English Royal Air Corps. For several years all Americans flew under the command of either the French or the English before the United States entered the war.

Soon after America joined the war, the American military also recognized, that in addition to aerial reconnaissance, the airplane could be used as an offensive weapon by attacking the enemy with machine guns or bombs. Before the end of the war in November, 1918, the American military decided they needed to build their own air corps. At Ellington Field alone, there were about 5,000 men serving in various capacities and 250 aircraft available for training and practice. Lieutenant Knapp continued his training until he was discharged February 12, 1919, at the Air Service Depot, Garden City, Long Island, New York. He married in 1920, and re-enrolled in Cornell University where he obtained his B.S. and M.S. degrees. He joined his father in the Knapp Fruit Orchard business outside Port Byron.

This story is told by his daughter, Ruth Knapp Gieschen, Lees Summit, Missouri. Although his military flying days were over, Lieutenant Knapp never lost his zeal to serve his country. He stayed in the air corps reserves for many years. Knapp was a proud booster of the American Legion, and worked to get benefits he believed the veterans deserved. He died May 31, 1976, and is buried in a family plot in Mount Pleasant Cemetery, Port Byron, N. Y. He was one month short of being 83.

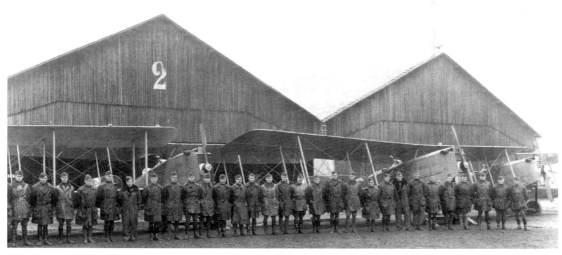

2nd Aeronautical Flying Unit – Squadron was located "somewhere in France.
(Photo courtesy of Ruth Knapp Gieschen)

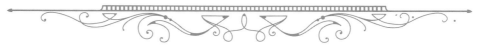

TAKE TO THE SKIES OR STAY ON THE GROUND?

Lt. Frederick Lovell Simonin
(Photo courtesy of Ann Richards)

Frederick Lovell Simonin enlisted in the Signal Corps, not to wave signal flags, but to learn to fly an airplane because at that time, aviation was classified as part of the Signal Corps. On March 23, 1916, a full year before America declared war on Germany, hundreds of young men were hurrying to recruiting offices to fill the aviation training openings that Congress had just authorized and funded. The army had begun to recognize the effectiveness of the airplane in conducting a war and wanted to build the aviation section. Frederick was one of those eager young men. His granddaughter, Ann Richards, Harrisburg, Oregon, tells his story.

The new Aviation Section grew from a force of 60 officers and 260 enlisted men in 1914 to 297 officers and a reserve of 2,000 Enlisted Signal Corps troops in 1916. This was when Frederick interrupted his studies at the University of Pennsylvania to accept a commission as a 2nd Lieutenant in the new corps. As part of his aviation training, he attended the Georgia Institute of Technology at the United States Army School of Aeronautics.

The Aviation Section was a new creation of the military, and its curriculum and a training schedule had to be developed immediately. Materials were written and implemented by Colonel Townsend Foster Dodd, who was considered one of the "original military aviators" listed by the War Department in 1913. (http://firstaerosquadron.org/first_aviators.html)

Colonel Dodd's experience was minimal due to the few times the United States had used airplanes in combat. He had taken part in aerial combat during the brief Vera Cruz incident in 1914. Two years later in 1916 he was part of the "Punitive Expedition" led by Gen. John J.

Pershing which pursued Pancho Villa into Mexico. On the basis of such limited experience, Dodd was assigned to produce the training manuals used at Carlstrom Field, Florida, where Frederick was based.

While Frederick was training in Florida, his first wife, Gladys, died of the influenza in 1918. This left Frederick with the care of their eight year old son, Charles Frederick. The father had orders to be shipped overseas soon. However, the military had a ruling prohibiting a parent to leave an orphaned child behind. Immediately his overseas orders were cancelled.

Frederick, who had enlisted for four years, spent his time training others and practicing flying at various air bases in the States. He reached the rank of First Lieutenant before his discharge from active duty on February 4, 1919. He had two more years of duty as a reserve officer, but he decided to extend it by serving in the air reserve for another 13 years before retiring. He spent those years training pilots and flying newer versions of planes at various air bases in the United States.

He married again, to another Gladys. They had two children, Suzanne and Robert. Numerous military papers left with the family when he passed away tell of his years with the air corps. Some of the papers related to the difficulty he had in obtaining his military pension. This problem was one that many other servicemen experienced. Frederick died September 16, 1964, and was buried in his home town of Philadelphia, Pennsylvania.

Even though he missed the experience of flying in combat, Frederick witnessed many important changes to the airplane. He also contributed to the development of the Aviation Section, especially in pilot training. The airplane had evolved in only two years from performing air observation duties to its new role as a fighter plane. A year after that, it became capable of making bomb attacks in the battles of St. Mihiel, Meuse-Argonne, and Verdun. It became a part of the offensive army of the army.

The Signal Corps in the 1930's would advance the invention of radar to play an entirely different role in military strategy during and after World War 1. The Signal Corps and the aviation arm were divided into two separate branches in 1947 after World War II, because their roles in the military became totally different. Frederick may have longed to be one of the early fighting pioneers of the sky, but his 19 years of service on the ground helped bring many innovations and new ideas to the Air Force.

For some air men, their job "was to fly like eagles," for others, it was to "keep your feet on the ground." The two phrases accurately describe Frederick's service to his country.

ANTI-AIRCRAFT GUNS

In 1914 Vickers developed a "pom-pom" anti-aircraft gun for the British. The British also planned to build anti-aircraft towers around nine ports in defense against attacks by the German Zeppelins. AA batteries attached to searchlights were set up around the edges of London. The royal Navy adapted field guns to fire in the air, as did the Germans. These tactics eventually stopped the Zeppelin raids in 1916.

(Eight WWI weapons invented)

A GOOD MECHANIC — FRANK SPURRIER

Lives of pilots in World War I depended upon the skills and knowledge of the mechanics who serviced the small fragile crafts that soared in the sky. And sometimes, it was solely a master mechanic's intuition that provided the answer to a problem that needed fixing. There were no repair manuals then.

Pvt. Frank Spurrier was considered one of the best mechanics at any airfield. Pilots who had him service their plane considered themselves to be lucky. His only child, Dr. Marjorie Sirridge, of Kansas City, Missouri, tells the story of her father. Frank was born in 1888 in Fairfield, Iowa, and had to leave high school early. However, he was able to get a job at a local garage learning to repair cars. At that the time Americans owned over four million cars, compared to the world's combined total of only about 750,000. Cars needed mechanics, and Frank, a farm boy, was eager to learn all he could about the various kinds of motor vehicles. (Chronology Wall – NWWIM)

The plane the Wright brothers invented in 1903 signaled the beginning of the air age, improvements came rapidly. However, flying was still a relatively new experience in 1914 when the war started. The care and maintenance of these planes were unfamiliar to both pilot and mechanic. There were no training schools for pilots, and no repair manuals available for mechanics. Learning the job as a mechanic required mostly having a combination of good common sense, familiarity with tools, and an awareness of the principles of how machines operate. Frank eagerly accepted the challenge to become a good mechanic.

In earlier years on the farm, Frank had enjoyed fixing the few mechanical tools the farm owned. He was especially interested in the tractor and how it worked. Unable to graduate from high school because he had to get a job to help support his mother, he convinced a local mechanic to hire him. Some years later, when he was 29 and the United States declared war on Germany, Frank volunteered for the Army. This was his opportunity.

When Private Spurrier arrived at an unnamed French airfield (censorship forbade him mentioning the name) in 1917, he was probably among the first American mechanics to service the planes American pilots were flying. They flew either French or English planes until near the war's end, when the American airplane industry Americans finally geared up to produce planes. About 60 American-made planes were ready to be shipped to Europe for the AEF when the Armistice was signed November 11.

Frank knew the principles of mechanics and had excellent skills working with tools. It was his imagination and sense of aviation principles that enabled him to be able to maintain and repair the different makes of airplanes. He had to know the strengths and weaknesses of each plane; which motor required its own exact blending of oil and gasoline; and which engine would cut out in a steep dive. The planes were made by various factories and each plane had its differences.

Unknown to friends and family back home, Frank had secretly married Miss Fannie Watson two months before he enlisted. So it was a great surprise when, in 1919, only two weeks after he returned from France, they announced their second wedding anniversary!

As was customary with many veterans, Frank rarely talked later about his days at war. It was only in his older years, that he began to tell some stories, especially about French friends he had known. He had one army friend who became a lifelong friend, and they corresponded for years. Frank's daughter, Marjorie Sirridge, became close friends with the friend's daughter. The girls visited each other, but the two men never saw each other after the war. Letters were the links to their friendship.

Frank's two years in France taught him how to check over a plane that just landed, refuel it, tighten the wires that held the wings in place, and prepare it for the pilot to hop in and take off. All this was done in a matter of a few minutes. The pilots, on a good weather day, operated on a tight time schedule and made repeated flights that day. The fatigue from constant flights may have affected some of the pilots and been a cause that hastened their deaths.

These flimsy planes with wing span of about 22 feet played a vital role in the conduct of war. No ground officer wanted to start an attack without knowing the observations the pilot made about the enemy's position and size. Aircraft was replacing the cavalry as a scouting unit. Pilots knew Frank's skill would enable them to fly a well serviced plane and complete that important reconnaissance report.

After the war he took a position with the Kingman, Kansas Municipal Light Plant. Later he was offered a promotion to superintendent of the Kingman plant. That was his position up to his unexpected death on May 5, 1950, when he accidentally came into contact with a powerful electrical cable carrying 13,200 volts of electricity. It was ironic that Frank, with his skills as an aircraft mechanic that undoubtedly saved the lives of many pilots, would die in such a tragic accident.

He was born in 1888 in Fairfield, Iowa, died at age 62, and was buried in Kingman, Kansas. Frank was one of the men who made flying safer for American pilots who took to the skies in a well maintained plane.

HERE COME THE MARINES — U. S. MARINES ENTER WAR

In two well known battles the United States Marine Corps established a reputation that continues today. At Belleau Wood and Chateau Thierry the Marines fought side by side with the American Second Division, but it was the ferocious fighting of the Marines that attracted the attention of newspaper reporters, and thus the world at large.

The Fifth and Sixth Marine Regiments were said to have bested the Germans by using "hand to hand fighting, nets, even their teeth" to such an extent that the Germans applied the name of "Devil Dogs" or "Teufelhunde" (in German) to them. This statement cannot be verified, other than as hearsay, although the popular literature repeats the story time after time.

This honor permits all current and future members of the 5th and 6th Marine Regiments to wear the special braided cord wrapped around the left shoulder. It is called by the French name, "le fourragere." In addition to this signal honor, seven Marines received the United States Congressional Medal of Honor for their service in World War I. (www.wwvets.com/marines.html)

Although the Marines are a separate service branch, they are attached to the Navy to use as land troops for special operations. Other duties include: To control minor incidents that could become disruptions; handle cyber command; assist civilians after hurricanes or other natural disasters; provide security for embassies; provide the Presidential Support Squad; and make amphibious landings in any place or climate.

The Marine Corps was established November 10, 1775, and has served in every war that the United States has participated in. From 1900-1940 their assignments were limited to small wars and counterinsurgencies. (hqmc.marines.mil) The saying, "Watch out, here comes a Marine," is taken seriously by other service men and bystanders. When the Marines come, everyone soon finds out they are serious minded about their assignment.

NOTE: Before World War II, only army personnel were eligible for the Purple Heart, except those Marine units attached to army units, as was the situation at Belleau Wood. Those wounded Marines therefore qualified for the medal. Approximately 75,000 Purple Hearts were issued before 1941, the majority going to World War I veterans.

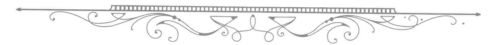

SOME FAMOUS NAMES
of
PERSONS WHO SERVED IN WORLD WAR I
(ranging from movie stars to leaders in the military and in the arts and religion)

Humphrey Bogart, movie star • Walt Disney, movie producer
Charles deGaulle, president of France • Ernest Hemingway, author
Bella Lugosi, movie star • Fritz Kreisler, concert violinist
F. Scott Fitzgerald, author • Walter Brennan, movie star
Field Marshall Montgomery, Commander British Forces in WWII
General George Patton, Commander US 3rd Army, WWII
General Douglas MacArthur, Commander, US Forces in Pacific, WWII
Harry Truman, 33rd U.S. President
General Rommel, German Commander, WWII
Fiorello LaGuardia, Mayor of New York • Pope John XXIII
Adolf Hitler, dictator of Nazi Germany
and
Benito Mussollini, dictator of Facist Italy, WWII.
(World War One – A Peculiar History)

VICTOR CANDLIN, A "DEVIL DOG," AND HIS GOLD STAR MOTHER

Victor Candlin, who died in war at age 20 with French medals:
le "fourrege" on left and Croix de Guerre with oak leaf cluster on right.
(Courtesy of Elaine Joselyn)

As already noted, the name "Devil Dogs" is reputedly what the Germans called the Marines who opposed them at the battle for Belleau Wood. The name came from their courageous response that was "like a bulldog" or "Teufelshunde," in German. One of those Marines was Private Victor Gladstone Candlin from the 6th Marine Regiment. Fighting alongside the 5th Marine Regiment the Marines showed the ferocity and tenacity it took to clear out the Germans in control of the area. Out of respect for their courage and their responding "like a bulldog", the Germans named them "Teufelshunde'" meaning "Devil Dogs."

The French also honored the Marines by renaming the area, "Bois de la brigade de Marines," meaning "The Marine Brigade Woods." The experienced German troops, some of Germany's prized soldiers, admired the spirit of these untried troops, even though it meant the Germans had to give up the area they had held for almost four years. The direction of the war was turning, and some five months later, it would end in victory for the Allies.

The 5th and 6th Regiments advanced to other fierce battles at Chateau-Thierry, Somme Py, Blanc Mont, St. Mihiel, and ended by fighting in the Meuse-Argonne sector. Victor's story, told by his great – niece, Dr. Elaine Joslyn, Kansas City, Missouri, was handed down to her by relatives. Victor was 20 years old, and a Marine through and through. His character was rated "excellent". It was at Belleau Wood, where the famous Marine challenge was issued by Captain Lloyd Williams, who when told to retreat, exclaimed, "Retreat, Hell. We just got here." (Asprey)

Side by side with the 5th Marine Regiment, the 6th was attached to the AEF Second Infantry Division. They were there as immediate responders to the infantry's call for "help from the Marines." The Fifth Marine Regiment had 2,824 officers and men, and the Sixth Marine Regiment had slightly more at 2,901. In addition, the Sixth Machine Gun Battalion of 809 officers and men had been assigned to the fight. The Second Division had about 25,000 troops but the Marines had an advantage with the 1903 Springfield rifles they used. These fine rifles enabled them to be such excellent shots that they could hit targets at 600 yards with a maximum range of 3500 yards. It was also recorded that in addition to their machine guns, they engaged in hand to hand fighting.

The Fifth and Sixth Marine Regiments were cited at least three times by the French army, making them eligible for the French award, le "fourragere," and three Croix de Guerre. All Marines today in those two regiments are entitled to wear le "fourragere" on their dress uniform as a result of the actions of their World War I predecessors.

However, the price in casualties was high. During the month of June, 1,062 Marines were killed and 7,252 wounded. These numbers came from the fighting at Hill 142; in the villages of Bouresches and Vaux; and in Belleau Wood, where unknown German machine gun nests were hidden among the dense woods and big rocks. These are the first four of eight battles involving the Marines. At least four Congressional Medals of Honor were awarded in these battles. (Asprey)

According to official Marine records Victor was wounded on October 8, 1918, on the Champagne Front, north of the village of Somme Py near the city of Reims and the strategic Blanc Mont Ridge. The nearby beautiful old Reims cathedral had previously been badly damaged by the Germans. The Marines began fearsome attacks on October 3, the first day of the Blanc Mont campaign. The Fifth and Sixth Marine Regiments were closely involved in those attacks along with more than 54,000 AEF Infantry soldiers during the first part of the battle. It lasted slightly more than two hours, and ended with the Germans still controlling the western ridge of Blanc Mont. More fighting continued until October 9, when the Americans were finally victorious in driving out the Germans. Blanc Mont Ridge and its chalky ground was in Allied hands now, and Victor fought until almost the last day of its capture.

Severely wounded, Victor died on October 17, 1918 in a hospital. The cause was noted as "death gunshot wound" (GSW). (Marine Corps Records.) His grave is in the Meuse-Argonne Cemetery. He was buried temporarily at other sites because the Meuse-Argonne cemetery was not built until years later. Of course, there were many times when the Army's rule of quick burial could not be obeyed, and dead bodies of both Allies and Germans littered the fields for days. His records indicate that he was rated "Excellent" as to his character.

His mother, Clara, was devastated by the death of the youngest of her eight children. She lived in the small town of Greeley, Colorado, and after the announcement of his death, she was presented a small pennant with a gold star. This indicated she was a mother of a soldier who died in the war. She previously probably had a pennant with a blue star, signifying a living soldier. Later, Mrs. Candlin became a member of the newly formed Gold Star Mothers Association, officially organized in 1928 after years of planning.

The main goal of the organization was to allow mothers, at government expense, to visit the graves of their sons in Europe. Mrs. Candlin worked in the organization which petitioned Congress in 1927. Successfully achieving their goal, the pilgrimages for the mothers began in 1930. (See story on "Gold Star Mothers," page 53.) These pilgrimages were emotional and heartbreaking, not only for the mothers when they found the graves, but for all who witnessed the events. However, the visit enabled many mothers to find closure to the death of their son or daughter.

Dr. Elaine treasures an object handed down to her that belonged to her great-uncle. It is a child's rocking chair from the early 1900's, one that Victor had sat in. She has placed a doll from that time period in the chair as a remembrance of her great-uncle. He was the young heroic Marine she never knew. She donated all the papers and the passport used by Mrs. Candlin to the National World War I Museum in Kansas City, where they will be preserved for research and possible display. Victor's sister was Elaine's grandmother, Fannymaude Louise, who married John Welsh. They lived in Colorado and had a daughter, also named Fannymaude, and a son, Robert

Everett Welsh, Elaine's father. He served in the Navy in World War II patrolling the Aleutian Islands and Alaska.

In the fall of 2014, Dr. Elaine and her husband, David Joselyn, visited Victor's grave and paid their own homage to her unknown but beloved great uncle. (Note: The writer had the opportunity to visit the grave site of Victor and place a small rose-bush by his white marble cross for the family. See photo on page 51.

MORE INFORMATION ABOUT THE MARINES

©International Film Service.
MARINE CORPS INSIGNIA.
The above photograph shows the insignia worn on the arm and cap by all marine men. "Always Faithful" is the translation (meaning) of the Latin inscription shown on the ribbon.
(Photo Courtesy the USMC)

1. Here is an explanation of the Marine insignia of an eagle atop the globe, which is wrapped with an anchor. The eagle on top symbolizes the United States. The globe showing the Western Hemisphere refers to Marines serving in all parts of the world. The "foul" (a specific type) anchor refers to the navy of which the Marines are a part. It was officially adopted in 1868.

2. Iron Mike – The nickname of a statue of the World War I Marine, located in front of the old post headquarters, now the Marine Corps Museum, in Quantico. There is also a statue of Iron Mike in the forest near Verdun. It is made of beautiful black marble.

3. Semper Fidelis – means "Always Faithful," and is the Marine Corps motto. "That the Marines have lived up to this motto is proven by the fact there has never been a mutiny in the Corps."

4. Marine Colors – are scarlet and gold and were selected by General John A. Lejeune, the 13th Commandant, who also served in World War I as a commander of the Army's 2nd Division participating in the early Marine campaigns. The color of forest green is the unofficial color of the corps.

5. Quatrefoil – The cross shaped braid atop the barracks covers of the hat of the Marine Officers is of French origin and has been worn ever since 1859. Its first use is remembered as being a way for Marines in the masts of ships to distinguish their officers from the sailors during a sea battle. (Conner)

Grave site of Victor Candlin in Meuse – Argonne Cemetery
(Photo Courtesy the USMC)

CASUALTY RATES AMONG NATIONS

- *65 percent of Australians serving in the war were killed or wounded, the highest proportion among any nation.(World War One Facts)*
- 11 per cent of France's entire population (which includes civilians) were killed or wounded in the Great War. (World War One Facts)
- Of British troops who were casualities, 58% were wounded by artillery shells; 40% killed by rifle or machine gun fire; 1 percent killed by bayonets. (Office of Medical History)
- The Marines at Belleau Wood suffered 55% casualties with 1,062 deaths and 3,615 wounded.
- The 2nd Division had much lower losses of 743 dead and 3,637 wounded. (USMC)
- In early 1915 German zeppelins made frequent raids on London, and total resulting deaths by the war's end were 2000 civilians. The first raid on Paris on March 21, 1915, killed 23 civilians and injured 30. In 1916 the British had developed new incendiary bullets which could pierce the outer skin of the Zeppelin and cause the inner gas bags to leak and catch fire. A British pilot, William Leefe-Robinson, became an instant hero when he shot down the first dirigible over Britain on September 2, 1916.

(World War One – A Very Peculiar War) and *(the firstworldwar.com)*

UNITED STATES OF AMERICA

———

WAR DEPARTMENT,

WASHINGTON, D. C.

This is the OFFICIAL CERTIFICATE OF IDENTIFI-
CATION for the War Mothers and Widows Pilgrimage
to Europe in 1931, issued by THE SECRETARY OF WAR.

Clara Candlin

has been granted Government Transportation to
Europe and is entitled to this Certificate in accord-
ance with special regulations issued by THE SECRE-
TARY OF WAR.

J. L. DEWITT,
The Quartermaster General.

R. E. Shannon

DESCRIPTION OF BEARER

Residence _1110 Tenth St, Greeley, Colo._
Date of birth _June 3, 1855_
Place of birth _England_
Age _____ years; Sex _Female_
Height _5_ ft _0_ in.; Weight _____ lbs.
Hair _Grey_ Eyes _Blue_
Complexion _____
Scars, etc. _____
Occupation _____

(Signature of bearer)

Passport used by Clara Candlin on gold Star Mother trip to France
(Courtesy of Elaine Joslyn)

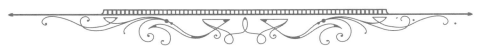

Almost 80,000 British women served as ambulance drivers, cooks, and auxiliary nurses. After 1915 they were allowed near the front lines if they were 23 years old or older.

Dorothy Lawrence disguised herself as a man and joined a tunneling company, but her identity was discovered when she fell ill. As a British journalist 20 years old, she was forbidden to write about her experiences.

Another Englishwoman, Flora Sandes, joined the Serbian Red Cross as a nurse. Then she joined a Serbian fighting unit and fought the Austrians, but was wounded. Later promoted to Sergeant Major, she became a hero to the Serbians.

A Russian woman, Maria Bochkareva, with permission from the czar, formed "The Battalion of Death," which fought from the beginning of the war. Maria was wounded twice and decorated for bravery three times. Captured by the Bolsheviks, she was shot by a firing squad on May 16, 1920, for having been a soldier in the czar's army.
(World War One – A Very Peculiar History)

A GOLD STAR MOTHER'S TALE

(above left) Private Roy Richardson, 139th Infantry, 35th Division, died in World War I.
(bottom left) Medallion presented to mothers who participated in the 1930 trip to France to see the graves of their sons.
(right) Margaret Richardson stands at the grave of her son, Roy Richardson, on a trip in 1930 with Gold Star Mothers sponsored by the U.S. government. (Photos Courtesy Nancy Arthur)

The words, "after Grandma's trip" or "before her trip," were how time and place were measured in the Richardson household. The word, "time," referred to Grandma's trip in 1930 to France as a Gold Star Mother. She went with hundreds of other Gold Star Mothers to see the graves where their sons were buried after they died in World War I. The grave Grandma wanted to see was that of Roy, her oldest child.

After she returned from the trip, she would not, or perhaps, could not, talk about what she saw, or how she felt. She and other mothers were like many soldiers in that respect. The soldiers rarely told their families about their war related experiences. Grandma was Margaret Richardson, and it is her granddaughter, Nancy Arthur, Raymore, Missouri, who relates this story.

After visiting the cemetery where Roy was buried, Grandma seemed never to recover from the trip. Perhaps, actually seeing the gravestone verifying his death, made her accept that the notification of his death was true. For many years before, she may have hoped the telegram announcing his death had been a mistake.

"Grandma was never the same after the trip. All she told us was about her roommate on the ship, who was a mother from Portland, Oregon," Nancy Arthur explained. Her grandparents lived on a farm near Odin, Illinois, with their four other living children. They were Ralph, Ruby, Reba and Ruth, who was Nancy's mother. Nancy and Grandma "were very close," she adds, but she never recalled Grandma talking about her trip to see Uncle Roy's grave.

Nancy has vivid recollections about life on the farm. There was no electricity, so they had a large battery to power their radio. Frequently they had to take the battery into a nearby town to get it recharged. The farm also had two wells in which they cooled food. They put milk and butter in one well and watermelons in the other. Nancy loved to spend time on the farm with her grandparents. Nancy was born and lived in nearby Centralia, Illinois, where her grandparents moved in their later years to be with her family. If Grandma starting to tell about something, it always began by her saying first: "After my trip…" or "before my trip." That was Grandma's way of measuring the time when events happened.

Grandma had kept a diary about the trip which Nancy once had the opportunity to read. It was mostly about the gourmet food Grandma had on the trip. There was nothing about seeing the grave stone. That stone was the evidence that Roy would never come back. Did Grandma continue to deny Roy's passing, her granddaughter wonders. Grandma wouldn't speak about it, nor could she even privately write about it. The diary unfortunately disappeared during Nancy's latest move to another apartment. Nancy keeps the hope she will find it someday. Men were not allowed to go on these trips sponsored and paid for by the government. "But Grandpa was never the same either, for he took up smoking," Nancy added, "and never quit."

Although a group of American Legionnaires and their families had made a similar trip in 1927, they were not officially sponsored by the government. Until then, the government had not allowed families to visit the cemeteries. They did give the family a choice of leaving the body in France or bringing it home for reburial in a place of their choice. About half the families left the bodies in France where they had been buried, the rest chose to have the bodies brought home which the government did.

THE FORMING OF THE GOLD STAR MOTHERS ASSOCIATION

Grace Darling Siebold, founder of the Gold Star Mothers Association, in trying to overcome the grief created by her son's death in the war, started visiting wounded veterans in the Washington, D.C. area where she lived. There she also found other grieving mothers. She convinced them to provide assistance to wounded soldiers who were hospitalized far from their homes. The body of her son, Lieutenant George V. Siebold, an aviator, was never found. He had been shot down in his plane just several weeks before the war ended. (Heiman) and (American Gold Stars Mothers)

The idea was born of forming a group of mothers whose sons were killed in the war. The group took its name from the Gold Star pennant that was given each family when a death occurred. The Gold Star pennant replaced the Blue Star pennant the family received when the young person signed up for service. The Gold Star Mothers was started in 1928 and officially incorporated in 1929.

Legislation authorized by Congress resulted from the lobbying done by the Association and other groups. The summer of 1930 saw 230 widows and mothers sail to France to visit the cemeteries where their sons were buried. Meanwhile, families of soldiers who died of disease while serving in France were offered the choice of having the body returned home or remain in the cemetery where he was buried. The organization is still active today with at least 150 chapters across the United States and a membership of 10,000 to 11,000. There are 60 active chapters which include husbands. (Budreau)

(This is a copy of the letter sent to permit Mrs. Richardson to make the Gold Star Mother pilgrimage.)

WAR DEPARTMENT
Office of the Quartermaster General
WASHINGTON

March 21, 1923.

Mr. W.T. Richardson
  R.F.D. #1
   Odin, Ill.

Dear Sir:

The Quartermaster General desires that you be informed that the permanent grave of the late Private 1/c Roy R. Richardson, Company F, 139th Infantry, is Grave 40, Row 25, Block G, Meuse-Argonne American Cemetery, Romagne-sous-Montfaucon, Department of Meuse, France.

This is one of the permanent American military cemeteries to be maintained by this Government in Europe. Each grave will be marked by a headstone of white marble, of suitable design, with name, rank, division organization, date of soldier's death and State from which he came. The headstones will be placed at all graves in connection with the improvement work now in progress, as soon as possible and without waiting for special action or request on the part of the relatives.

In effecting removal, the utmost care and reverence were exacted and more than willingly accorded by those performing this sacred duty. The grave of the deceased will be perpetually maintained by this Government in a manner befitting the last resting place of our heroes.

Very truly yours.
(signed) H. J. Conner, Asst.

ROLE OF THE YOUNG MEN'S CHRISTIAN ASSOCIATION IN WORLD WAR I

Soldiers depositing money in banks operated by YMCA in France
(National Archives)

Shortly after American soldiers' feet touched French soil, they were followed by the feet of hundreds of workers from the Young Men's Christian Association. These workers were prepared to set up numerous facilities so soldiers would have a place to go and relax when not serving on the front lines. The YMCA had begun its wartime work in the American Civil War of 1861-1865 and served again in the Spanish-American War of 1898.

On the day the United States officially declared war against Germany, the head of the International YMCA notified President Wilson of its intention to provide services. Fund raising campaigns began in which six other welfare groups participated. Eventually the seven organizations raised a total of $192 million dollars. In today's money, that is more than two billion dollars. (Measuring Worth.) And this was just the beginning of fund raising by these groups.

People rushed to apply for positions with the "Y", as it was commonly called. From over two million applications, a total of 25,926 workers were chosen to fill jobs at home and abroad. About 20 % of the jobs were reserved for women with most of these jobs slated for abroad. In the United States the YMCA operated canteens at training camps; helped soldiers traveling to camps or overseas; and assisted wounded men in hospitals. The YMCA workers also assisted groups of entertainers in the United States and France, or provided the entertainment themselves, if they had the training and experience to sing or dance. In some canteens, movies were shown every night, or as often as available. Even the most boring of movies was a welcome relief from the occasional inactivity of trench life or constant danger of enemy night patrols.

It was excitement, adventure, and a genuine caring for the "wellbeing of our brave soldiers" that energized most workers. The desire to provide for men's needs in a Christian atmosphere was uppermost, especially among the young women volunteers. Many wrote home how easy it was for a soldier to fall in love with them. But the girls recognized the men were homesick and weary, as they sometimes were themselves, so few romances flourished. Besides, the rules were strict.

Officially, the duties of YMCA workers were to "provide recreation, library services, Bible study, and religious services." In numerous canteens, often consisting of only a small hut or even a tent, the women served hot chocolate and donuts to raise the spirits of tired, dirty, and cold soldiers. They provided thousands of sheets of stationery with the Y's red triangle logo. (Kautz Family Archives) Sometimes the workers wrote letters for illiterate soldiers or hospitalized service men too wounded or ill to write. Reading and writing lessons were provided in the more safely located canteens where classrooms could be set up. For all these services and more, the soldiers highly praised the YMCA workers, and many letters expressed gratitude for the "Y" making available a place where the soldiers could go for recreation.

The YMCA agreed to operate the Post Exchange for the army and sell personal necessities as well as candy and cigarettes. It was in this capacity that the organization received some criticism. Some soldiers complained, saying prices were too high, and the operators were making a big profit. The troops had assumed that some items were free, but that was not the situation. The soldiers were charged for those items instead, thus providing a source for complaints. After the war many of these complaints were investigated. While a few allegations proved true, for the most part, the YMCA was declared to be guiltless of the accusations.

In addition to working with AEF troops, the YMCA also provided services for prisoners of war on both sides. The "Y" stayed in Europe several more years after the war ended, not leaving until after the Army of German Occupation disbanded. The last soldiers were shipped home in 1923.

YMCA workers carrying supplies to troops in the field
(National Archives)

SOME ACCOMPLISHMENTS of THE YMCA:

Opened and operated: 26 R&R leave centers, 1,500 canteens, 4,000 "huts", 2 million AEF soldiers were served.

Other activities: 80,000 scholarships awarded to veterans, 5 million POWs on both sides were provided with humanitarian services.

Casualties: 33 YMCA workers, 29 men and 4 women died in the war. (The Service of the YMCA and Red Cross in WWI)

MILITARY AWARDS:

319 citations and decorations, including French "Legion d'Honneur," Order of the British Empire, and the U.S. Distinguished Service Cross, and Distinguished Service Medal.
(The Service of the YMCA and Red Cross in WWI)

Although some soldiers were lucky to receive a pass until midnight to visit the nearest village and enjoy themselves, for others, nighttime meant there were dangerous duties to perform. That was when night patrols were made by both sides. Night also was when teams of stretcher bearers crawled across shell holes, dead horses, broken rifles, and shattered bodies of both friend and enemy. Darkness provided the opportunity to bring in the wounded lying in open sites dangerous to reach in daylight. The medics could only hope the soldiers were still alive and had not died from shock or loss of blood or limbs.

Some soldiers were beyond anyone's help if they fell or slid down slimy banks of great craters. The weight of their gear and the height of the crater made it impossible for them to climb out. Unless some of their men came along with ropes and harnesses, they were doomed to die, suffocating in the deep pool of mud. Often they begged their comrades to shoot them and put them out of their misery. Would it be considered a Good Samaritan act or would it be murder?

It was rare that an American had the moral will or strength of mind required to provide that "coup de grace." One story tells about an American officer who saw a young German soldier with half his face shot off begging for relief. The captain tried to shoot but couldn't end the German's misery. His sergeant then took the officer's pistol and performed the shot.

(World War One, A Very Peculiar War)

"MR. TIPTON, MEET CAPTAIN WHITE"

Rejected by the Army for vision problems, Charles M. Tipton, Sr. was determined to serve his country in some capacity in World War I. He found a position that often took him near the front lines, but the weapons he used for his service differed from those of the soldier. His job with the Young Men's Christian Association, was to address the fatigue and distress of soldiers visiting his facilities. He did this by extending a kind heart, a cup of coffee, donuts, stationery, and reading materials. Sometimes the troops attended lectures or religious services he provided.

The YMCA, also known as the "Y," was assigned the duty of maintaining soldiers' morale and opening their hearts to salvation. Over 25,000 American civilians were employed by the "Y," both stateside and overseas during 1917-1919. Mr. Tipton's official title was Business Director of the "Y" team assigned to the AEF's 78th Division. This division would see much action in the few months before the Armistice was signed. They fought in Alsace-Lorraine, St. Mihiel, and the Meuse-Argonne up to the exact day and hour of the signing.

During his work of providing rest and recreation for the 78th Division, Mr. Tipton became acquainted with a Captain Wellstood W. White, who commanded the 303rd Artillery Munitions Unit, 78th Division. His men had the dangerous task of delivering ammunition to the front lines. This work had special hazards, for not all accidents occurred at the front lines.

One example was when an explosion occurred while delivering the ammunition. A man in the ammunition caravan, not realizing the danger he might cause, thoughtlessly lit a match to

Captain Wellstood W. White, 78th Division, AEF
(Courtesy of Charles Tipton, PhD)

check the gasoline level of his truck. The resulting explosion demolished most of the caravan, injured many soldiers, and left Captain White with a hearing loss in one ear.

Captain White also was responsible for the moral training and morale of his troops. Here Mr. Tipton came to Captain White's rescue. In YMCA canteens with Bible lessons and "Y" stationery available for letter writing, soldiers had a safe place to relax and recuperate from the stress and noise of bombardments. This story is told by Mr. Tipton's son, Charles M. Tipton, Jr., Ph.D., Professor Emeritus of Physiology, at the University of Arizona, Tucson, Arizona. A granddaughter who is also a great niece, (by marriage, as noted later in story) Mary Elizabeth Tipton Yong, teaches elementary school and lives in Lees Summit, Missouri.

Captain White and Mr. Tipton became friends through their work assignments. Because the celebrated 78th was known as "The Lightning Division," it became the point of the wedge in major battles. This means the Division led the charge into the trenches of the enemy. This effective tactic, "the wedge," if performed correctly, usually was highly successful in winning the battles.

Both men took seriously their responsibility to strengthen the character and help maintain the morale of the courageous 78th. YMCA canteens became a place of recreation and refuge for the battle hardened troops. Soldiers found companionship with other soldiers in the friendly "Y" sites. Sometimes the canteens were located in a small building, but more often in a tent or even a dugout surrounded by sandbags.

Mr. Tipton was Business Manager for a staff serving over 25,000 soldiers in a war. In addition, because of his civilian experience in accounting, he also managed the Accounting Department also. The good will and hard work shown by Mr. Tipton and his staff were praised in a letter written by the newly promoted Major White on April 4, 1919. Because Major White and his men were one day unexpectedly scheduled to leave France for the States, he was unable to say goodbye to his wartime friend, Charles Tipton.

The letter he wrote said it all: "From all I can learn, no other Division in the A.E.F. (sic) received such good "Y" service. I thank you again…" Major White was going home, while his friend, Mr. Tipton, with his staff, was headed in the opposite direction to continue serving AEF troops in the Army of the Occupation in Germany. The men saw each other again in 1919 at Major White's home in Maryland. Mr. Tipton spent some time there recuperating from the rigors of his job with the "Y" in France and Germany. He possibly was experiencing what was then called "shell shock," from the symptoms he exhibited. However, besides receiving healing and relaxation, he also found a bride in Major White's younger sister, Mary Louise White.

They were married in 1923, and lived in Evanston, Illinois, where they had four children. What had started as a casual wartime friendship between two men, ended up becoming an important family relationship as the two men became relatives. Little could they have guessed in 1918 what would be the outcome of their friendship.

"Captain White, meet Mr. Charles M. Tipton of the YMCA."

"Mr. Tipton, meet Captain White of the 78th Division, AEF"

(Mr. Tipton's son says his father's symptoms were more typical of what is known today as Chronic Fatigue Syndrome.)

COFFEE, TEA OR CHOCOLATE?
The Story of Frances Gulick and Other Volunteers

The soft, high-pitched voice asking the soldier what was his preference came from a woman. A woman, but not a nurse, was near the front lines. The woman was dressed in a dark bluish gray uniform with a hat and muffler bundling her against the winter wind. She was one of more than 5,000 women hired by the Young Men's Christian Association (YMCA) to staff their canteens in parts of France. (American Legion Monthly.)

The YMCA canteens or "huts" served thousands of soldiers daily in a variety of ways. Not just mixing hot chocolate and passing out cigarettes, but teaching illiterate soldiers the rudiments of reading and writing. Other duties included sewing on buttons and service stripes; writing letters for soldiers; or checking up on their families at home if the soldier believed they might be experiencing problems. The list goes on.

At this time the military had no provision for anyone other than chaplains to care for either the spiritual or moral needs of service men. The "Y," as it was popularly called, attempted to alleviate these needs through offering reading material and pamphlets; lectures on health and safety; and religious literature and services. The Y staff worked in "canteens." The buildings in time became a general store for soldiers, or post offices, gyms, clubs or theaters.

There were at least 4000 huts and tents designated for religious services. Canteens and post exchanges numbered more than 1500. Although these latter two were operated under policies and restrictions established by the Army, there were the usual complaints. The canteens sold razor blades, tooth paste and other personal items. Overcharging for items, or requiring soldiers to pay for items the soldiers thought should be free of charge were the most common complaints. These complaints were investigated after the war and most proved to be groundless. But even the good intentions and actions of the Y staff were sometimes questioned.

"R & R" (Rest and Recuperation) were two initials dear to the heart of every serviceman. The YMCA stepped up to make these leave days restful and free from the daily routine of each soldier. The facilities of the 29 leave centers for R & R were used by nearly two million officers and enlisted men during the war. Entertainment in the form of movies was available at the canteens nearly every day. Other types of entertainment provided by nearly 1500 professional artists and musicians found a capacity audience at each performance.

For the young American woman the work as a Y volunteer provided adventure and a unique experience. Several have written about their days and months in France. One such volunteer, Frances J. Gulick, wrote about her assignment to the First Division at Gondrecourt, calling it "the worst mudhole in France," in November, 1917.

She had been transferred from Alaska where she had worked the previous two winters in a dance hall that did not sell liquor. "What would Gondrecourt be like?" she asked herself. Gondecourt was located in northern France in what was mostly the British sector, and she thought she would be meeting British soldiers and possibly some French who had seen action on the front lines. What "beneficent influences" were she and her fellow staffer, Ethel Torrance, expected to exert on these battle worn fellows?

Once she reached the camp, she learned that Gondrecourt now was a large training center for newly arrived Americans. There were few of the exhausted British who had almost three years of fighting to their credit. British and French were there, in a training capacity instead. She quickly changed her expectations and adjusted to a new set of needs from the Americans.

The men from the newly constituted American First Division were the first AEF combat soldiers to arrive in France. For this, they held an honored position throughout the war. They had been stationed in France for the longest time, and their courageous fighting helped to build the reputation of AEF soldiers. Frances Gulick formed many friendships with the men and was greatly saddened after the war to learn that so many soldiers in the First Division had been killed.

Finding shelters or places for the girls to sleep during their tour often proved difficult, calling for imagination and ingenuity. Frances slept on a pallet in the canteen by the piano until the night the Germans sent a shell through the piano. Another time she and a married couple spread their blankets in a fruit orchard and slept through a French artillery bombardment that fired over their heads. Motorcycles roared by in haste to deliver important messages, but the tired staffers slept through all the noise.

An informal rule developed that the driver of a lorry should be smoking a lighted cigarette to warn others of his presence on the road. Frances did not smoke, so she solved this problem by picking up a soldier on a pass and giving him a cigarette to light up. Her wits, good sense of humor, and these kinds of experiences made her tour in France a highlight of her life. Her Y career ended with Frances and four other friends being invited to march with the First Division in a parade in New York on September 10, 1919.

A week later on September 17, Frances and the girls joined the First Division in its last wartime parade. She said she had left "something of me (that) would belong forever to the First Division." The YMCA probably left similar feelings with many veterans. After the war ended, the YMCA recognized the need for veterans for advanced education. The veterans were offered 80,000 scholarships. This plan became the basis for the GI Bill of World War II.

As a neutral charitable organization, the Y also remembered their duty to the five million prisoners of war in POW camps maintained by both the Allies and the Central Powers. YMCA services were provided to as many prisoners as possible under the circumstances. (The Service of the YMCA and Red Cross in WWI…)

After the war ended, there were over 1.5 million AEF troops remaining in France. It took weeks to process them for shipment home. Hundreds of ships were required to transport them. In an effort to relieve the soldiers' boredom from drilling and daily duties, a military committee organized the first ever and only "Inter Allied Games."

There were 22 sports competitions in which more than 2,000 athletes entered. It was to be held in Paris, but there was no facility large enough for the 25,000 anticipated soldiers and civilians who would attend. So the YMCA donated money to build a 25,000 seat stadium and named it after General Pershing. After the games ended, it was donated to the people of Paris. This was probably the single largest expenditure of funds raised by the YMCA.

Although the volunteers did not serve on the front lines, their work often carried certain risks of war. As a result, their efforts were recognized by the United States government as well as the French and British, with 319 citations and decorations awarded to YMCA workers.

While the YMCA was the biggest and best known of charitable organizations, there were other groups that provided money and assistance. These included The National Catholic War Council, Jewish Welfare Board, the Young Women's Christian Association, The Salvation Army, and The American Library Association. Also a group of small agencies joined together to form the War Camp Community Service. By combining all their efforts, these groups raised a total of $170,000,000. Today's equivalent in dollars would be more than two billion ($2,000,000,000). (Measuring Worth.) The American public was generous toward their boys. (Ellis)

The "colored troops," (the term used to refer to the African-Americans in those days), were still segregated in France. To provide YMCA services for them, there were black YMCA volunteers and staff. They set up canteens for the black troops, staffed by blacks, with the same goals and services as the white canteens. The largest hut in France was built at the port of St. Nazaire, where the hundreds of colored soldiers stationed there daily unloaded many tons of supplies.

Among the many services the YMCA provided the African-American troop, was a money order station. The soldiers sent as much as $2,000 daily to their families back home. The soldiers also had a library and a classroom. It was here for the first time in their lives, that many men finally had an opportunity to learn to read and write. African-American women volunteers were allowed to socialize with the soldiers, whereas in the white canteens such visiting was discouraged, even forbidden.

Some canteens had small trucks which carried hot chocolate and donuts to at least 14 locations near front line areas where there were no huts or tents. The ever popular movies were reserved for the established canteens. In some places white women, if no African-Americans were present, "gave a service that was necessarily perfunctory." This did not include such personal services as sewing on buttons or service stripes or even talking to a homesick boy. However, this slight change of policy, allowing white women even to be present, was a milestone in racial relations. Previously not even black women could be present.

Another service rendered by some YMCA volunteers was when great numbers of causalities arrived at the aide stations. The YMCA workers might be asked to assist in the initial treatment and cleaning of the wounded. The changing of dirty, bloody bandages was not a daily practice for the YMCA volunteers, but when they were needed, they came and served.

In future wars the YMCA and YWCA continued to be present, but many of their jobs and services were provided by military personnel. This included assistance by the military in helping families at home and abroad. The familiar inverted red triangle with a strip of blue across the center and the letters YMCA is still found today at many military camps and forts. The cheerful, uplifting services of YMCA volunteers are welcomed wherever they make an appearance.

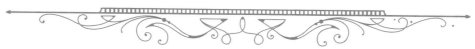

NEW IMMIGRANTS HELP A NATION FOUNDED BY IMMIGRANTS

Without the enlistment of almost one million new immigrants, General John J. Pershing would never have achieved his goal of having four million men in uniform by the end of 1918. Immigrants swarmed to recruiting offices and draft boards, with the states of New York and Pennsylvania leading the list. New York immigrant registrations totaled 784,439 while Pennsylvania followed with 495,000. Illinois, chiefly the Chicago area, was third with 318,039 men. Not all those who registered were drafted on this first round of drafting.(Sasse)

The first day of draft registration, June 5, 1917, drew 1,239,865 "unnaturalized" foreigners who were from other countries besides Germany. There were 113,823 naturalized Germans who registered. "Unnaturalized" meant men who had previously declared their intention to become citizens but had not gone through the process.(Ellis)

Recruits who spoke or understood little, if any English, were sent to special classes for instruction. This tutoring continued in France by the YMCA and other not-for-profit groups. The immigrants had to be quick learners as the non-com instructors did not speak any language but "army" English. Some officers spoke French or German, but few could converse in the other languages spoken by the immigrant soldiers such as Serbian, Croatian, Czech, Polish or Baltic languages.

THE OTHER SIDE OF THE COIN
A German Soldier's Story Told by His Son

Ghent Oertel, Raymore, Missouri, told about his father's role in World War 1 as a medic in the German Army. His father, George Rheinhold Oertel, was trained as an engineer, and had invented many patented items. He served on the Eastern Front as a medic along a long line of border countries from Poland in the north to Kiev south in the Ukraine.

His medical treatment was not limited to wounded German soldiers. One day a Russian peasant drove up in a wagon with his wife suffering labor pains. They needed medical help quickly so George helped the wife deliver a baby. Ghent doesn't remember if it was a girl or boy, but it was a brief change of activities for his medic father. George had served previously in 1906-08 in a reserve unit in Poland as Germany required their soldiers to undergo frequent military training until they were 45 years old.

Life before the war, Ghent was told, was full of good times. His parents met in 1912 in Berlin, the capital of Germany. There was money to be made and spent, coffee shops in which to sit and talk, and high fashions for men and women to buy and wear. Life was pleasant. His parents met on a street car, the scene of many such meetings in those days for young people. His mother refused to give her name. She was too modest. At her stop, George got off also and carefully followed her to learn her name and place of residence. The next day on the street car, he gave her a poem, "Little Fisher Girl," a play of words on her last name of "Fischer" meaning "fish." Charlotte Johanna Fischer was impressed by the cleverness of young George and allowed him to court her.

But plans for marriage were delayed when World War I broke out on July 28, 1914 and George received a telegram to report for duty within five days. Family objections arose to an immediate wedding. He might be killed, leaving her a young widow. There might be food shortages and sickness. In fact, by the end of the war, thousands of German civilians died of starvation, tuberculosis, and other diseases. There was no medicine available to civilians, and even supplies to troops were low because of the successful British blockade of German ports. The blockade continued until after the peace treaty was signed on June 28, 1919. This blockade of humanitarian aid by the British is still controversial today.

Limited humanitarian efforts were made through the International Red Cross and other international groups. However, the aid was not large enough to sustain the German population, and they suffered terribly. Finally, after the war ended, the couple decided to risk all the problems and arranged to marry. The bride wore a white dress sewn with myrtle flowers. In Germany myrtle is the flower for brides. Her veil was made from a curtain by her Aunt Martha.

Life after the war must have had some happy moments, but the chaos of unstable governments, the depressed economy, and disastrous inflation made their lives miserable, Ghent said. He wonders how people managed. His uncle died, and his death was listed by the coroner as from "starvation." Fortunately, George was "a keen student of the times," Ghent declared. His father said again and again, "Germany lost the war and will never rise again." The family was buying food directly from farmers at inflated prices and cooking weeds to eat. His father predicted the rise of a dictator and knew he could not live under that kind of a leader.

Finally an opportunity came from relatives in the United States for them to immigrate. Ghent had been born in 1920, and was five years old when they set off for America. They landed in Ellis Island, where the reception from immigration officials "was terrible," Ghent says. Fortunately their papers were in order. Otherwise the family would have been refused admission and sent back to Germany.

From Ellis Island they took a train to Seattle. For five days and four nights, they sat up on wooden benches facing hostile passengers. The open hatred, expressed through words and even spitting, was a surprise for Ghent, and difficult to understand. "You killed my Uncle Charlie," a young boy yelled at Ghent's father. "No, son," he answered, "I healed men on both sides." But it was useless to protest, and Ghent learned to ignore being called "the Kaiser's brat." His father repeatedly said that hatred had no place in their thinking if they were to live a good life in the United States.

The job in Seattle for his father didn't work out, so the family rode the train for a long trip back east to Rochester, New York, to another job for the father. That was where Ghent and his younger brother grew up. Father was a strict disciplinarian and expected all Ghent's grades to be A's and he had an even greater goal for Ghent in high school. Ghent was to win the Steuben Medal in German. It required knowledge of German literature as well as speaking and writing in German. Ghent said he had an excellent teacher in the best high school in town. As expected, with hard work and determination, Ghent won the prize. His parents were ecstatic.

His mother was able to get employment because she had received an exceptional education for a girl, and learned three languages. Later, Ghent and his family became successful Americans. As for Ghent, he became a graphic designer, an occupation to which he devoted his whole life. Part of his success was due to the two volume work on identification of colors he compiled and published, entitled "*200 Contemporary Colors.*" With 200 pages of entries, he ended up with 22,000 separate color variations. It is still the standard work in that field.

Although of immigrant background, the Ghent family achieved the American dream. Was it really an American dream, or was it the dream of other peoples too?

(Note: Mr. Oertel passed away several weeks after he gave this interview. His family generously donated the scrapbook of more than 400 photographs taken by George Rheinhold Oertel in his service as a medic in the German army to the National World War I Museum.)

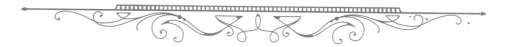

AMERICAN ACES AND THEIR "HITS"

There were 23 American pilots who each shot down at least six or more enemy planes, thus entitling them to be called an "Ace." Five victories were the minimum.

PHOTOGRAPHS OF THE EASTERN FRONT BY A GERMAN SOLDIER

A. Wounded German soldiers at convalescent hospital

B. Medical tents set up in churchyard

C. Listening to record of Karl Lindstrom's music in the field
(The numbers refer to a certain company or battalion.)

D. Medical teams prepare to move to front to get wounded

E. German medical wagon to transfer wounded

F. Learning how to repair and assemble rifles

G. Local Polish boys

IMMIGRANT SOLDIER MAKES GOOD, THEN LOSES IT ALL? OR DOES HE?

Charles Brunntraeger on his mount in Kripp, Germany, at a remount station
(Family photo)

Private Charles Michael Brunntraeger, in the 1930's or 1940's decided for several reasons, it was time to change his last name. He chose "Shipman." A surviving family member, grandson Neil Brunntrager of St. Louis, Missouri, is not sure why his grandfather made this decision. Neil, who tells this story, has no plans to change his name. Was it a reaction to a long delayed prejudice against German names or perhaps the rise of the Nazis to power? Anyway, before his participation in World War I, his grandfather had opened several bakeries in New York and was successfully making and selling delicious German bread recipes, when the United States declared war on Germany.

Michael felt a duty to defend his new country. Michael joined the United States army in the SOS (Service of Supply) of the Quartermaster Corps. He was familiar with horses and pleased to be assigned to a remount station in Kripp, near his old home in Germany. Being a natural speaker of the Bavarian dialect also helped ensure his position.

Earlier he had service in Koblenz, a huge transportation hub where its famous ancient fortress still stands. Kripp was one of the four remount stations maintained by the AEF in Germany. Evidently there were no adverse reactions from the townspeople against Michael for being a member of the victorious AEF army.

Neil, the grandson, has a picture of his grandfather in his American uniform mounted on a horse. After about six months' duty in Germany, Private Brunntrager returned to the United States where he was discharged in 1919. He moved back to New York City, where he established three more bakeries, possibly including the famous German rye bread on his menu. By then, he probably had decided he had spent enough time caring for and feeding horses. Now it was time his American customers received his attention.

Tragically, one of his sons died in 1916 before Michael enlisted in the service. Even more sorrow was to come later when four other children died in the terrible flu epidemic that spread across American in 1918-1919. Misfortune remained his constant companion it seemed, when the economy went into the Great Depression. He lost all his bakeries, but he did not give up. He somehow obtained the money to buy a medallion licensed taxi cab and drove private passengers. The medallion is a special expensive license required by New York City to be able to own a taxi.

This German –American citizen served in the army of his new country, built a thriving business, but one that failed in the Depression. Perhaps his greatest loss may have been the lives of his children, but he never gave up hope for the future. Michael died in 1972 and was buried in St. Louis.

He modeled a life for new American immigrants to imitate-- – a life of courage, imagination, and hard work.

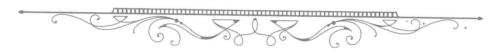

UNEXPECTED ENDING ON TRIP TO VISIT AMERICA

Edwin, son of Heinrich, riding a tractor with Heinrich's great grandson in the background, plows the fields their ancestor, Henrich, bought almost 100 years ago when he came to Iowa as a displaced German in World War I.
(Photo taken August 8, 1997, courtesy Darlene Uthof Cherland)

For Heinrich Willem Uthof, the trip to the United States in early 1917 with four friends, had an unexpected ending. They were Germans training to be cabin boys and waiters on German ocean cruise ships. This was an honorable profession at that time in Germany. Though they were assigned to a ship that was going from Germany to New York, they were young, ambitious, and had no worries.

They knew their native country, Germany, was at war with Europe, but they thought they would be safe in the United States when the liner reached New York as the United States had not yet declared war on Germany. This story is told by Heinrich's son, Ray, and his wife, Betty, who live in Fenton, Iowa.

But one day in April, 1917, when the ship was docked in a New York harbor, the unexpected happened. Imagine the astonishment the boys and all the passengers felt when United States Navy officials showed up, announcing they were impounding the ship and all its passengers. The United States had just declared war on Germany. The surprised and worried passengers were not imprisoned, but they had to stay within the boundary where the ship was docked.

When the war ended one and one-half years later November, 1918, they were released. Not wanting to return to Germany, they were told if they knew someone who would give them a place to work, they could accept the job. Heinrich and some of his ship mates decided to search for jobs.

Conditions were terrible in Germany with civilians starving and dying because of the British embargo on food and medicines. Crops had not been harvested because all the able bodied men were in the army. Many were still prisoners of war in camps in France and England. Heinrich and his friends saw many opportunities to live a better life in America, so they decided to stay.

One man knew a farmer in the area of Lotts Creek, Iowa, and contacted him. That farmer knew other farmers who needed workers because many of their farm hands were serving in the army. The farmers agreed to provide jobs for the hapless German men. Heinrich had only eight cents in his pockets when he met his new employer in the midst of winter in Iowa. An Iowa winter can be very cold. So Heinrich went to a clothing store in Fenton, bought clothes he needed, and put them on his account. Fenton was near the farm where he would be working.

This was probably in early 1919, and for several years Heinrich worked as a farm hand. He met Lydia Caroline Elise Mueller of German ancestry, and they were married January 26, 1921. They farmed in Seneca near Fenton and then bought 160 acres of farmland south and west of Fenton. They had five children, of whom Ray is the only surviving one. A granddaughter, Darlene Cherland, and her husband, Steve, now own the farm.

True to his word, Heinrich became an American citizen on September 23, 1921. Two of his friends who had been cabin boys, and a third friend went to New Jersey to live, and the fourth friend moved to Wisconsin. Ray says that in Fenton, Iowa, where they lived, the Lutheran church for years would honor its German residents by having a service in German one week. The next week, the service would be spoken in English. The mother of Lydia, Heinrich's wife, gave the land to build St. John's Lutheran Church in Fenton. For these immigrants, having their own church was important.

Betty and Ray tell of visiting Germany to see the house where his father, Heinrich, was born. It was in a small town in central Germany made by combining two towns, Btundersen and WolfHagen, into another small town, even though several kilometers separated the towns. They met many relatives there and enjoyed the visits immensely. One young man from Germany came to Iowa to firm up the friendship two years ago when Heinrich's great-granddaughter was married. A relationship has been established between the two branches of the families as a result of more visits to the old country. Ray and Betty's daughter and six grandchildren visited recently in Germany to see their newly discovered relatives.

One wonders what Heinrich would think about the consequences of his decision to stay in America and become an American citizen. Germany and the United States had been enemies in two World Wars but changes in world politics have occurred so that now, families from the two countries have become friends. Heinrich most likely say "Yah" and nod of his head, signs of approval. Heinrich was born April 23, 1884 and died January 1, 1987. His wife, Lydia, was born January 26, 1899, and preceded him in death in 1937.

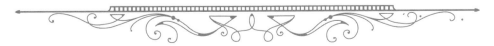

TEACH YOUR LIEUTENANT HOW TO RIDE A HORSE — YOU'LL BE GLAD YOU DID

Rolla Runner
(Courtesy of Norma Lewis)

Having his horse shot out from under him did not deter Private Rolla W. Runner from completing his ride carrying an important message. Rifle fire raged all around him as he galloped across the fields in France in the fall of 1918. The family doesn't know the rest of the story; they just know he finished the trip. Rolla's story is told by his daughter, Norma Lewis, Raymore, Missouri.

He was in the Headquarters Company, 129th Field Artillery, 35th Division, which fought horrendous battles in the Argonne Forest area. They struggled to win the village of Exermont and finally had it under control, but the Germans later counterattacked and drove the AEF out. Nevertheless, the forest and hills nearby needed to be recovered from the Germans, who had occupied them the past three years. So this time the 1st Division successfully attacked. (Eisenhower). Thickly wooded forests and steep hills flanked by large open fields made this one of the most dangerous places to fight. This was also where Capt. Harry S. Truman's Battery D was located. His battery consisted of four French 75 mm artillery guns, more than 100 horses and about 200 men.

After the Armistice was signed, Private Runner became one of hundreds of American soldiers who was infected by the influenza epidemic just as he was about to be sent home. This meant he had to be hospitalized and stay in France, while his buddies went home without him. He was greatly disappointed because he would not be permitted to board a ship until he completely recovered. Perhaps his only consolation was there would be no more dangerous horse rides any time soon.

Adding to his difficulties, he had no way of notifying his wife about his delay in arriving. A letter would have been carried by ship, just like the troops, and would arrive at the same time he would have. The trip sometimes required 10 or 12 days to cross the Atlantic.

His wife, not knowing of his illness, was waiting at the train station for him. She was shocked and greatly upset when his buddies told her he was ill in France. "It was a terrible disappointment to Mother," her daughter, Norma, adds. But eventually Rolla recovered and returned home to Kansas City. He was discharged May 3, 1919, having served almost a year to the day overseas. After recovering from the flu, he may have been assigned to the Occupation Army serving in Germany for up to six months before he could be shipped home. Norma doesn't know for sure but that could explain his extended stay in Europe.

Private Runner was the only one of the three sons of Blanche Cameron Runner and Warren Tinsley Runner to be inducted. Like most Missourians, he trained at Camp Doniphan, a military base just outside Ft. Sill, Oklahoma, near Lawton. He was later transferred from the Headquarters Company, 2nd Field Artillery of the Missouri National Guard to the Headquarters Company of the 129th Field Artillery, 35th Division. Hundreds of Missourians made up this division. Then the National Guard was integrated into the regular army to achieve the higher number of troops the larger divisions now required. At the time he was inducted, he and Nannie Roberts Runner were newlyweds. When he told her he was in the army, the couple decided she would accompany him to Camp Doniphan and work as a cook for the nurses. That way they could be together until he shipped out.

Once he was in France, his early experiences at home with horses qualified him for the dangerous duty as messenger. But it also enabled him to befriend an officer, Lt. Thomas C. Bourke, from Kansas City. The lieutenant was supposed to lead his men on horseback but he had never ridden a horse, so Rolla became the one to teach Lieutenant Bourke how to ride as an officer in grand style. From that training experience they became lifelong friends.

One reason the Runners settled in Kansas City after the war was because it was the home of the Lieutenant. Norma recalls how every Christmas season, the mother of Lieutenant Bourke would drive up in her chauffeured limousine. She always brought toys and food to Norma and her family. The Bourke family was a prominent, wealthy Kansas City family and never missed a Christmas bringing those gifts to Norma. Mr. Runner always had a job throughout the Depression, sometimes thanks to his old friend, Mr. Bourke. Mr. Runner retired from the United States Department of Agriculture as a meat inspector.

Norma appreciated the special bond between her father and Lieutenant Bourke. The bond lasted all the years until 1964 when her father died. Mr. Bourke was the first person to sign the guest book at the funeral home.

It was his way of honoring a lifetime friend, who had taught him how an officer should ride a horse. Head high, chest out, back straight. Just like the real infantry officer Lieutenant Bourke was.

ARMY MESSENGER TO RURAL MAILMAN

Doughboy with all required equipment, often weighing 60 pounds or more
(National Archives)

Delivering messages from trench to trench was George Fred Harrouff's assignment in AEF in World War I. Those messages could mean the difference between life or death for the soldiers in the trenches around Verdun, where George was stationed. Verdun is located in the Argonne sector where some of the toughest action of the war occurred for Americans. George was small, weighed about 125 pounds, and a fast and courageous runner. He had just the right qualifications to be a messenger. Each company had several men designated as messengers in the event that extra men were needed to get the messages through.

One story tells about a fourth runner being sent out, after the first three failed to reach their assigned posts. It was a perilous job and many runners lost their lives carrying messages. There was always an alert German sharpshooter waiting to see a runner take off. Some messengers rode horses, others rode bicycles, and a fortunate few had access to the rare motorcycle. Often the messengers ran through open fields, dodging rifle fire or machine guns to the AEF command post or headquarters which might be quartered in a chateau, a village house, or perhaps just a dugout. One of his daughters, Herwanna Sayre of Raymore, Missouri, knows his story.

Her father was born near McPherson, Kansas, and lived there until he was eight years old. Then he and his family moved to Washita County, Oklahoma, where he was drafted into the Army in 1918. The family was forced to move to Oklahoma because George's father had co-signed a note for a neighbor who absconded, leaving the Harrouff family to pay off the note. In the process they lost their farm which had been attached as part of the note. So they decided that in the open land of Oklahoma they would find a place to start a new life.

George was called "Fred" because his father's first name was also "George". To help out, Fred regularly sent some of his army pay home to his family. Once he sent $500 for his father to buy a farm across the road. It had fruit trees and seemed a good buy. That was a large sum for those for those days. He must have saved for many months on his army pay of about $30.00 per month or had other resources.

While he was in France, is parents took in a boarder, the new lady principal at the nearby small rural school. She and Fred exchanged letters, and when he came home in 1920 they fell in love and were married. They lived with his parents on the farm for the next four years. A daughter and two sons were born. But Fred was anxious to be on his own with his new family.

In 1925 the family moved to Lawton, Oklahoma, where his in-laws lived. Fred's last child, Herwanna, was born there in 1926. She explains her unusual name, that it was the name of an Indian princess who was the first Christian convert at the nearby Mennonite Mission. The daughter of the missionaries also was named Herwanna, so there were three little girls with that royal name, our narrator says.

Fred had previously taught school before he entered the service, but his combat experiences left him nervous and anxious. He became withdrawn and shy, or as Herwanna describes it, "somewhat on edge." He had brought some souvenirs home, as did many soldiers. They included a gas mask which he never would say whether or not he had worn it and a gold watch with a cover. He most probably wore the mask many times, because the Germans sprayed various types of gas in his sector many times.

After his discharge, Fred tried several jobs. He later took a job delivering mail and this seemed to satisfy him. Shy as Fred was, he liked to have a good time with all kinds of people. He delivered mail to the black military families on his route and enjoyed visiting with them. During these days, this was unusual for a white man to be friendly on a daily basis with blacks. "It was like a ministry to him, to be accepting of all people, especially on the mail route," Herwanna added. Fred's wife was a social person, a good cook, and a leader in the church, all qualities Fred lacked. But by complementing each other, they had a good life. His wife lived until 1986.

Fred's father, George, had a habit of writing in a diary. It was unique because he began writing it when he was 15 and continued until he died at 95. These little volumes were a family treasure and were carefully stored in a big trunk in the attic of his farmhouse. Herwanna has read them all. The first ones were written in beautiful handwriting, then as the writer aged, the writing became more difficult to decipher. Topics ranged from what kind of seeds he planted to his applications for patents of inventions he made. Eighty years of his life and those of his family were recorded for posterity. One volume was donated to the Kansas State Archives in Topeka, Kansas.

After Fred retired from the post office, he spent peaceful time fishing and playing dominoes with his old buddies at the post office. He also kept a farm in Oklahoma, leasing the land to an oil company instead of farming it himself. Smart thinking on his part made him keep the mineral rights. The lease money rose from $1.00 per acre to $2,000.00 per acre. At the same time, he leased the land to a couple who raised cattle on it.

The daring, small runner with the swift legs that enabled him to perform one of the soldier's most dangerous assignments, was able to find peace and live a useful life despite his terrible war experiences. For many soldiers who had fought under the same horrendous conditions, this was not always the case. Fred considered himself a lucky man.

Herwanna doesn't know why he had the ability to live peacefully despite his harrowing experiences in the war. Perhaps, it was because he was able to accept all people including blacks (who were called "colored" then.) Perhaps he had learned how to accept his own condition of edginess. Maybe he felt compassion for the "colored," because he knew personally what suffering was like. Herwanna supposed this gave him his ability to identify with and accept other humans in all extremes.

George "Fred" Harrouff spent the rest of his life delivering understanding and empathy every day, free of charge, along with the mail he faithfully handed out to his rural route customers.

HE WENT IN A BOY, AND CAME OUT A MAN

Howard Adolph Cook
(Courtesy of Yvonne Paysinger)

Like many American soldiers in World War I, Howard Adolph Cook, "went in as a boy and came back a man," his daughter, Yvonne Paysinger, Raymore, Missouri, says of her father. He left high school one semester early so he and a buddy could join the army on January 18, 1918.

He was assigned to the Truck Company Number Two of the First Corps Artillery Park and completed basic training at Ft. Logan, Colorado. Howard sent home a postcard picture of an artillery battery. Written on the other side is the message that he passed everything OK, but had trouble with his eyes. The card was postmarked Wichita, Kansas, which meant the army accepted him despite eyesight problems.

Howard was born November 18, 1899, in New Knoxville, Ohio. His family of German ancestry had come to Kansas by train to homestead at Bluff City, Kansas, in Harper County. Howard was seven years old then and went to the nearby grade school. But when it came time for higher education, Howard and his lifelong friend, Jack Jay Sanborn, moved to Wichita, about 60 miles away because there was no high school at home. They boarded with a family friend. In their senior year, they joined the army in the middle of the school year, missing their last semester of high school. They were assured by the school they would receive a graduation diploma.

More education and training awaited them in the army because General Pershing was making major changes to modernize the army. He wanted to bring it up to the same standards the Allies used. The United States army had scarcely changed its tactics and weapons since the Civil War. Consequently, training needed to be updated also. The war being fought in Europe now was vastly different from any war previously ever fought.

General Pershing made many innovations and changes in the former order and ranks of the established army. Order and ranks refer to the type of units and their sizes. One of the more unusual was the formation of the First Corps Artillery Park. It was sometimes referred to as CAP and was composed of six truck companies with 150 men each and a depot company of 305 men. This depot company was the largest company in the army. In addition, there was an ordnance company of 57 skilled mechanics, a 48-man Headquarters Company, and a medical detachment with 1000 trained medics.

Now that trucks had become an essential part of military equipment, General Pershing had to assign units of men and equipment to maintain them. In his brief episode in Mexico pursuing Pancho Villa, the general had recognized the usefulness of this new vehicle, the truck.

The truck company trained together at Camp Jackson, South Carolina, then moved on to Camp Merritt, New Jersey, from where they sailed to Europe on May 22, 1918, on one of the Great Northern line ships. The sailing was uneventful, for which some men were grateful, while others may have been disappointed at not sighting a submarine. (www.vets.com battlefield) They landed May 31, 1918, at Brest, a French port, and marched out of the city to what was supposedly the old prison camp of Napoleon Bonaparte. After a week or so there, they were loaded into the famous French "quarante hommes or haute chauvaux" cars (40 men or 8 horses) en route to St. Nazaire.

They were scheduled to arrive at the Chateau-Thierry front on July 13 as part of the effort to block the Germans from reaching their targeted city of Paris. This was part of the last determined effort of the Germans to win the war. All roads and towns leading to Paris were stationed with Allied troops. The action started. Fighting was fast and furious as huge artillery shells carpet bombed (See Glossary) ahead of the troops. Howard's company had 300 trucks into which they loaded ammunition bound for different battle fronts on the Marne River. The Depot Company was assigned to open several dumps for both heavy and light artillery, which required two sizes of shells, the 75 mm and the heavier 155 mm. These included were shells such as shrapnel, heavy explosive, and several kinds of poison gas shells in the two sizes.

The medical attachment was bombed frequently by German planes which ignored the huge red crosses painted on their tents. In an article by the Evansville, *Indiana Courier*, and quoted in Heiman Blatt's *Sons of Man*, Blatt says "(in) the city of Chateau Thierry… the dead were dying in the streets everywhere. It was assigned (sic) we shall never forget." Because of the German shelling, the trucks were driven at night, and it was then that most of the movement of men and machines at the front occurred. Even in the dark, the trucks were often targeted by German artillery, and when hit, the load of shells made a gigantic explosion. That is why medics rode with the trucks.

During the daytime the trucks and soldiers were hidden as much as possible from the roving observation German airplanes. Unfortunately, in this part of France, Allied planes were in short supply and could not provide the necessary observation of the enemy or strafe and bomb German trenches. The Germans commanded the skies most of the time. Still the Depot Company was able to establish at least six ammunition dump sites, continuing as far as Fismes on the Vesle River. This was the eastern front of the German-held territory. Dumps were storage buildings from which the artillery, in coordination with the infantry, could order the type and size of ammunition and shells needed for the next attack of defense.

Trucks such as the ones the used by the CAP made regular deliveries of the ammunition ordered by each battalion or fighting unit. Sometimes an artillery battery supply was limited to firing only seven or eight shells per hour if ammunition supply was scarce or deliveries were late. It was important to fire as regularly as possible, even at sporadic intervals. Otherwise, the Germans might suspect the battery's ammunition supply was depleted, and they would take the opportunity to launch an attack. Capturing or blasting gun batteries often determined the fate of the battle. The mathematics used to determine range and elevation that Captain Truman had joked about, turned out to be no joking matter, especially when firing ahead as in a rolling or curtain barrage. (See Glossary.)

The CAP was praised by Lt. Col. E. P. Walker for its "conduct under all circumstances and conditions as soldiers. That you are, and your discipline has been excellent throughout, more than one Visiting Officer has remarked it was the best organization… they had seen, and I trust you will keep up the good work."… "Good luck to you all." The letter came as the CAP was departing for six extra months of additional duty in the AOG (Army of Occupation of Germany.) The company must have been pleased with the letter of praise from a commanding officer, even though their new assignment meant six more months of service, this time in Germany.

Among other mementos that Yvonne possesses from her father, is a copy of the poem, "In Flanders Field," written by a Canadian surgeon, Major John McCrae, who served in Belgium in 1915. She laughs as she recalls hearing her father dramatically recite the poem. It is one of her fondest memories of him. Howard married his sweetheart, Genevia Britten, in 1921 and they opened a café which turned out to be unsuccessful. They moved to Ponca City where they had two daughters, then eventually moved to Wichita, Kansas, where he became involved in the Veterans of Foreign Wars (VFW).

In 1968 he was selected the "All American Commander" by the national VFW. Some of the activities of his post included selling more than 2,000 poppies; sponsoring the Drum and Bugle Corps; a Junior Rifle Club; Voice of Democracy contests; and planning ceremonies for various veterans' holidays and military funerals. His post named, "Over There Post," was the fourth largest in the nation. He died in 1972 and was buried in Bluff City, Kansas, near his family's farm.

Yvonne looks back over her father's life. She thinks about his leaving home as a high school student and volunteering for the Army. She is proud that he undertook a demanding and dangerous job of driving trucks carrying ammunition over French roads that had dissolved into pools of mud. Lastly, in spite of all the dangers, he returned home safely and uninjured. It was these challenges and accomplishments that consequently changed Howard, the young farm boy. He did, indeed, "come out like a man."

POEM, "IN FLANDER'S FIELD"

A Canadian doctor, Major John McCrae, wrote this famous poem in May, 1915, after a German shell exploded near him in a Flanders, Belgium, field hospital killing his associate and others. This was during the battles of 2nd Ypres, and the British public welcomed the poem's hope and inspiration at this difficult time. Major McCrae died of pneumonia a year later.

ST. MIHIEL — THE RESULT OF GOOD PLANNING BY AEF

Gateway to St. Mihiel Cemetery where 4,153 American soldiers are buried
(Photo by Nancy Cramer)

The St. Mihiel Salient was the first of three important battles the AEF fought as a entire American army in World War I. Finally General Pershing achieved what he had long requested-– AEF troops fighting under American officers. Always before, the AEF had fought along with either British or French troops under the command of those officers. Now the AEF went into battle as a separate American force, led by its own AEF officers.

The Salient, its perimeter measuring at least 65 miles, was a large high outcropping of rock and soil. The Germans had seized control of it from France in 1914 and defended all three sides of it so successfully that the French could never retake it. The French had tried for three years in desperate attempts which resulted in about one million deaths for both sides.

This situation would change in September, 1918, when the long anticipated deployment of large numbers of American troops entered the battle zone. The German soldiers were experienced and well entrenched, in contrast to the mostly inexperienced Americans who were now assembling for battle in enormous numbers. Most notably, the American General John J. Pershing, had an audacious plan that General Foch, the Allied Supreme Commander, reluctantly approved. Pershing would make use of all the American services in the battle.

This included 600,000 infantry and support troops; 2700 artillery guns; airplanes; and masses of tanks, led by Colonel George S. Patton. The artillery began firing at 1 A.M. on September 12 with a heavy barrage. Then at 5 A.M. the attack began with guns firing at a rate of the infantry advancing one hundred yards every four minutes. The troops were moving at a fast pace. The German barbed wire was old and rusty and easily crossed. There had been a lack of rain and the ground was dry, conditions were ideal for a rapid advance.

Colonel Billy Mitchell, of postwar fame, headed the AEF air corps. In order to keep the Germans unaware of the Americans' preparations, he had led airplane attacks into enemy territory the night before, hitting targets in the rear. These included bridges, aerodromes, and railroad crossings. In the daytime his planes conducted surveillance, noted large troop formations, and strafed troops and moving vehicles when possible.

As for Colonel Patton, who was to become an important military commander in World War II, he excelled in launching aggressive attacks by his tank corps. He led the 1st Tank Brigade at St. Mihiel and at the Meuse-Argonne until he was wounded on the first day. (Eisenhower). This was the first time in warfare that all four forces had been united in one massive attack. (Note: This is also the first war in which airplanes and tanks were developed enough to be of combat strength.)

Rail communications between Paris and the eastern part of the western front were seriously endangered by the continued presence of Germans in the Salient. This was another reason it was essential for the Allies to regain the Salient. The attack would take place simultaneously on two fronts. The French V Corps would besiege the western face while the American IV Corps (1st, 42nd, and 89th divisions) and I Corps (2nd, 5th, 90th and 82nd Divisions) attacked the southeast face.

French artillery, combined with AEF artillery, provided the First Army with over 3,000 guns. British and French aircraft reinforced the AEF airplanes so there were nearly 1,500 planes, the largest force ever assembled in World War I up to that date. The Germans soldiers were badly outnumbered by the Allies, and large groups of them began to surrender. A total of 13,250 prisoners had surrendered by the end of the St. Mihiel campaign.

However, the plans for the attack had inadvertently been published in newspapers, so the Germans were aware of the awesome force that was soon to breach the Salient. Many Germans started retreating to set up a defense in the rear at the Hindenburg Line.

The remainder of the troops put up a stiff defense at the front, and the Allies took many casualties due to the Germans skill and bravery. During the 30 hours of fighting, 460 German guns were captured by the Allies. However, many units of Germans, because of their prior knowledge of the attack, fled with their guns from the Salient early in the fighting, thus keeping them from Allied seizure.

On the second day, the weather turned windy and rainy, creating the muddy conditions for which World War I was known. Other factors slowing down an Allied advance included the Germans' well planned series of trenches, newer rolls of barbed wire, and concealed machine guns. These factors seriously hampered the ability of the tanks and trucks to move men and supplies. But the weather and road conditions also restricted German movement, and in many cases the Germans were forced to leave valuable artillery behind. German commanders decided to continue moving back to consolidate near the Hindenburg Line. The Allies later found a written German order confirming this. It was the beginning of the end of the war. General Pershing's tactics are still studied today in military classes. These principles he originated are considered to be most valuable:
- Thorough and detailed planning, although the final orders were kept to only eight pages.
- Each Corps had been given a specific sector with defined boundaries within which to operate.
- Leaders of small units could operate on their own while following the orders' intent.
- Leaders could influence what happened on the battlefield by following their own leadership style. This was especially demonstrated by Colonel Patton, who led his men from the front lines, instead of from the rear as was usually done by high ranking officers.

Simultaneously while capturing the St. Mihiel Salient, General Pershing and his staff were in the midst of planning the next engagement for the AEF. It was to be the battle for the Meuse-Argonne sector, named after the famous lengthy Meuse River and the heavily forested Argonne. In the meantime, the AEF paid a high price with about 7,000 to 8,000 casualties in the battle for the Salient, including nearly 1800 deaths. The Americans captured 13,250 German prisoners, while the German casualties were less, at about 5,000, killed and wounded. However, many Germans had surrendered rather than take a chance of dying or being wounded. Overall, the numbers for both armies ran unusually high for a two day battle. (VFW Magazine, 2004)

The psychological aspect for the French and Americans in the capture of the Salient was probably the most important element of the victory. The Yanks had come to win, and to win big. To the admiration of their Allies, the Yanks fulfilled their expectations. (www.historyofwar. org/articles/battles-st-mihiel.html.)

FIRST AMERICAN OFFICER DIES IN WW I

Lt. William T. Fitzsimons, first AEF officer
killed in war
(Courtesy NWWIM Archives)

First Lieutenant William T. Fitzsimons, Jr., Kansas City, Missouri, was the first American officer to lose his life in World War I. The tragedy of his death is enhanced by the fact that he had already spent the years 1914-1915 treating British wounded in an English hospital and several months in Belgium caring for soldiers.

During his two year service abroad, his skill and knowledge were in great demand, especially in the spring of 1915, when the British were incurring the greatest toll of dead and wounded in their entire military history. The first day of the First Battle of the Somme ended with 20,000 British dead and 40,000 wounded. Such a record made the English weep.

Lieutenant Fitzsimons returned to his home in late 1915 to set up his own private practice. But, as a graduate of Harvard Medical School, the doctor, with some Harvard colleagues, made the decision to go to France and work in the hospitals for the Allied wounded. (kuhistory. com/articles/a-death-in-france.) It was about the time that Congress declared war against the Central Powers. Lieutenant Fitzsimons and others sailed across the Atlantic, landing in France from where he sent the obligatory printed card home which said: "Have arrived safely." He added: "Very busy, Much to do." He then signed his name and reported for work.

An outrage occurred soon afterwards. Lieutenant Fitzsimons and others were victims of a violation of the internationally accepted war dictum when his tent was hit by a bomb from a German airplane flying overhead. He was killed instantly. The bombing occurred even though the hospital tents were clearly marked with gigantic red crosses. He had the dubious honor of being the first American medical officer to die in the war. Also killed in the attack were several enlisted men and orderlies, as well as some patients.

The War Department immediately sent the customary telegram to his home announcing his death. (Note: There is some confusion as to the actual date of the bombing. Some sources claim September 4 and others state September 7. Military records occasionally are not clear.) However, most likely, the post card which came by ship, arrived after the telegram had arrived bearing its sad news.

His grieving family established a memorial in the form of a fountain at the end of one of Kansas City's many boulevards. The memorial reminds anyone who sees it of the terrible loss that one Kansas City family suffered in the early days of America's participation in World War I.

Army Hospital 21 was established in Aurora, Colorado, in 1918 to treat many war casualties who had been exposed to chemical weapons (poison gas) in Europe. The hospital in Denver, Colorado, had long been recognized for its ability to care for tuberculosis patients and it was believed that these practices could be applied to treat other lung problems, especially those caused by exposure to poison gases. Soldiers who suffered from being "gassed" would be sent to the new Aurora hospital. It was opened in the fall of 1918, and in 1920 it was formally named Fitzsimons Army Hospital, in honor of Lieutenant Fitzsimons' death and his sacrifice. (www.en.wikipedia.org/wiki/Fitzsimons_Army_Medical_Center)

Memorial fountain in Kansas City, Missouri, honoring Lt. William T. Fitzsimons
(Photo by Nancy Cramer)

ANIMAL STORIES

The first seeing eye dog was named Buddy. He was the pup of a war dog.
The original Pooh Bear (of Winnie the Pooh fame) was a mascot for a Canadian unit.
Rin Tin Tin, a German shepherd dog, was born in a trench in 1918 and was rescued by an American soldier. He became famous in the movies and starred in more than 40 films.
Stubby, an orphan dog, was adopted by an American who smuggled him to France where he became the mascot of the 102nd Infantry Regiment. He made a number of heroic rescues of wounded soldiers and saved his regiment from a mustard gas attack. He was decorated for valor by General Pershing himself.
(WWI Facts)

WAYNE MINER KILLED ON LAST DAY OF WAR

On a terrace above the memorial to Lieutenant Fitzsimons is a memorial to Private Wayne Miner, also from Kansas City, Missouri. He was in the 806th Pioneer Company, which was composed mostly of African-Americans. In the early hours of November 11 before the Armistice was scheduled to take place, he was among the four men who volunteered for the dangerous job of carrying machine gun ammunition to the battle front. During this task, he and several other soldiers were killed. He was the last man from Kansas City to die, possibly one of the very last of all AEF soldiers to die in the war. He was a courageous and dedicated soldier and was recommended for the Distinguished Service Cross, which unfortunately, he never received. An American Legion Post in Kansas City was named in his honor.

SON OF CLOSE FRIEND TELLS OF TRAGIC BOMBING

Additional information provided by John McGuire, son of Dr. Clarence Archibald McGuire, a close friend of Lieutenant Fitzsimons, tells this version of the German bombing at Base Hospital 5. The bombing took the lives of Lieutenant Fitzsimons and several soldiers, as well as wounding other medical personnel that day in September, 1917:

Dr. McGuire and Dr. Fitzsimons had been friends since boyhood, when the latter lived in Kansas where his father owned and operated a store. Upon the death of his father, his wife, Mrs. Fitzsimons, moved with her children to Kansas City where she set up a household. Fitzsimons later attended Harvard Medical School, while his friend studied at the University Medical College of Kansas City. Fitzsimons, upon graduating, decided at the outbreak of the war in 1914, to go to England and help the medical teams in the hospitals. Later he spent some time in Belgium, where he served in British hospitals. In 1916 he returned to Kansas City to set up his own practice, but instead, heard of plans made by Dr. Harvey Cushing, famed brain surgeon, to organize a hospital unit to go to France.Other such hospitals were being organized by university medical schools so there would be a total of almost 70 active base hospitals in France. (Cart)

Dr.McGuire and Dr. Fitzsimons joined Dr. Cushing's staff, eventually staying temporarily in a Red Cross hospital on the coast of northern France. One night soon after they arrival, the narrator says, his father was lying on a cot in his tent next to Fitzsimons' tent, when a soldier on duty to watch for aircraft, yelled, "Dirgible overhead!" It was only about 100 to 200 feet above the tent hospital. Fitzsimons rushed outside, lit his pipe, and called to his friend, "Clarence, come look at this. It's fantastic!" Just at that moment the pilot dropped a bomb, perhaps seeing the lit pipe.

The bomb hit Dr. Fitzsimons, whose body was instantly blasted into pieces. The shrapnel from the bomb also riddled the blanket covering Dr. McGuire and pierced his back. The medics picked out as many pieces as they could, but Dr. McGuire carried some of this shrapnel all the rest of his life in his back. Several other soldiers were killed in the bombing, although the tents were clearly marked with the Red Cross symbol.

Dr. McGuire told his son that the date of the incident on the fountain was incorrect, and for some reason, never did take his son, John, to see the fountain monument, nor otherwise ever mention it again. Perhaps the memory of the bombing was too painful for Dr. McGuire to visit his friend's memorial, accompanied by his own son.

Dr. McGuire sent his own medals from World War I to Fitzsimons Hospital in Colorado in honor of his friend, the first AEF officer to die in The Great War.

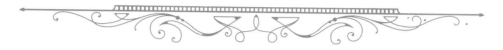

U.S. MEDICAL CARE BECOMES MODERNIZED

Perhaps it was the carnage and the number of casualties that spurred many advancements of medical care for the 237,135 wounded American soldiers during WWI. (1916-1918 Gray & Argyle) One of numerous innovations included transporting x-ray machines in ambulances or wagons to field hospital units. Another was the beginning of surgical reconstruction of facial and jaw injuries.

Other innovations included establishing laboratories containing sophisticated equipment to perform multiple procedures in testing blood, sputum, milk, and water. Wounds could be tested for various bacteria. A military lab was equipped to perform the same tests as the best civilian hospitals provided in the United States.

Further advances included the use of several kinds of anesthesia and numbing medications before surgery. This made obsolete the slug of whiskey from a bottle, which often formerly had served as anesthesia. Even on the battlefield, before the wounded soldier was taken to an aid station, the medic's job was to lessen the soldier's pain by administering morphine on abdominal wounds or other serious ones.

Surgery on lesser abdominal wounds had improved greatly and therefore, was more successful. Lowering the rate of infection was essential to recovery, and two simple procedures made this possible. They were thorough hand washing, and the use of sterilized instruments, both of which are routinely practiced today. Rubber gloves were first used in 1890's by a surgical nurse in Baltimore. They became popular in Baltimore, but were not widely used for some years, and probably not in World War I. (Caroline Hampton Halsted)

A new technique used washes to flush dirt and pus from gashes in the flesh and greatly helped to cut the rate of infection. This was perfected by Dr. Frances Ivens in her meticulous work on gas gangrene patients. She frequently cut off the dead tissue to prevent more formation of infection. (Dr. Grace Holmes, oral interview)

The dangerous bacteria that caused "gas gangrene" had lived in the French soil for hundreds of years. It came from the frequent spreading of cow manure for fertilizer. The French were immune to it, having lived on the land for centuries. Also, the soil had never been as deeply exposed as it was when the artillery shells blasted deep craters in it. Once the soil was disturbed by the shelling, the bacteria, which had long been hidden, were exposed to air, and proved deadly to soldiers of non-French heritage.

These are but a few of the innovative and successful practices initiated at Base Hospital #28 and the others. Base Hospital #28 had the best recovery record of all 22 AEF base hospitals. Of nearly 10,000 admitted patients, only 69 failed to survive. Some of those soldiers had wounds too severe to have been saved even today. This was in the age before antibiotics and the more sophisticated medical procedures used today. (Base Hospital #28, NWWIM)

The number of American battle deaths quoted in a 1919 book, *American Part*, with its figure of 48,909 deaths is close to the currently accepted figure of 50,500. The latter figure is higher because of the difficulty caused distinguishing between the deaths of patients who previously had influenza, but later died of pneumonia. The influenza may have created conditions weakening the body's resistance to infection and could not resist the onset of pneumonia. This later count brought the total AEF deaths to 116,700, for the two million AEF soldiers serving on French soil.

Much of the higher survival rate is due to the quality of training of American doctors and nurses who volunteered for overseas duty immediately after the United States declared war on Germany. By Armistice Day the number of AEF soldiers mobilized and serving in both France and the United States totaled 4,743,826. Had the war continued, the medical teams could have anticipated thousands of more patients. (The Great War. Resources. WWI Casualties and Deaths/PBS)

With unusual foresight, two Kansas City, Missouri, physician leaders had begun preparations to plan a military hospital for France, just five days before the United States declared war on Germany. The doctors formed a group which funded and staffed what became known as Base Hospital #28. Base hospitals were located near the sea coasts and constituted what is called a "general" hospital today. That means all types of medical services were offered there. These specialized services often meant the difference between life and death for the wounded soldier.

Dr. John Fairbairn Binnie and Dr. Lindsay Stephen Milne, members of the University of Kansas School of Medicine, near Kansas City, Missouri, headed the planning committee. They began meeting April 1, 1917, and continued regular sessions at the newly built Christian Church Hospital in Kansas City. (Dr. Frederick Holmes) An estimated 15% of all United States physicians signed up for duty in France as medical officers in the AEF. In addition, 8,510 graduate nurses volunteered their services, as did specialists from all areas of medicine. Waiting in the States were 3500 more nurses ready to be mobilized at the time the war ended. Laboratory experts and technicians set up labs in France which were comparable to hospital laboratories in the United States.

For the first time in the history of war, medical treatment in the battlefield became as competent as modern medical care at home. Other large base hospitals included #21 from St. Louis, Missouri, located in northern France where British soldiers fought and sent their casualties. As for #28 Hospital, because of its close proximity to the AEF battle areas in eastern and southern France, it served mostly AEF wounded. Train loads carrying up to 600 wounded men, arrived numerous times daily for Base Hospital #28 to process and begin specialize treatment.

However, the hospitals treated all injured patients, regardless of nationality or army. Many soldiers of various nationalities and rank were able to return home alive and on the road to recovery, thanks to the skillful doctors and nurses from the United States of America.

Serving the injured in war zones was not without its hazards. Of the total number of 1,499 American doctors, five were killed in the line of duty, four died of illness, and two were taken prisoner.

Removing an injured soldier
from the trenches.
(Public Domain, courtesy VFW Magazine, 2004)

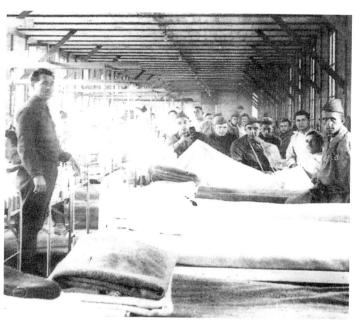

Scene from Hospital Ward at Base Hospital #28
(Courtesy of NWWI Archives)

It is estimated that more than 760,000 German civilians died in the war and in the months afterwards. This was due to the effects of diseases such as tuberculosis and influenza, malnutrition and actual starvation. This was despite the efforts of the International Red Cross and other humanitarian groups that were limited by the effects of the British blockade of German ports.

(Office of Medical History)

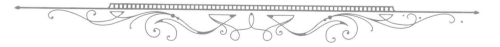

DANGERS OF TRENCH FOOT AND GANGRENE

One of the most common reasons to answer "sick call" was a bad case of frostbite. Soldiers were required to stand for hours or even days in trenches filled with water, snow and ice. Standing in one position or unable to move actively around in the trench, created problems for blood circulation in the soldier's feet. This in turn caused other medical problems. A common condition, referred to as "trench foot," was also one of the most painful and dangerous medical situations, often leading to gangrene. Modern antibiotics, not available for another 20 years, might have cured the gangrene. Instead, amputation was the usual solution in the most severe cases.

Constant exposure of the feet to moisture and cold air; inability to change wet socks for dry ones; tight fitting boots; and poor nutrition were among the many causes contributing to trench foot. It is one of the infantryman's biggest worries, other than bullets or shells. Frost bite or trench foot was noted in medical literature as far back as 2000 years ago, describing the soldiers of the Greek general Zenophon, who developed many cases of trench foot as they marched through Armenia's high elevations in pursuit of the Persians during 400 B.C.

Napoleon's men suffered grievously in their Russian campaign in 1812. Many died from the side effects of gangrene. So did soldiers in the Crimean War of 1854-6. Many advances in the treatment of wounds and disease were made in World War I, but trench foot was not one of them. If the bottom of the trenches had boards on the bare earth, this would have lessened the incidence. However, even when these "duck boards" were in place, they were useless when large quantities of rain or melting snow made pools of water the soldiers had to stand in. Sometimes pumps could be used if the trench was a reserve one behind the front line where the noise would not signal to the enemy what activity was taking place. If the enemy heard the pump's noise, they might decide to attack while the soldiers' attention was diverted.

Soldiers often arrived at their assigned trench, exhausted by the heavy packs they carried and the deep mud they slogged through. They had to report to communication trenches half a mile farther from their assigned trench, requiring a further expenditure of energy. More rest during the march if possible, would have helped. When periods of trench duty were shortened from 72 hours to 48 hours, this extra time helped reduce the outbreak of trench foot.

In the first stages of frost bite, the appearance of the foot may change only a little. However, the soldier usually experienced great pain. After that the foot became numb and was red and hot. Once the ailment was in the severe stage, the foot became grossly swollen and blistered and toes turned purple or even black. Despite this, with proper care, many toes healed and did not need to be amputated. But sometimes the disease was too far advanced. The foot died and had to be removed. Large doses of aspirin usually relieved the pain. If the feet remained cold, massaging helped, as did wrapping the foot in soft cotton. Feet that felt hot were left exposed to the air and not bandaged. Blisters were punctured and treated with an antiseptic.

Doctors learned when soldiers reported to a unit hospital, that often they had not changed socks or even taken off their boots for over 14 days. Boots were not even unlaced to relieve the pressure on the feet. Sometimes soldiers wore two pair of socks for warmth, even though the boot size permitted only one pair. This second pair added undue pressure to the feet.

The greatest incidence of trench foot occurred on the Western Front in Flanders near Belgium and France. It also became a serious problem in Gallipoli and Macedonia. Weather conditions aggravating the problem included heavy rains which soaked clothing and sudden drops in temperature which created frost. For two months starting in December, 1914, almost 5,000 cases were reported. However, after a strict regime of foot care, change in trench flooring, and better nutrition, the numbers were considerably lower. (Dr. Miller, Editor)

History tells us "that an army travels on its stomach." That may be true, but the infantry travels on its feet. Careless or inadequate treatment of the feet can cause a man to suffer loss of toes, a foot, or even a leg. In World War I, the procedure of amputation became a last resort. Not only did the limb of an amputated part require many months to heal, but the soldier suffered excruciating pain at times throughout his lifetime. Worst of all, an amputated limb damaged the emotional well being of the soldier, often making him an invalid in his mind as well as his body for a lifetime.

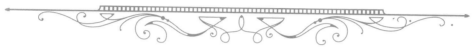

INFLUENZA — THE WORLD'S WORST EPIDEMIC TO DATE

The "Spanish" flu, misnamed and misunderstood, created the world's worst epidemic up to that dreadful time in 1918 when it first infected soldiers at Camp Funston, Kansas, now the site of Fort Riley. Where it came from and how it chose a remote Army training camp has puzzled epidemiologists for almost one hundred years.

While the knowledge of its source remained unknown, still more frustrating was the knowledge of how to treat the infected. This was especially true of persons who later became victims to pneumonia, which often accompanies a weakened immune system. There were no antibiotics then to treat pneumonia.

Still more puzzling, was the evidence that the flu infected mostly children and young, healthy adults. It had a lesser effect on the elderly, quite the opposite result when most illnesses strike. The best treatment the medical corps could provide was bed rest, good food, and constant care.

AEF military records show there were 316,000 diagnosed cases of influenza among soldiers and 53,000 diagnosed cases of pneumonia. Almost 20,000 died from the pneumonia, usually two or three days after being infected. Often, whole companies of men (about 200 in one company) were quarantined or confined to quarters to prevent the spread of the contagious influenza. It was especially difficult to isolate and treat victims on board the crowded troop ships crossing the Atlantic. With hundreds of men bedded in the close quarters of the ship, it was almost guaranteed that every soldier would be exposed to the flu and possibly become sick.

Fortunately, the flu which appeared suddenly in September, 1918, lost its momentum among the troops by November, 1918. The number of cases dropped dramatically. This was the first of three rounds of infection that plagued literally the world's population. Estimates of deaths range as high as 60 million sickened people worldwide, although the lower number of 15 to 20 million seems more likely. There was no accurate recording of deaths among civilians, due to the difficulty of reporting, especially in the rural areas of Asia and Africa. (Dr. Grace Holmes)

FATHER KNEW BEST

Hallie Oliver Young (left), shooting rifle (right) from kneeling position
(Courtesy of Joan Mills)

This is how the family tells the story. According to his daughter, Joan Mills, Kansas City, Missouri, just days before he was to ship out for France, Hallie Oliver Young, was diagnosed with a serious case of the influenza and his parents were notified. Hallie and others in the same near death stage of the flu, were moved from the hospital tents and laid outside on cots because of a shortage of beds. It was thought they would die soon, and the beds could be better utilized by another soldier. This was on or about April 27, 1918.

When his father, Richard Young from Coffey County, Kansas, received this news, he immediately got on a train and rode day and night to New York. Somehow he located his son's unit on Ellis Island. Mr. Young stubbornly convinced the Army doctors that he could care for his son, and Hallie would recover. Whatever happened and how the father was able to accomplish it, the outcome was that Hallie and his father began the long journey home on a train. Hallie's army days were over. The rapidly spreading influenza epidemic attacked thousands of American soldiers in both the United States and in France, as well as hundreds of civilians.

Joan Mills tells the story as the family remembers it, but with some missing details such as how the father actually managed to get his sick son out of the army camp, and how did the father get them on a train and care for him during the trip? This would have been at least a three to four day trip, and other passengers might suspect that Hallie was seriously ill. Or perhaps the father obtained a private seating. This information, interesting to know, has been lost to the years.

Hallie recovered, as his father had predicted, with no obvious effects from the flu. He was thin in stature but that was "because he moved fast," his daughter said. He wanted to get ahead in the business of farming, so he took some business courses in Kansas City, Missouri, and used them to improve his financial knowledge in operating his farm in Westphalia, Coffey County, KS. He also was self taught by reading farm journals, business magazines, and *The Saturday Evening Post*.

His parents were members of the Free Methodist Church, and his mother disapproved of card playing, movies, and women who wore makeup. Hallie didn't go to church often because he said all they wanted to do was take up collections. His objection became a source of disagreement with his mother.

Hallie lived to be 66 years old, 40 years longer than the army doctor had predicted, when he died on February 19, 1958. His father's action in bringing him home in 1918 most likely saved Hallie's life. Perhaps his father's strong will power and a streak of stubbornness paid off. Sometimes it takes a bit of stubbornness to make the impossible become the possible.

His father knew what was best for his son, and he did it. It paid off.

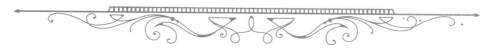

Registration certificate for Hallie Oliver Young
(Courtesy of Joan Mills)

CAN'T SHOOT DOWN THE FLU BUG

Walter Longhenry, left, and friend, doing pushups in basic training
(Courtesy of Lew Longhenry)

Proving his marksmanship ability on the training camp firing range was no challenge for Walter Henry Longhenry. His target papers, when shooting at a range of 500 yards, were perfect almost every time. His son, Lew Longhenry, Raymore, Missouri, has a dozen of these rare targets to prove his father's ability. Noted on the score sheets were wind speed and direction as well as other weather conditions which might have influenced his scores. But despite disadvantageous conditions on occasion, Walter scored high. Lew tells more about his father's service in WWI.

Walter was drafted May 28, 1918 in Boone County, Iowa. He was assigned to Company G, 88th Infantry Division and designated to use a 30.06 caliber Springfield BAR light machine gun. These had recently been added to the AEF arsenal. Lew has a number of empty clips that match a BAR bullet. He does not know if they were from his father's gun shooting at targets, or if his father picked them up elsewhere.

His father's pay book is among other reminders of his father's service. Tiny neat handwriting meticulously records each monthly pay period and other incidentals, such as "nothing due for clothing." The pay book opens 11/30/18 and his pay is written as $33.00 for one period, $36.00 for another, and the last pay at $33.00. This was paid upon his discharge at Camp Dodge, Iowa. Lew can't explain the differences in monthly pay.

Even though this amount beginning at $30.00 per month may seem low to the reader, the American Yank was the best paid soldier in Europe. Walter took several deductions so his net pay was lower. A sum of $6.60 was deducted each period for the $10,000 insurance policy each soldier was eligible to purchase as a death benefit. Because Walter was single with no dependents, probably his parents were the beneficiaries. Special extra allowances were available for soldiers who were married with dependents.

It is the irony of fate that excellent marksman as he was, Walter never had a chance to serve in the front line trenches. He became a victim to the ravaging "Spanish flu" soon after his arrival in France. The story the family tells is, that Walter was in the field, wrapped up in the great coat issued for cold winter wear. He headed for the latrine but on the way, he passed out. He was taken immediately to a field hospital, where he woke up hours later. It took weeks for him to recover from the illness.

Numerous other soldiers of the 88th Division spent their fighting days in the hospital. The enemy they had to fight now was the highly infectious influenza. Walter wrote that there were a total of 6,845 soldiers in the 88th Division suffering from the flu. Soldiers with the flu were more susceptible to pneumonia, and 1,041 cases of pneumonia were diagnosed. There were no medicines such as antibiotics available, and consequently many soldiers with pneumonia died within a few days. For the others with the flu, it was rest, good food and the warmth of a hospital room with a comfortable bed that eventually cured them. (Note: An American division in World War I had about 28,000 soldiers, including support units. French and English divisions usually had fewer men, about 20,000. The 88th had nearly 8,000 men sick with the flu, or almost 35% of its men away from the front lines.)

Those 35% were badly needed on the front lines because the 88th Division was stationed in the large Argonne sector where relentless fighting took place. Many AEF soldiers were killed, and the seriously injured filled even more hospital beds. This time, the German airplanes, seeing the large Red Cross painted on the roof, spared the hospital buildings from bombing raids. The symbol indicated it was a hospital, and this time the red cross symbol was respected by most of the enemy planes who passed over the target.

(Note: It is now known that the influenza virus started at Camp Funston, Kansas, near the present day Ft. Riley, and was transmitted by those soldiers exposed to it, but did not show any symptoms yet as they carried the virus to France when they shipped out. There is no agreement by historians on why it was called "Spanish" flu.)

Among other items the family has inherited are rare copies of two small military books. They are "Infantry Drill Regulations, 1911" and "The Soldier's Foot & Military Shoe." Both books were essential to the infantryman, but few copies have survived because of the thin delicate paper and its' slightly thicker paper cover. Walter also saved a copy of the small newspaper, "Tars and Tripes," (the actual name) dated May 4, 1919. It was issued to all soldiers while crossing the Atlantic on their return trip home to be discharged.

An item in the collection that must be handled carefully is a jagged three inch long piece of shrapnel from the metal shell casing that exploded from the heat when fired. Shrapnel shells were some of the most dangerous explosives. They created serious wounds including amputation of limbs and even decapitation. If a piece hit the abdominal area, there was only the slightest chance that the victim would survive.

A landing slip marks his arrival in 1918 at LeHarve, a western port of France. All soldiers were required to fill out a post card addressed to home, saying they had arrived safely in France. Also a part of the collection is a map of Haute Alsace-Badricout, France, where Walter's unit was stationed. It was also where he was probably hospitalized. Ultimately nearly two million AEF soldiers landed at various French and British ports during 1917-1918.

It was an impatient Pvt. Walter Edward Longhenry who waited six months for his discharge to come through. An important factor in issuing discharges was the number of ships available for transport. After he finally arrived in the States and was mustered out June 4, 1919, Walter returned home to Boone County. He picked up the plow he had left behind and never ventured far from Iowa again. He had completed eighth grade before joining the army. That seemed enough schooling for him to raise a family and run a farm. Most important to him, was that in his later years he still could pick off a squirrel at 100 paces. Lew laughs as he tells this.

He died in 1986 at age 92, leaving his family this valuable box from his military days. Lew and his brothers and sisters decided recently to donate the contents to the National World War I Museum. There it will be carefully preserved, perhaps some items displayed, and everything made available for historical research.

Walter, the sharpshooter, failed to shoot down the "flu bug." Perhaps it was a good thing he missed. Serious as the flu was, it may have otherwise saved his life. If he had been on the battlefield, he would have been assigned as a sniper or scout with his 30.06 BAR machine gun. That was a dangerous duty, no matter how good you were at shooting.

Flu bug or German machine gun. Not much of a choice. But for Walter, the flu bug won.

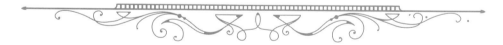

DIED OF TYPHOID AS BULGARIAN PRISONER

Boban Zarkovch's Serbian great-grandfather died of typhoid while a prisoner of the Bulgarians in World War I. Boban, a former Serb who now lives in California, tells stories about his great-grandfather, and when Boban himself met a "Solunlac." There had been a disastrous typhoid epidemic in Serbia in 1914-15, with nearly half a million civilians and soldiers dying in Serbia, Romania, and Russia. Requests from the Serbian government for international help were generously answered by many nations.

The English government sent the Scottish Women's Hospital group and other medical teams to Serbia. France assisted the International Red Cross, while Americans sent money and American Red Cross medical teams. This was the world's worst typhus epidemic up to that time and was believed to have started during the 1912 Balkan War when an Austrian prisoner, sick with typhoid, was interned. The extremely contagious disease is spread by bacteria carried by lice. It can be eliminated in one site, but as long as people traveled or moved around the areas, the lice, which attached themselves to people's bodies and in the seams or lining of clothes, would spread the disease. The lice bite the skin and inject the harmful bacteria.

For years, doctors had no evidence as to what caused the disease. Finally, a doctor during this epidemic isolated the bacteria and was able to prove that lice were the culprit. The first step was to thoroughly clean the hospital rooms and homes where sick people lived. Next, it was necessary to wash their clothes in boiling soapy water, and then scrub their bodies with hot water and strong soap to rid them of the lice.

Lice were especially prevalent among soldiers who lived in trenches day after day. The Allied soldiers about once a month would go to local French washer women who boiled their uniforms and under garments in soapy water. Meanwhile, the men took group showers outside. They were sprayed with a powdered disinfectant. This helped temporarily until the eggs, laid in the seams of the garments, began to hatch in great numbers. Even the boiling soapy water could not destroy all the eggs. When they hatched later, the routine of biting, itching, scratching and lice hunting started all over again.

Bohan also wrote about once having met a "Solunlac." This was the name given a Balkan soldier who fought on the "Solunski front" from 1916-1918. (The Salonika front.) The Solunlac soldier that Bohan met was then in his 90's and unable to tell Boban much about his experiences in the terrible battles against the Bulgarians. Much of the fighting took place in mountainous areas where the Bulgarians had installed machine gun nests and heavy artillery. The Serbs and other Allied soldiers had to climb ladders sometimes to reach the high mountain crevices where the guns were hidden. The mountain rocks and small trees cleverly concealed machine gun nests. It took the grim determination of the Serbs to clear out gun emplacements from the various rock levels and overhangs.

By now the Serbs were filled with the desire for revenge, not only for their own suffering during the march to freedom in 1915, but for the many stories of Bulgarian atrocities against the Serbs' families and their priests. The Serbians held the priests and the church in great reverence. A priest, if available, blessed the men who were leaving for an attack. A great enmity had existed between Serbia and Bulgaria for many years, and World War I only deepened the hatred when Bulgaria joined the Central Powers.

The epidemic was miraculously brought under control. It required hard work cleaning and scrubbing every house and habitat; boiling clothes daily; and using disinfectants. The military assisted by limiting the movement of soldiers in not granting passes and restricting the soldiers from moving from the camps to the villages. Fortunately there was no fighting going on at that time, as the Serbs had surprised both the Allies and Central Powers by defeating the Austrians in 1914. The Austrians immediately retreated to Austria and their homes before the lice started spreading again. Typhus usually resulted in a painful, ghastly death, especially if the victim was in poor health to begin with. Today there are medications to take when traveling where typhus is endemic. Those medications also help to cure the infected.

A century ago there was nothing more than aspirin and vinegar compresses. In one small Serbian village a chapel was built to honor the children who had died of typhus. In the novel,

Reach to Eternity, by Dobrica Cosic, the Serbian author wrote that after one bite from a louse, (scientific name *Typhus exanthematicus*) people often lost their will to live. The international medical teams, by eradicating the lice, helped restore the Serbian spirit. Serbian soldiers' morale was high when the Austrians, along with German armies, attacked later in 1915.

However, this time the Serbians were greatly outnumbered and lacked enough artillery and shells to defend themselves. They retreated over the Albanian mountains where the French and Italian ship evacuated the survivors to the Greek island of Corfu. The soldiers who were physical able, were taken to the Greek city of Salonika and continued to fight the Bulgarians on harrowing snow covered mountains. The Serbs along with English and French troops, achieved victory when Bulgaria surrendered in October, 1918.

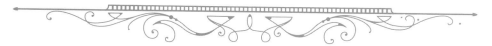

AMERICAN NURSES ON DUTY

"Nurse, I Need Help!"

(Kansas City STAR newspaper sketch of Nurse Grace Simpson in Uniform)

Just as their men stepped into wool khaki colored army uniforms, hundreds of young American women tied on starched white aprons and covered their hair with caps to nurse the more than 200,000 wounded who were in AEF hospitals. The nurses arrived in France by the trainloads at the military hospital receiving stations. They were assigned to their hospitals, big and small, across the entirety of France.

Stories from their diaries and letters home tell of heroic actions as well as the long days and weary nights spent taking care of the wounded. Some soldiers had injuries so serious it was amazing they lived even to reach the hospital much less survived. The women who cared for the wounded were trained nurses, some with graduate degrees and experience in working in the finest of United States hospitals. There had been no difficulty in obtaining the number of nurses needed. By war's end in November, 1918, more than 3400 American nurses, back in the United States, were available to be transported to France if needed.

However, because of the cessation of hostilities, there was no longer the need overseas. Many of those already in France, stayed months longer at their assigned hospital to care for the most serious cases. Like their soldier brothers, many nurses did not return until mid 1919 when their nursing services were no longer needed abroad. American nurses, although not officially members of a service unit integrated into the AEF, were recognized by various governments for their dedication to duty and acts of sacrifice. The Distinguished Service Cross, second in prestige to the Medal of Honor, was awarded to some nurses.

As a result of numerous examples of hard work and the expenditure of arduous hours in World War I, the Regular Army Nurse Corps would eventually be established as an official branch of the United States military. This was after the nurses had proved themselves again in World War II. The recognition was made in 1947 when the military finally acknowledged the value of skilled nursing services given to the wounded. The English nurse, or "Sister" as she was called, also provided the same high standards of conduct in World War I, but was already officially a part of Queen Alexandra's Imperial Nursing Service then. It remained for another cataclysmic war to open the eyes of the American military and honor their invaluable women nurses.

One outstanding example of nursing care, well known in Europe but scarcely heard of in America, is the story of the medical teams provided by the Scottish Women's Hospital. Completely staffed, funded, and administered by British women, this group provided essential nursing services to hundreds of Serbian troops in the two Balkan wars of 1912 and 1913.

The Scottish Women's Hospital staff was requested to return in 1914 when Serbia was struck with the largest typhus epidemic in history to that time. The hospital group eliminated the cause of the disease, and saved what lives they could with the primitive medical knowledge of the time. However, it was the next year in 1915 when their heroic actions during the retreat of the Serbian army, made them famous throughout Europe. It has remained the source of unending gratitude among the Serbian people. (Note: They will be part of the author's next book about the historic retreat of the Serbian Army.)

Nursing in World War I was not for the weak or faint hearted. The strength and stoicism of hundreds of American nurses proved that. Just like their army brothers did, these nurses made the rest of the world recognize and admire the sons and daughters that America sent to rescue Europe from the grip of the Central Powers.

AUNT BESSIE, A RED CROSS NURSE

Few details are known about David Joselyn's Great-Aunt Bessie L. Hilton and her service as a Red Cross nurse in World War I. David knows she came from her home in Lebanon, Missouri, to train at the former University Hospital in Kansas City, Missouri. According to an article in the *Kansas City Star* newspaper on May 24, 1918, she joined the group of 72 nurses who departed Kansas City that evening for France. They were assigned to Base Hospital No. 28 in Limoges, France. The hospital was originated, sponsored, funded and staffed by a group of Kansas University doctors who began assembling it in early 1917. David Joslyn is from Independence, Missouri, and told this story.

A send-off party was held at Union Station in front of the Red Cross booth in the station lobby. The unit was presented with a service flag in a special ceremony. Like many other cities, similar ceremonies were held when the units left for hospitals in France. The nurses wore a dark blue uniform with a military coat and cap modeled after those worn by American soldiers. They also wore the caduceus insignia indicating medical corps on their lapels.

A year earlier on April 24, 1917, ten nurses from Kansas City had left to join Base Hospital No. 21 which had been organized by Washington University Hospital of St. Louis, Missouri. They were part of an emergency team which treated mostly British soldiers in the German's last effort offensive in the spring of 1918. This hospital, which handled the most critical cases, was located near Rouen in northern France.

One nurse, Miss Westman, commented for the newspaper: "There were three weeks when none of us had any rest. We could hear the guns at the front and the wounded poured in upon us almost faster than we could handle them. As fast as we could, we patched them up and sent them on, mostly to England." Base 21 Hospital served many severely wounded men who could not be moved but needed care for months after the war ended. Consequently, it was not until May, 1919, that the hospital team packed up and left for the States. It had provided medical service for 60,000 soldiers, mostly British but also some Americans. (KC Star 9/5/1938.)

According to more *Kansas City Star* articles in 1918, there was a continual flood of applications for nursing training and appointments to serve in the war. Applications of 20-25 per day were processed at the United States Student Nurses' Reserve. Another article lists 340 Kansas and Missouri young women accepted into training but whose names had not previously been published.

Young women answered the call for volunteers for World War 1 as readily as did the young men to the army. The call for help from the Allies created a flood of American women eager to perform their profession as nurses.

THIS PHOTOGRAPH AND INFORMATION WAS RECEIVED JUST BEFORE THE FINAL EDITION OF THE BOOK WAS COMPLETED:

David Joslyn informed the author that he had received from his twin sister, the full uniform and kit bag of their great Aunt Bessie. The sister had possessed the items and upon learning of David's interview, sent them to him to donate to the Museum. These photographs show the uniform jacket, unusual in style and perhaps specially ordered and pants which button at the because a dress would be difficult to wear in a field hospital under battle conditions. The initials and numbers on the satchel probably refer to Bessie Hilton #120, a number assigned to her. The bag unfolds full length and has pockets in which clothing and other items can be stored.

(Photos by Nancy Cramer)

POISON GAS — A TERRIFYING WEAPON

The gas siren whined loud and clear. Each soldier had 60 seconds to locate and put on his gas mask before the invisible weapon would find its target in his body. Here is a personal account that describes one of those unexpected attacks. It is presented in the author's own words and spelling.

In the *Centennial History of Missouri*, by Walter B. Stevens (1921), Maj. Norman B. Comfort described a German gas attack. *"The German is cunning. He knew of our last relief and gassed us terribly. Our present sector is especially adapted to mustard gas, named 'yperite' because this species was first used at Ypres, pronounced 'ep' with a broad 'e'. It is a nasty insidious gas and the most difficult to combat. They pepper our paths with three mustard shells. A white powder lies all around the bursted shell. The color can easily be detected but at first seems harmless and smells like so much lime. The atmosphere becomes permeated and (is) so much heavier than air, it stays in volume close to the ground.*

"Our particular sector is more or less wooded and shrubbed. It is damp, moist country, and when the sun shines, which is really the exception in 'Sunny France,' or has been in the eight months I have been here, a vaporous steam rises. One by one our eyes become red as fire. Men commence vomiting and soon the respiratory organs become affected. The rubbed portions of the body which are tender become raw by friction and the torture grows excruciating.

"We, of course, wore our gas masks in the alert position constantly, donning the masks at frequent times, depending on the wind. The mask itself, is an infernal device, however, and many a time I've argued with myself as to which death would be more agreeable, the gas or the mask itself. It is heavy. The eye glasses become clouded so you can't see. There's a plug in your mouth that chokes you and pincers that crush your nose to smithereens. Sometimes you sleep this way (with the mask on) and awake strangling to death because the plug has slipped out of your mouth. For eight months now, except in the back, (reserve areas) are my pistol and tin hat that have been near my head and the mask has hung around my neck. We never move an inch without those three articles."

Such horrifying attacks affected at least 71,345 American soldiers, with 1,462 dying from the gas. However, these numbers can be misleading. Because being gassed seriously weakened the body's defenses to disease, when men were exposed to the influenza virus, their resistance to the disease was lowered. Consequently, they may have died of pneumonia or tuberculosis and other diseases. Baseball's star pitcher, Christy Mathewson, died prematurely in 1925 at age 45 from tuberculosis, having been gassed in World War I. (Doughboy Center).

It took an average of 60 pounds of mustard gas to kill one soldier. In a new book, *Gas! Gas! Quick, Boys!* writer Michael Fremantle gives details of the importance to the war effort of "chemicals and chemistry." He states that "between 60% and 70% of all combat casualties were caused by shells," either fired from the rapid repeating artillery or sometimes dropped from airplanes or balloons.

One of the most serious incidents occurred at the first Battle of the Somme in 1916 when 30 million shells were expended in four months. That equals 150 rounds per minute. Fremantle explains that while the amount of shells fired was new to warfare, the chemicals had been developed in the 19th century. It was the combination of advancements in both chemistry and in the manufacturing processes that created the disasters. No longer did Germany have to depend upon Chile for nitrate import, which had been blockaded by the British. In the meantime, Fritz Haber, a German chemist, discovered how ammonium could be produced from hydrogen and nitrogen in the air to produce mustard gas. (Fremantle)

Just as it required 60 pounds of mustard gas to kill one soldier, so could 500 pounds of high explosive powder, or 5,000 rounds of ammunition do the same damage. Mr. Fremantle quotes statistics showing that 65 million gas filled shells were fired during the war. On one single night, July 12, 1917, about 50,000 rounds of mustard gas were fired at the British at Second Ypres.

The Germans were the first to use gas in the form of 110 tonnes (sic) of chlorine on April 22, 1915, in battle fields near Langemarck, Belgium. The unsuspecting British had no warning and consequently hundreds died or were sickened by the chlorine. In mid-May, 1915, the British and French retaliated with their own version of phosgene-chlorine mixture, code-named "White Star." Special brigades were formed and trained in the use of the different gasses which were delivered in either artillery shells or hand grenades. Also, training was provided in use of flame projectors (throwers.) Weapons had emerged which were unimaginable a few years before. Special troops were designated with the rank of Chemist Corporal. (Special companies RE of 1914-1918)

American troops felt the first use of the dreaded mustard gas by the Germans in 1917. Mustard gas, being difficult to detect at first by sight or smell, also was insidious because it could be absorbed into the ground and lie there waiting for days or weeks. A change from a cold to a warmer temperature releases the deadly gas. A skin burn can be caused by just one drop of the chemical sprayed on people standing within 10 cubic meters. (How Stuff Works).

Mustard gas was widely used near the end of the war and many AEF soldiers were exposed to its dangerous effects. It is estimated that one million soldiers and civilians were injured by the use of poisonous gas, and more than 100,000 people died from exposure to chemical weapons. World War I was a war that used large numbers. Big numbers of killer agents brought unbelievably big numbers of dead and wounded. Poisonous gasses, as a weapon of war, would not be used again until the Iraq-Iran war of the 1980's.

A verse selected from the well known poem by the famous World War I British poet, Wilfred Owen, *Dulce et Decorum* est, addresses the terror of an impending gas attack:

> *Gas! GAS! Quick, boys!—An ecstasy of fumbling,*
> *Fitting the clumsy helmets just in time;*
> *But someone still was yelling out and stumbling,*
> *And flound'ring like a man in fire or lime…*
> *Dim, through the misty panes and thick green light,*
> *As under a green sea, I saw him drowning.*

Owen sees through his clouded glass goggles of the mask the greenish colored gas surrounding and enveloping the hapless soldier who can not put his mask on in time to prevent breathing the poison. Owen had been cited for bravery and was in line to receive the Military Cross. He was killed in battle on November 4, 1918, just a week before the signing of the Armistice. This poem was one of only five that were published in his lifetime and is considered one of his best of all his writing. He wrote this after experiencing a gas attack.

HE ALMOST LOST HIS LAST BATTLE

Dawson Clark, Sr.
(Courtesy of Deloris Clark)

Dawson Clark, Sr. fought many battles in World War I, but he almost lost his last battle – that one was with mustard gas. He was gassed when he and his unit, Company I, 325th Infantry Regiment were shelled with mustard gas somewhere in the Meuse-Argonne campaign. Clark's story is told by his daughter-in-law, Marcia Clark, Raymore, Missouri. She nursed him during his later years and remembers him sitting in his chair, and smoking a cigar, against his doctor's orders, and coughing and coughing, again and again.

After his return from the war, Private Clark was sent to a Veteran's Administration hospital, where he met his future wife. They were married but later she developed cancer and died. Although he was on total disability, he tried his hand at commercial photography for a while. However, his lungs kept filling with fluid, and he would have to be hospitalized for three months at a time. He was a recipient of the Purple Heart as were many gassed veterans.

Deloris married his son, Dawson Jr. on April 3, 1955, after a six week courtship. Dawson, Jr. was an alcoholic, as was his father but both joined AA and gave up the drinking. Tragedy, however, still seemed to shadow the family . Her brother-in-law was blinded by a dynamite explosion in Wadena, Iowa. Nevertheless, the blinded man made his mother a beautiful wooden cabinet despite his lack of sight.

A surgical technician before her marriage, it seemed natural that Deloris would assume the task of caring for the two men. Her father-in-law, Dawson Sr., had his bedroom upstairs and would ring a bell sometimes as often as five times a day to summon her help. At the time Deloris was mother to two little children, and time after time, she would climb the stairs to find out what her father-in-law wanted.

He had been urged by his doctor to exercise because that would help clear his lungs. However, he seemed overwhelmed by his disability. Walking or other exercise was not on his agenda. Instead, about the only time he showed interest in something was when his monthly disability check arrived. Then he would go to the American Legion where he was a member and play cards. He never talked about his wartime experiences to Deloris. Perhaps he shared them with his Legion buddies. This was nearly always the pattern of most veterans. They were reluctant to tell their families about their memories or experiences in the war.

The family, therefore, knows little about Private Dawson's army life. Any papers remaining are with another branch of the family or have been lost. Research shows that the 325th Regiment was attached to the 82nd Division which was active at the fighting at St. Mihiel, Meuse-Argonne and Lorraine. The soldiers fought on an almost daily basis from August through November 1, 1918, just before the Armistice was signed. If the Regiment was not fighting, they were marching to another site, or in reserve, ready to be called into action. An example of such call to action reads:

Oct. 17 – The 2nd Battalion, 325th Infantry, was ordered from bridge reserve to accomplish this mission {cover the valley of the "Agron and village of Champigneulle} with fire…after progressing only 500 meters beyond the lines of the 326th Infantry… it came under heavy fire. Under brigade orders, it retired…" (82nd Division Documents)

The next day at 4 A.M. the 325th relieved the 78th Division on Cote 182. Two days later with little opposition, the 325th formed a new line on a ridge which formed a strong point. Always moving, sometimes in between other units, and pressing forward as General Pershing demanded, the troops were on the road except when enemy fire was the strongest.

Sometimes troop movements were slow and difficult. Massive numbers of men, roads crowded with hordes of refugees, hemmed in by huge artillery trucks, made travelling from one post to another slow and difficult. Units and individuals became lost from each other. Stragglers emerged from numerous wooded areas and joined up with any AEF unit they found. At other times three or four sets of orders would be issued within a few hours times, often countermanding each other. The challenge of moving thousands of men, horses, and artillery guns on the only three primary French roads in the area was further complicated by road conditions. The engineers could not keep up needed repairs in roads that were muddy and carved with holes filled with water and debris. This movement of men was one of Pershing's biggest headaches.

The Meuse-Argonne territory was thick with woods and wandering streams amid the ridges and valleys. Maps were often inaccurate or issued late. Commanders often had no time to study them before sending orders to attack. For the men and officers of the AEF it is remarkable that they fought as well as they did. Inexperienced, poorly trained, facing heavy artillery bombardment, and not knowing if the shells contained explosive powder or gas, which meant stopping to put on the ever present mask, the men encountered many unknowns. This is a partial explanation for the high loss of lives and numbers of wounded.

The 325th had 1,170 wounded, of whom 94 later died, while 239 were killed in action in the 49 day fighting. (history.army.mil/documents/wwi/82div.htm) The total number of Americans casualties was 120,000 for the taking of the Meuse-Argonne sector. (Sullivan) Perhaps Private Clark had good reasons for not telling his family about his time in France. A farmer, he had been inducted into the army on Feb. 22, 1918, at West Union, Iowa, and was discharged 16 months later at Camp Dodge, Iowa, on June 26, 1919. He died on February 5, 1964, at age 70 in Wadena, Iowa, where he is buried. His wounds, seen and unseen, resulted from only a few months spent in France. Yet he bore them the remainder of his long life.

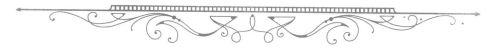

BRYAN TEDDER

"Served with honor in the War"

Bryan Tedder with unknown lady
(Loaned by Gail Long)

Two family photos show a tall lanky young man holding the reins of his horse, and in another photo he is standing in the company of a young lady, possibly his sweetheart. This rural American soon joined thousands of other Midwestern men in putting on suits of khaki and binding their legs with the puttee wraps that kept water out of their boots.

These "Rookies" traveled by the hundreds to Camp Doniphan, Oklahoma, for months of basic training. There they formed the various units of the 35th Division. Private Bryan Tedder was assigned to the 137th Infantry which was made up from former National Guard units. He later was transferred to the 69th Infantry Brigade. His story is told by granddaughter, Gail Long of Nine Mile Falls, Washington.

Arriving in France at the rate of 300,000 soldiers per month, the soldiers headed toward the battlefields later made famous by the horrendous fighting that occurred there. Americans at home were to become familiar with these names: Alsace-Lorraine, St. Mihiel, Argonne Forest, and Verdun, known also as the Meuse-Argonne offensive. For three years the French and Germans had fought over Verdun, a large sector of land in northeastern France. German control was never wrested away. German casualties were 330,000 dead and wounded while the French suffered a similar number of 378,000 dead and wounded. (Ousby)

However, in the fall of 1918 the influx of energetic, enthusiastic, and mostly inexperienced American doughboys began to change the direction of the war. Among those AEF soldiers was the 69th Infantry who participated with the French in the retaking of Verdun, despite terrible losses on both sides. Verdun had been captured by Germany in the Franco-Prussian War of 1871, and had become a symbol of disgrace to France. To win back control of Verdun from Germany was one of France's goals. The 1918 French victory at Verdun wiped away many years of shame.

After arriving in France, Bryan was stricken with the flu, as were hundreds of soldiers. He was hospitalized and when he recovered, he rejoined his unit on the front just in time to be among hundreds of the 69th Division who were gassed by the Germans. The 69th Brigade, part of the 35th Division, was assigned to be the leading column of support and reserve columns. They faced the German First Guard Division, considered the best in the German army, and the Second Landwehr, a less formidable unit of former soldiers over 35 years old.

On September 26 at 2:30 A.M. the AEF began a three hour intensive artillery shelling to destroy obstacles in the Americans' path to the Germans to take control of the Grange-le-Compte sector in the Argonne zone. The preliminary heavy artillery barrage was the usual firing pattern before the infantry began an advance.

At other times the barrages could continue five to six days without ceasing. (Pypes Family papers). Casualties were high on both sides. For the 35th Division their losses were 1,480 deaths, 6,001 wounded, and 167 captured, huge losses incurred during one large important battle. An American division had about 25,000 to 28,000 men including all its units on the front and in the rear as support troops. This number of casualties amounted to almost 30% of the 35th Division.

Like many soldiers, Bryan afterwards spoke little of his army days. He did tell his granddaughter, Gail Long, about spending days in tents with the floor so filled with mud it never dried out. He told her about being gassed, probably by a gas filled German artillery shell. The distance was too far between the lines for the enemy to creep up and use gas canisters, as they had early in the war. The gas used was either phosgene or chlorine but not mustard gas, fortunately for Bryan. Mustard gas was also used in the Argonne and could cause immediate death or serious injury to the inner parts of the body, if large enough quantities were used. If small quantities were expelled, it could cause an otherwise early death from complications.

Bryan was discharged April 23, 1919, at Camp Funston, Kansas, and returned home to marry his sweetheart, Mary Imo Hamilton, on February 2, 1920. He had brought her an embroidered pink handkerchief from France as a symbol of his remembrance. They farmed near Hutchinson, Kansas, and raised two daughters, Helen Ada and Mary Ellen, and one son, Bryan Jr. The soldier, Bryan, Sr., was born in Lone Jack, Missouri, on June 16, 1896 to Jesse Tedder and Ellen Bryan Tedder. They had eight children. One died in infancy and another one died as an adult of appendicitis. Granddaughter Gail has a small United States flag that belonged to her grandfather when he was at Camp Doniphan, and also the Bible he carried in France. Bryan died August 10, 1966, in Hutchinson of lung cancer. Men who had been gassed were more susceptible in later years to respiratory diseases. This medical fact was unknown in 1918 because gas had never been used in warfare before. Diagnosis and treatment of the after effects became new challenges to the medical profession.

His family has a certificate that was sometimes awarded to veterans. It portrays a woman as Liberty, knighting a kneeling soldier. (See Introduction of book.) Bryan was injured twice, once by influenza and then by being gassed. Catching the flu, a previously unknown illness, was something unexpected. But being gassed was something Bryan might have anticipated to happen because he had a new gas mask issued to him. In spite of these injuries, he probably just hoped he "would serve with honor."

Granddaughter Gail agrees that he endeavored to do his best, calling him "one of those everyday honorable men." She adds, "Who happened to be my grandfather." Truly spoken with pride.

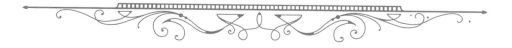

MEDIC FOR VETERINARY CORPS

John Martin Miller

Private John Martin Miller
(Courtesy World War I Bonus Case Files,
State Historical Society of Iowa, Des Moines)

Private Martin's application for his veteran's bonus, filed January 22, 1923 was for the amount of $178.00 for 344 days service in the Veterinary Corps. He served from July 22, 1918, until June 30, 1919, another Iowa farmer answering the Army's call.

There is limited information in Private Martin's military file. Perhaps his file was one of those that burned in the 1973 fire at the National Archives in St. Louis. However, a photograph from the Iowa Department of Veteran Affairs exists showing him to be a handsome, proud looking, serious young man, dressed in civilian clothes as if ready to begin his day of work.

According to the information with the photograph, he was born May 22, 1889, in Dudley, Iowa. He entered the army on July 22, 1918, and was sent eventually to Veterinary Hospital No. 2-A somewhere in France, after veterinary training at Camp Lee, Virginia. Hospital 2-A may have been in the general area of the Verdun sector. It had an animal capacity for 1,000 animals. (The Army Veterinary Service During the Great War, WWI).

An internet article, "The Army Veterinary Service during the Great War," shows a photo of troops at Hospital #2 but does not identify the site. As might be expected with priority shipping of 300,000 combat troops each month, the moving of veterinary personnel overseas was low on the priority list. In April, 1918, there were 132 veterinary corps officers in France, but a serious shortage existed of enlisted men, considerably affecting the care of animals. Eventually there were more than 9700 enlisted men, who provided with an extra force of 2,000 laborers, were able to maintain a reasonable form of care. Sometimes, men from the remount stations were called in to supplement the manpower shortage.

By the end of the war, there were 15 AEF veterinary hospitals working with a total animal capacity of 12,000. This still was far too few hospitals and medics, because the horses were worn out by now, and suffered from slow healing wounds and starvation. The medical personnel had to resort to using picket lines, corrals, paddocks, and similar facilities to provide space for the animals. Additional shipments of animals were delayed from their sources in Portugal, Spain, and France. This shortage of draught animals created huge problems in the important movement of artillery and infantry especially from St. Mihiel to Verdun in October and November, 1918.

For the horses of the Army of Occupation of Germany, facilities were built in two large cities, Koblenz and Trebes. Knock-down type stables could be shipped as temporary quarters. When the army sent home all its troops from Germany, most horses in good enough condition were sold to the public.

The veterinary corps received much criticism as to how it initially handled the veterinary services for its animals. The men were poorly prepared, had inadequate facilities and training, and did not even understand the importance of removing sick and wounded horses from the battlefields. Help from the Cavalry and Remount Stations was invaluable, especially in evacuating horses and mules. The French and British recognized this lack of preparation of these valuable animals and criticized the AEF until the latter provided adequate facilities and more manpower was available.

Living, healthy animals were as valued as much as manpower and imperative to the success of battles. Strong, well cared for animals were necessary to pull the artillery guns, wagons, and ambulances. By the end of the war, fortunately, the Veterinary Corps had organized itself into a good operating unit, and the mistakes, errors, and carelessness were a thing of the past. (Veterinary Hospitals) But lessons learned were lessons remembered, and the Veterinary Corps was no longer the last unit for its needs to be considered by the military command.

Unfortunately for the untreated and injured horses of World War 1, their suffering was remembered only by their caretakers. Often, the sympathetic caretakers were unable to provide the help the sick animals required. Meanwhile, trucks and other motorized vehicles were replacing the horse and mule power wherever possible. While mules were found to be more capable of hauling artillery guns and wagons out of mud than trucks, the pulling was arduous for a poorly fed and overworked animal. So their lives were considerably shortened by this work.

It is estimated that more than 800,000 British horses died on the Belgian Front. (Horses in World War One) Reliable figures for mules and horses of other armies are not available.

The Great War had many victims, and thousands of horses and mules were among the most helpless victims of all. It may have been painful also for John Martin Miller, a farmer, to witness the suffering of these powerful mules and often beautiful horses.

THE POLAR BEARS

Americans under British command fought in Vladivostok and in Siberia from 1918 to 1920 against both the Bolsheviks (Reds) and the White Russians (anti-Bolsheviks) as a joint force with Japanese and the Czech rebel soldiers. They were not removed from their stations until August 25, 1919. The AEF were called "The Polar Bears" and their shoulder patch shows a white bear. Of the 2,000 Americans, 244 died and 308 were wounded.

REMOUNT STATIONS — WHAT IN THE HECK ARE THEY?

For most of World War I, horses and mules provided the power that moved the Army. They were as necessary then to the AEF, as trucks are today to the modern military. The remount station was where horses and mules were examined and treated. They were eliminated if they had a highly contagious disease that might infect other animals in the stable. The station served as a clinic or hospital for sick or injured animals as well as a place where they could recuperate from surgery or injuries.

The United States, when war was declared, was as unprepared for horse power as it was for manpower. The U.S. Veterinary Corps was established on June 3, 1916 as a part of the National Defense Act which instituted many imperative defense programs. The French and the British from the beginning of the war in July, 1914, had purchased thousands of horses and mules from the United States. Missouri was one state which provided at least one million mules for the Allies. (Meyer)

In 1917 the United States had 72 veterinary officers but no enlisted men to care for all the transport and riding animals they would need the next two years. At war's end 18 months later, all these figures had changed radically. The Veterinary Corps numbered 2,312 officers and 16,391 enlisted men. The army compiled rules and policies for recruitment, training procedures, and equipment that related to the large numbers of animals under their care.

Because mules could handle the muddy and rough French terrain better than trucks, mules were in high demand. As of October 30, 1918 it was estimated that the AEF had at least 165,000 in its use. Missouri bred mules were highly desirous as stated in Duane Meyer's book, *The Heritage of Missouri*. He wrote the "He (the mule) kept the artillery right up to the front… went without his oats… waded through mud and over filled-in shell holes." The mule "took his share of gas and shell shock, slept out o'nights in… rain and cold." "He pulled and pulled…" "The mules at times was the soldier's best friend."

The soldier who drove the mules was called a "mule skinner," and he had to deal with the stubbornness of his team, probably using a lot of profanity in the process. For many tasks, the mule was preferred because it could stand up longer, travel longer distances, and required less feed. Mules would take routes that horses refused to take, such as crossing a stream on a log and climbing rough, narrow paths.

Mules would avoid holes in the planks of a bridge or other places, thus not breaking a leg. Horses were unable to sense the danger there and consequently many were injured, often resulting in "putting them down," or in other words, shooting the injured horse whose broken leg would not heal properly.

The sergeant major supervised all activity in the mule camp. This included shoeing the mules, getting coal for fuel for the blacksmith, repairing equipment, and selection of "skinners" (drivers.) For each battalion there were two teams of four mules for transporting food to the trenches or camp. Each team of four mules had approximately 3,000 pounds to haul, so rarely did one see a team of only two mules hitched to a supply wagon.

In addition to pulling wagons, animals were hitched to crudely built ambulances and kitchen wagons. Much of the driving had to be done at night because of danger of being shelled. No lights were allowed and roads had disintegrated into deep ruts or pools of water. Occasionally mules because of their greater strength were used to pull a horse that was drowning in a river or had fallen into a shell crater and could not climb out without assistance.

Teams of from eight to 12 animals dragged the heavy artillery from site to site. Some of the bigger guns were so heavy not even 16 animals could move it, so Ford tractors were brought over from the United States to do the transporting. German guns, such as the Big Bertha and the Paris Gun were of such size and weight they had to be moved on railroad cars.

The veterinary corps served as the medical corps for the animals. The doctors had to detect diseases, prevent, and treat them. The most common disease was mange which affected 47% of the animals. They were treated and most returned to work. Losses of animals due to gas attacks were high. The animal's mask was not very effective, and the soldier had to put his on first, exposing the horse or mule for a longer period of time to the gas. (The Army Veterinary Service…)

Total AEF losses of animals during the war are debatable and inaccurate. At times the feed was so limited many animals starved to death. Many animals gnawed the wagon wheels or frame, or stretched to chew on a tree limb trying to satisfy their hunger. The average horse required about 12 pounds of oats and 10 pounds of hay. Shipping and distributing this amount of food for just one artillery battery of 100 horses created mammoth problems for the Quartermaster Corps. Multiply that by even 50 batteries and the situation is almost unsolvable at times.

The injured ones were transported to the veterinary hospitals by trains because of the severity of their wounds. Officers performed surgeries whenever possible, but many animals were too weak and exhausted and had to be put down. For an animal lover, this "coup d' grace" was an emotional time. All numbers are broad estimates and most are far too low. It was also difficult to keep track of the animals killed by explosions or gas. (The Army Veterinary Service…)

Some men raised on a farm wanted to get far away from the obstinate mule. But for others, their love of animals was such that they were pleased with an assignment to care for the powerful four legged creatures. Despite importing extra horses from Spain and Portugal as well as the

United States, by war's end the Allies experienced a great loss of animals and had to substitute other means of power.

Despite the great losses of both horses and men in cavalry charges against machine guns, some commanders continued to order them until the last days of the war. This was illustrated by the Germans' use in their last desperate struggle in what was known as "The Hundred Days' Offensive" which began in spring of 1918. However, war tactics had changed dramatically, and the use of cavalry charges was being slowly eliminated with the exception of battles on the Middle East and Eastern fronts, although, some cavalry charges took place twenty years later in the early days of World War II when the Germans attacked Poland and Russia.

Soldier leading horse loaded with artillery shells out of the muddy field
(National Archives, Courtesy VFW Magazine, 2004)

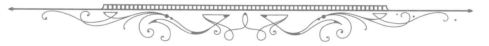

PROLIFIC IS HIS MIDDLE NAME

Private Loren Goddard, 168th Infantry, 42nd Division (Rainbow), First Army, was a prolific letter writer. The fifty or more original letters that exist today are carefully enclosed in their fragile envelopes. Niel Johnson, widower of Goddard's niece, Verna Gail Johnson, Independence, Missouri, has carefully preserved them in archival boxes, along with newspaper articles and photographs of the handsome young soldier. Mr. Johnson and his late wife carefully researched the Goddard family, including the two members who fought in World War I.

The cache of letters that Loren's mother and sister preserved is only a portion of Loren's correspondence. He mentioned answering letters to numerous other relatives and friends, writing as many as 13 letters one time. This created a dilemma for him as he didn't want to use the same message in each. But with strict army censorship rules, not much could be written that would be different to 13 separate readers.

Loren Goddard
(Courtesy of Niel Johnson)

This writer became curious as to what Goddard was NOT writing about, when he repeatedly said, "Well, there's nothing else to write." Censorship certainly was one reason he failed to reveal what he was assigned to do during the almost 18 months he served in France. But perhaps there were other reasons.

Perhaps there was a reluctance to reveal the gruesome details of war he had witnessed, the shelling that blew up bodies and destroyed property. Possibly he wanted to keep a hand on his feelings, and check his revulsion to the war. The 42nd Division was involved in some of the most ferocious fighting of the war. This reluctance to tell about their experiences was true with most men who were stationed in action zones. In every letter Loren writes claims he is "in the best of health," even when he was in a hospital "severely" wounded as his discharge paper describes his condition, or when a bad cold hung on for weeks as did such a cold when he was in Germany.

Goddard, of Fairfield, Iowa, was a member of Company M, 168th Infantry of the famed 42nd Rainbow Division. Composed of men from more than 26 states, the men's home states stretched " like a rainbow across America," hence the nickname "Rainbow." The 42nd was engaged in 12 battles from February 21, 1918, until November 11, 1918, when the Armistice was signed. It was one of the few divisions that saw most of the combat in the war.

Goddard was wounded three times and spent a number of days in military hospitals. He always returned to the front lines after each recovery. Goddard was first wounded on March 9 , 1918, by shrapnel. The official record records his injuries as "severe." His second injury was possibly on July 28 when he and hundreds of other soldiers were gassed. His third injury, also tagged as "severe," occurred on September 12. Mr. Johnson has preserved hometown newspaper articles noting each time Loren was wounded.

Loren's first letter in the collection is dated February 9, 1918, "somewhere in France," and was written soon after he arrived. The next one on February 15 enthusiastically described a football game between Companies M and K. It was scoreless until the last fifteen seconds of the last quarter. Suspense was broken when one Company M soldier "drop kicked a 30 yard goal."

The next letter is dated March 3, 1918, and was written six days before his first wounding in France. He commented on how "great it is for site {sic} seers" but he "will take the U.S.A. any time. The states has it on this country to the tune of 99 ¾." Official censorship forbade Goddard from writing details about his wounds, how and where they occurred. However, after the first wounding of March 9, he could not refrain from proudly writing that "the Huns are minus 4 of their number caused by my {30}, which is sure a good old rifle." Surprisingly, this remark was not deleted by the censor.

Loren went on to say that others of his outfit "all got their number (of Huns) but I did not have quite the chance they did, as I am used in a special connection with the regiment and was not where I could connect with the enemy at all times." This is his first mention of the "special connection," but he never told what it was. Was he a scout, a forward observer, or a messenger?

A May 19th letter, next in the collection, mentioned he was in the "casual camp," usually a place of recuperation. The trip from that camp back to his company was by train. Loren and the other 31 soldiers on the train stopped off at several "fair towns and cities," enjoying visits there. He added he "has not wrote {sic} to Willard," his brother in a different division, Company M, 133rd Infantry, 34th Division. Loren assures his mother he will soon write Willard. (Note: The 133rd was at that time in the States where Willard served as a trainer for new recruits.)

Loren's first wounds were from shrapnel in the arm and leg. The last wound, termed "severe" is not described, although he was wounded once with a bullet in his wrist. This third wounding he received in the well – publicized offensive the Meuse-Argonne in which 1.2 million American soldiers took part. The fighting actions of the 42nd made headlines in many newspapers.

Months later, in February, 1919, his mother wrote that she had received her allotment only once, and that was in November, 1918. Loren assured her he would look into it if the allotment did not start to come regularly. He often asked about the health of his sister, Marie, if she had overcome her nervousness and was she taking up her music again. Another family member, Harry Jolly, was also among the 54 men from Fairfield, Iowa, who all enlisted at the same time. Jolly was related by the marriage of Loren's father to Jolly's mother. Loren's parents had divorced some years ago but details are scarce.

Because his mother was divorced, Loren was able to send an allotment only to her and not to both parents, as many soldiers did. Loren appealed to the Y.M.C.A. for assistance in tracking down the missing monies. A July 8th letter was written on French letter head, "Le Foyer Du Soldat – Union Franco – Americaine," roughly translated as "Hall of Soldiers – French and American Together." In it, Loren mentioned hearing from his father, regularly, but not often. "Father is well as you probably know." He adds thankfully, "It was quiet that night," then added, "Our artillery has been pretty busy up until tonight. The Germans are sending over a shell or two…"

On July 19 Loren replied to his mother's statement that she had not heard from him yet. "I do not understand the reason for it as I have been writing you about once a week." He notes it had rained a lot, and was hot in France. He "did hear from Willard, who told what had been going on in our old company."

Another letter curiously reads, "You say the people are giving the (blotted out by censor) a lot of credit for the work {underlined} they have been doing over here. Well, all though {sic} we have not been in many scrapes, I sure do think we do deserve some credit for the work {underlined} we have done…" (Note: Some soldiers thought civilians back home were criticizing the troops for not fighting enough and letting the French and British bear the brunt of the attacks.) The letter continued to note that in the previous week there were many "fireworks" where he was stationed. "Things have calmed down now." "You understand what I am telling or trying to tell you." He saw Harry {Jolly} again after arriving at the present site. "I guess him and I are going through the war with damage done…I have a hunch that a Goddard is to {too} ornery to lose much in a small war."

He says he cannot get comfortable enough to make his writing legible. What does this mean? Is he lying on a hospital bed? His bravado approach probably was meant to reassure his mother, but perhaps he was reassuring himself also.

Loren's letter of August 7 reassures his sister he will be in the hospital only a short time. The wound is healing fast, and it has been only a week since he left the company. "They were having quite a time holding the 'Boche back'…" He was several miles away from the firing line "and "sure seems quite {sic} to me. It is quite a relief also. The Americans have been making quite a showing in the present drive by the Allies." ("Boche" is a derogatory name for a German.)

Loren was in a convalescent camp again on August 15th when he wrote a letter reassuring his mother that "the Kaiser is fairing {sic} badly, at least his men are…" He was also "building barracks that hardens us up a little before we are sent back to the lines." He says the work is easy but he was sunburned and in good condition except for his neck, "as the bullet entered a very vital spot." He worried about injuries to the rest of his company in the offensive against the 'Boche.' "

(Note: This likely would be toward the end of the massive Great Spring Offensive in which the Germans made one last desperate push to end and win the war before more thousands of Americans arrived in Europe.) (Banks)

In this letter his handwriting is clear and steady, more legible than in other letters. Loren indicates that a casualty list that would have noted his wounding on July 28th had not been posted yet. The date of July 28 fits into the time frame when the 42nd was attacking and pushing German troops back. Because of the enormous number of casualties, and the need for accuracy in the accounting for missing bodies, the AEF often delayed issuing the casualty lists for several weeks.

In a letter dated August 18, 1918, Goddard said that only one man from Fairfield had perished to date. The man was August Van Oyen. Jolly was believed either to be in the air corps up for a commission, or he was "shell shocked." According to the official record, of Ma?? 15 (month is illegible), Jolly was listed as "slightly wounded. Loren's letter continues, describing his wound. "The other wound bothers me but not enough to hurt…{using} a walker. I was lucky to come out as easy as I did. I was hit with a piece of shrapnel and right on the knee cap." He jokes, "the knee cap knows most of the sounds of a Boche bullet and is ready at any time to carry me to a shell hole…Sometimes it gets nervous too."

Because his mother is expressing often a worry for his safety, he tries to reassure her by advising her "to take life as easy as you can and don't worry yourself away over me. If I don't pull through, many of them (the others) will never see the states (also) … one thing is sure. I have done or tried to do my little bit and hope I have succeeded …"

In these surviving letters, this is the only time Loren mentions the possibility of his not coming back. Perhaps he has finally come close, for a brief moment, to reaching his breaking point.

Goddard's letters followed the typical pattern of many other soldiers' letters: 1) How are you? 2) I can't say what I am doing 3) I am very busy (or) Not busy now 4) I am fine (even if he is in a hospital and 5) Write often and I'll try to answer. In Goddard's case, he had letters from many friends and relatives, and he tried conscientiously to answer each one. An almost impossible job, he probably concluded.

Meanwhile, letters from home for Loren were piling up at his camp until he was released from the hospital. He was relieved to hear from Willard in August, 1918, and curiously enough, it was censored by the United States Marine Corps. Sometimes Marines were attached to army units, and this may have been the case with the company commander, a Marine.

Trying to match the date of Goddard's wounds with activity of the 42nd Division of about 28,000 men can be guess work at times. At the time of Loren's wounding on March 9th the Germans were spearheading a massive and successful campaign. All their forward motion came to a halt on August 8. The German Army's General Eric von Ludendorf called August 8 the "Black Day for Germany," as thousands of demoralized German soldiers surrendered when they lost the battle for the city of Amiens. The city was captured by the British, using additional Australian and Canadian troops. (Banks)

Loren's last wound was in his right wrist above the joint, probably from a machine gun, he wrote, adding that his mother would have heard where he was wounded before his letter came. He described himself as "some sort of a jinx," because every time he came back from the hospital, "the boys look for something to take place." "I must quit this kind of talk, which is of no interest to you, I don't think." This is the first time his optimism has left him, at least in the letters that are preserved.

After the Armistice was signed on November 11, 1918, at exactly 11 A.M., the fighting ceased. There would be no quick departure from France for Loren, as his 42nd division was part of the 250,000 troops assigned to the Army of Occupation of Germany. They marched or "walked" from their last location for several hundreds of miles through numerous villages and towns; their destination was the area of Wiedergissen, Germany. (Note: Correct spelling is Wiedergeben). It is bordered by Belgium on the northwest, and Luxembourg and France on the west. The explanation for the necessity of occupation, as the soldiers were informed, was that the Allies needed troops in Germany until the Versailles Peace Treaty was actually signed. The required signatures were affixed in a brief ceremony held in Versailles, France, outside Paris, on May 28, 1919. By then, only 110,000 troops remained in Germany and France. All AEF were finally withdrawn from Germany in 1923.

Loren heard from his brother, Willard. Only one letter from the Willard is among those preserved. Perhaps that is the one Loren refers to. In addition to the delay in Loren receiving mail from home, the weather was miserable as it rained almost daily. It was difficult for Loren and other soldiers to keep their spirits up while with the AOG. In addition, rumors were rampant as to a departure date. The rumors never proved true, and this didn't help the troops' morale either.

Loren finally returned home, went to work, but never married. His sister, Marie, married George Applegate. They had one child, a daughter, Verna Gail, who married Niel Johnson. Loren's mother opened a small business. With one exception, from October 30 to November 25, 1918, Loren had written once a week or more often. The October 30th letter he admits he "carried in {my} pocket for weeks," and was postmarked Luxembourg, Europe. There is no explanation except possibly he was in transit from France to Ahrweiler, Germany, in the Rhineland Palatinate.

For Loren, frequent letter writing may have been how he managed to connect with the family ties that sustained him through his 18 – month overseas ordeal. Writing may have staved off homesickness, especially when he was away from his unit and in the hospital. He had friends in the company and was fond of his brother, Willard, although their paths rarely met. Once home, Loren became a machinist in Cedar Rapids for many years. Later in life he suffered a stroke that affected one side of his body, and he retired in his early sixties. He left a helmet with a flag painted on it, which a relative proudly keeps.

Loren served as a member of the illustrious 42nd Division. This unit was one Pershing relied upon when he needed aggressive and experienced soldiers. It had been one of the first divisions to go to France with Pershing, so Loren and other members of the 42nd had "been there, seen it, and done it." Perhaps writing dozens of letters helped contribute to his positive attitude. It may also have been his way to endure the dangers of the battlefield.

THERE WERE THREE OF US

Willard Goddard, Loren's brother
(Courtesy of Niel Johnson)

Willard James Goddard decided to follow his brother, Loren, to war by also enlisting in the Iowa National Guard at Ottumwa, Iowa, on April 30, 1917, less than a month after President Wilson issued a call fo volunteers for the army. Willard was a member of M Company, 133rd Infantry Regiment for a year until the army combined the National Guard units. Then Willard and Loren were separated with Willard being transferred to Company K of the 308th Infantry Regiment, 77th Division.

Only 21 years of age, Willard must have quickly impressed the authorities with his leadership ability and was promoted to corporal about eight months after enlisting. The 133rd was reassigned along with the 134th regiments to make up the 67th Brigade of the 34th Division, which was known by its nickname, "Sandstorm Division." This was a reminder of the windy, sand blown training at Camp Cody, New Mexico. It also gained the name of Red Bull Division with the shoulder patch depicting a red head of a bull. Family lore has it that Willard spent many months there training raw recruits.

Then his division was shipped to France just one month before the Armistice was signed, so they were not involved in any combat. His story is told by Niel Johnson, Independence, Missouri, whose late wife, Verna Gail, was a niece of Willard's. Two letters from Willard have been preserved. The one letter has places cut out where evidently the censor thought important information was written. Willard described his trip over to France and was anxious "to get on line." He assured his readers he would go see Loren. Did that happen? There is no written evidence that he did. Perhaps it was because Willard was in southern France, many miles from Loren's station.

However, his brother, Loren, was a prodigious letter writer (his mother saved more than 50 of them). For whatever reason, Willard appears to have left most the letter writing to his brother. In a family where the mother and sister requested frequent communication in a written form, Willard seems to have fallen short in this regard. This made him the topic of many letters, "Where is Willard?" or "Who has heard from Willard?"

The other preserved letter that has not been altered by the censor was addressed to both Mother and Sister and announced he would be back in "old U.S.A" in April, 1919 sometime. He had received a letter from his girl friend and asked, "How is Addie treating me?" This was a curious request which he did not explain. Perhaps they knew – maybe he didn't write to Addie often either. He also inquired as to the size of Anamosa, Iowa. Addie had just visited cousins, the Jolly family, there. Willard wanted to know if it was big enough "to get around?" Willard intended to "go the rounds" when he returned. What that meant, he did not explain either. He closed with, "Your son and brother" and added for the third time, "I sure will be glad when we land on that soil again."

He and Addie were married July 28, 1919, three months after his discharge, so evidently Addie was treating him well enough. He had a job as typesetter, and then moved to Anamosa where he was employed as a lithographer. In the late 1920's they moved to Cedar Rapids, Iowa, where Willard Jr. was born in 1930. A sister, Lillian, had been born in 1921.

The Goddard-Applegate families, like many families in small towns, had sent their best and brightest sons to protect America and help their Allies bring an end to one of the most brutal wars in history. Some, like Loren, served the entire time that American troops were involved and many were wounded or killed. Others, like Willard who was younger, had less time to prove the degree of the sacrifice he was making.

NOTEBOOK RECORDS IMPORTANT FACTS ABOUT WAR

Private George S. Applegate meticulously kept a small black notebook, recording the route of his journey to France in 1918, and his return home a year later. A member of the 352nd Infantry, 88th Division, George Applegate served overseas during the last few months of World War 1. Many recruits at first were assigned to a depot which is a common assignment for Rookies, until they received assignment to a permanent unit. George's personal story is related by his son-in-law, Niel Johnson, Independence, Missouri. It is supplemented by information from the small notebook in which George occasionally wrote.

He was born in the small town of Andrew, Iowa, on July 12, 1891. A lineman with the Iowa Telephone Company, single and 26 years old, he registered with the draft board in June, 1917, in Davenport, Iowa. However, perhaps due to the essential nature of his civilian job, he was not called into the service until May, 1918. He trained at Camp Dodge, Iowa, which was only partially constructed when the recruits moved in. It lacked a water supply and electricity for several months. From there, George was sent briefly to the 163rd Supply Depot.

Apparently he trained as a signalman, although he did not receive the official certification for satisfactorily completing a special course in signaling until March, 1919. It was signed by William Weigel, commanding general of the 88th Division. As was customary, the Division

Members of Headquarters Company, 352nd Infantry Regiment, 88th Division, in France.
Pvt. George S. Applegate is in the middle of the back row, among those standing.
(Courtesy of Niel M. Johnson)

had its own signal unit, the 313th Field Signal Battalion. However, George ended up being assigned to the Headquarters Company.

His little black book contains names and addresses of 69 members of his company, each name written in that soldier's own handwriting. A company was made up of 250 men, so perhaps these were special friends. Or perhaps George simply didn't have time to get everyone's name. In his small cramped handwriting, George penciled in his journey from Camp Dodge for France, leaving on July 25, 1918. Arriving in France on August 16, they assembled at Semur (Cote d'Or) in the northwestern part between Angers and Tours.

The division, with the exception of its Field Artillery, received special training in open warfare at a site about 200 or more miles away in the Hericourt Haute-Saumur area near Belfort, France. This was the region of St. Mihiel in the Meuse-Argonne sector. Here they were placed under the command of the experienced 4th French Army and went on to relieve the 38th French division in Haute-Alsace. It was customary to place an inexperienced, newly arrived American unit under the command of either a French or British commander whose soldiers had seen years of battle. The French or British taught the Americans how to become better soldiers, while the Americans were fighting.

George lists village by village and town by town with the name and date of arrival. There were many forced marches, with the men carrying heavy packs weighing 60-80 pounds, on congested roads to the center of Haute-Alsace.

Then, on or about October 6th with only two ambulances for the entire Division of 25,000 men, the influenza struck the 88th Division. By October 18 there were 80 deaths. A total of 6,845 cases of flu and 1,041 of pneumonia were treated in the next few weeks. Of those men, 444 died later. However, soldiers who were healthy enough to return to the front line, carried out night raids and captured German prisoners. While many soldiers of the 88th division occupied hospital beds instead of bedrolls in tents, the men who remained healthy achieved as many of their objectives as their relative strength in numbers allowed. George does not mention becoming sick, so one can assume that being in the Headquarters Company, he was not as exposed to the flu as the average soldier who would have been in closer proximity to many men.

We do not know exactly what George's duties were, although his daughter, now deceased, recalls that he received messages at a switchboard and if the message was in French, he had a French soldier standing by to translate it. Perhaps he also strung phone wire and repaired switchboards and broken wires. Communication lines were always a frequent target of German artillery. Lines from exposed Observation Posts back to Headquarters or unit commanders were constantly targeted by the enemy and blown up or otherwise destroyed. Perhaps George was assigned the hazardous job of repairing them on the front lines where he was exposed to enemy snipers.

On November 3rd George's division left for several other towns, ultimately arriving at Bonnet on November 30. This is in the Alsace-Lorraine province, which the Germans had taken in 1871 as victors of the Franco-Prussian war.

In the interim, some of the 88th took part in the final battles of Meuse-Argonne when the war ended. The army staff was in the process of planning the attack on Metz, France, which Pershing determined would be the final blow to the Germans. Fortunately for both sides, the Armistice was signed and the attack was cancelled. It would have been as bloody as the Meuse-Argonnes because Metz was a valuable railroad hub. (Ellis)

The diary stops here and the next entry is April 11, 1919, noting that "Major Nelson sang at Bonnet." Evidently the division finally received its "marching orders" for they were packed up and had a final inspection by General Pershing, as was customary before departure of the troops. More train stops followed, more marching with the heavy packs, perhaps heavier if they had found some souvenirs, until they finally boarded a ship for home.

For the first few days they stood at the ship's rails until the seasickness subsided. At that point, the mysterious friend, "K.C.," rescued them from their discomfort with candy and cigarettes, as he had done on the trip over.

At last their ship docked at Hampton Roads, Virginia, where the Division went through another inspection after disembarking. At nearby Camp Hill, Virginia, they experienced the luxury of hot baths, delousing, and getting new uniforms. Feeling great, George and some friends went to a show in Newport News. But the next few days George recorded as having "nothing to do." George was less fortunate than his comrades who were able to start their homeward bound journeys earlier by using different routes. Kansas and Utah men were the first to leave, followed by those heading to St. Louis, and last of all, men going to Iowa.

Again the Red Cross or YMCA workers welcomed them with refreshments, especially the scarce delicacy of ice cream on arrival in East St. Louis. Soon George signed his name in the army for a final time, this time to his discharge papers. He boarded a train for Des Moines, Iowa. From there it was to Davenport, and home. Not forgetting his notebook, he dutifully inscribed, "arrived at 9:45 p.m."

Private George Steward Applegate is now private citizen, "Mr. George S. Applegate."
"Welcome home, George!"

George continued his work in communications as a lifelong employee of Northwestern Bell in Davenport, Iowa. He married and had one child, a daughter, Verna Gail Applegate. (Note: Little did George know that in a decade after his service, he would become a brother-in-law of Willard and Loren Goddard by marrying their sister, Marie Goddard.)

Certificate of Completion

USE OF MINING - HAWTHORN CRATER

Mining was carried on extensively after the first year or so of the war. One of the largest tunnels was 300 meters long or about 1000 feet, and took seven months to prepare. It was dug by the British 252nd Tunneling Company and was 22 meters (about 75 feet) underground.

When it exploded on July 1, 1916 at 7:10 A.M. a photographer happened to film it exploding. A crater 40 feet deep and 300 feet wide was created. It is known as the Hawthorn Crater and was the first of 17 mines to explode that day.

July 1 was also known as the beginning of the famous Battle of the Somme. For the bombardment that followed, 100 trains per day were needed to bring ammunition to front-line railheads during the peak time of artillery firing.

(World War One. A Very Peculiar War.)

THE " HARLEM HELL FIGHTERS"
African–Americans prove their patriotism in World War I

EAGER TO FIGHT: Men of the all-black 369th Inf. Regt. The "Harlem Hell fighters" distinguished themselves in France.

Highly decorated soldiers in France
(National Archives, Courtesy VFW Magazine, 2004)

When America declared war on Germany in 1917, there were four all-black regiments in uniform. Their communities were proud of these men and they became an example to encourage more African-Americans to volunteer. Many African-American volunteers, therefore, stepped up to enlist, and within only one week's time, the quotas for African – Americans were filled. No more enlistments were accpted.

However, later when it was necessary to re-institute the draft, the system of quotas changed radically. Discrimination once again became the rule, and African-Americans were in great demand to fill draft board quotas.

This was especially true in the south where discrimination was highest. Registrants were told to tear off a corner of their application. (Note: This was so the board could easily identify them.) Meanwhile, the draft boards, consisting of all white men, found all kinds of reasons for exempting white men, and all kinds of reasons for increasing the numbers of African-Americans.

Despite the deliberate attempts at discrimination, a positive step taken to ameliorate that discrimination is that by the end of the war, some African-Americans were serving in higher level positions such as chaplains, surveyors, truck drivers, chemists, and intelligence officers. The unfortunate news is that only about 10% were ever assigned to combat units, something the men had wanted, and had enlisted and trained for. So, the army in its effort to avoid sending African-American servicemen to France, thinking they might possibly incite racial problems, proposed a new department. This was called the Service of Supply (SOS).

The SOS would consist of 30% African-Americans, with the rest made up of Caucasians, a few native Americans, (Indians), and non – English speaking immigrants. Even in the Navy and Air Corps, Black-Americans were relegated to noncombatant jobs. No African-Americans were allowed in the United States Marines, and only 1% or 4,000 were accepted by the American Naval forces. (Mead)

Of the 400,000 mostly volunteer African – Americans, only 10% ever saw combat. This occurred when the French army, whose severe losses required the addition of two regiments, requested, almost pleaded with General Pershing to release two African-American regiments to the French. The Frenchmen were used to people of color because of the Africans who lived in the various French colonies of Africa.

The former African-American 15th New York National Guard was a strong, unified group that had practiced and trained for years before war was declared. In the Army reorganization, the 15th was to be part of the newly organized 369th Infantry Regiment of about 3000 men. This regiment was part of the 92nd Division under Brig. Gen. Charles C. Ballou.

All through basic training in South Carolina, where these men were consistently considered inferior, they experienced gross discrimination, physical battery, and racial slurs. Despite the fact they wore the same uniform as whites and answered to the same officers, they were shunned from the social activities of the white soldiers, and African-Americans simply were not accepted by the local population.

When situations did occur that were based on racial issues, the officers took over before violence and gun play began. Then an apology usually was issued, the whites reprimanded, and the whole incident smoothed over. Justice was meted to the guilty party, but if any punishment was delivered, it was to the African-American soldier and was excessive in its application. The military deemed it important to "hush it up," and be sure that the newspapers did not carry the story.

In France, the African-American 92nd Regiment had a disappointing record due to many reasons. This, in the minds of high ranking U.S. officers, confirmed their view of the inferiority of the African-American soldier. However, the French held a different view and rewarded these men for their brave actions and aggressive fighting when the 92nd came under French command. General Pershing had previously rejected a request from the French for the transfer of the 92nd to French command.

The 369th regiment was the first minority outfit to land on French shores in 1917, and to their great disappointment, instead of heading for training camps, they were put to work digging trenches, draining swamps, and building railroads. It was difficult to contain their feelings of betrayal. With great expectations they had enlisted and trained alongside white men to confront and attack the enemy. They, too, wanted the opportunity to defend their country. Belatedly, they realized it was not to be. (Mead)

Fortunately, one commanding officer, Colonel William Hayward, had faith in their ability to fight. He pleaded with officials and issued demands for a change in their assignments to the French. Even General Foch had to use his authority to get General Pershing to release the 92nd Regiment. Finally, Pershing relented. It was an eventful day when the 92nd joined the 16th Division of the French Fourth Army.

As the 92nd rode the train leaving the west coast at St. Nazaire, the soldiers were astonished by what they saw. It was their first sight of the after effects of the war. They saw ruined landscapes, deforested woods, and bombed houses. And most of all, everywhere they saw small cemeteries with rows and rows of white crosses. Once in the French camp, they were allowed to wear their own AEF uniforms but wore French helmets with the metal stripe down the center. They were issued the unfamiliar French weapons, and training started all over again.

Food was magnificent, but they unknowingly drank the day's ration of wine at one sitting. It was meant to be consumed during the entire day. The consequences were predictable and laughable for their French companions. After a few days of this happening, it was decided that the Americans' should lose their wine ration. They learned many things, but the proper French method of drinking wine was not something they acquired.

They learned how to use pigeons for communication, to operate French–made radios, wield the longer French bayonets, and fire the French Lebel rifle with clips holding only three cartridges, instead of the American Springfield with its five cartridges per clip. They mastered handling the grenade launcher and operating the French Chau Chat machine gun. It had problems to be reckoned with because it shook when fired and was difficult to aim and hold steady. But they overcame these obstacles to become first rate shooters.

Several African-American soldiers quickly made names for themselves. One was Lt. Jim Europe, the leader of the popular jazz band which was in great demand throughout the area. For years after the war, jazz bands entertained Europeans in great numbers. Jazz was "in," especially the kind played by African-Americans.

 Lieutenant Europe, however, got his initiation into night raids when he bragged to some French soldiers about his fighting ability. They decided to invite him to go with them on a night raid. As an officer, he carried only an officer's small pistol. The raid was successful, but afterwards, Lieutenant Europe set his own record in running as fast as he could back to the safety of the camp. Despite the fear he had exhibited that time, he had performed some deeds during the raid that distinguished him as a brave fighter. He received a citation for the night's work, gaining the admiration of his French comrades and fellow African-Americans.

At a later date another African – American, Pvt. Henry Johnson, made the record books for his actions defending his post and the life of a French soldier from an unexpected German night attack. Using first his rifle, and then his great strength with his fists, he finally resorted to the bolo knife he always carried. With great expertise, he took on the rest of the German attackers and finished them off with the knife. His partner was hit with shrapnel from a grenade early in the action, while Johnson suffered 21 wounds, most from bullets. It was estimated the two men fought off at least 24 Germans.

Their commander recommended them both for medals of valor and honor. As a result of their fighting, their wounds were so severe that they became crippled for life. Their story made New York newspapers and the Associated Press. Harlem was proud of these first heroes, but Harlem also had many subsequent heroes of whom to be proud. (Max Brooks.)

The 369th Regiment set another record for combat troops of all nationalities and races. It spent 191 continuous days on the front lines, without relief or rotation to a reserve trench. This was far more days than any other unit. Regular periods of relief from the front lines were customary.

The French awarded the Croix de Guerre to the whole unit, and 171 awards to individuals for bravery. The rank of sergeant was given to Johnson for his heroism.

In a separate incident Corporal Freddie Stowers of the 371st Infantry was awarded the Congressional Medal of Honor, the only African American to receive this honor during World War I. Other African-American units served admirably and were given suitable awards, making these regiments the most highly decorated of all AEF units.

Despite the numbers of medals honoring numerous heroic actions, once these troops returned to America, racial discrimination plagued them again. Forgotten or ignored were the valor and courage they showed when fighting the Germans. They were "blacks" once again. (Perisco.) After the war ended, the lynching of 135 African-Americans, including at least ten veterans, took place, with some wearing their military uniform. Many other violent acts followed the men of the 92nd and 93rd Battalions for years.

Altogether the 92nd Division experienced 1,637 casualties, while the 93rd suffered 3,534 casualties. Race riots greeted the returning soldiers in 26 American cities. It was not until President Harry Truman began desegregating the services in July, 1948, that equal treatment and opportunity were assured to African-American servicemen. This was done by an Executive Order and not by Congress. Finally, integration of the military had begun.

No longer were all African-Americans assigned to serve only as laborers and waiters. Many more courageous acts also were to come out of World War II actions in which African – Americans proved their worth as fighting men, time after time.

(NOTE: As of December, 2014, a petition spearheaded by Senator Charles Schumer of New York was finally approved by the Army to award Sergeant Henry Johnson with the Congressional Medal of Honor. Senator Schumer had wanted to have the medal presented on the 95th anniversary of the May 15th occurrence of Sergeant Johnson's action. Supporters have been working for decades for this award to be made. Evidence in the form of a dispatch of 1918 was found in 2011 which increased the basis for his cause. The dispatch read in part, "Notable instance of bravery and devotion..."

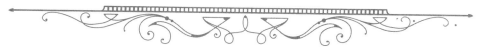

LITTLE KNOWN BUT HIGHLY IMPORTANT — THE ENGINEERS AND PIONEERS

Ever wonder who repaired France's torn up roads, rebuilt the blown up bridges, constructed shelters and latrines for a new camp when a unit of soldiers moved into an unused area? Who made docks large enough to accommodate ten ships at the same time? Or fabricated huge warehouses to store tons of goods including food, ammunition, clothing, and medicine? Unloaded and inventoried these goods, which were discharged at a daily average tonnage rate of 3,700 tons?

If that wasn't enough work for these construction men to do, they were trained by the infantry to fire rifles and serve on the front lines and in trenches when needed. These men, numbering 74,000 officers and troops, also assisted with camouflage, searchlights, and flash and sound range findings for the artillery. This was in addition to the traditional engineering responsibilities which required obtaining safe water supplies and proper disposal of sewage waste. These were the jobs the Engineers and a special attached unit, the Pioneers, were trained and expected to perform.

Unloading and storing goods brought in by the ships was the responsibility mainly of the "colored" soldiers, as they were called at that time. This job assignment created resentment in many of the "colored" troops, because they believed when they enlisted, that they were to be trained to take their place on the front lines. (Office of Chief Engineers)

It's the little known and unrecognized Engineers and Pioneers who contributed their strength and building skills to both the AEF and French civilians. The engineering department was formally organized in World War I after the end of hostilities. However, the 315th Engineers, a special unit on its own, was in existence when the United States declared war on Germany in April 1917.

The 315th Engineers was then attached to the 90th Infantry Division, which was part of the First Army of the AEF. The First Army was named as such because it was the first AEF combat force of an army size and became the first Americans to fight against the Germans.

Once in France, among the first jobs of the Engineers was to lay 947 miles of railroad tracks, the equivalent of the distance from New York to Chicago. The Pioneers were used for the first time in France on these jobs also, and then afterwards in the rebuilding of the shattered French nation. To construct temporary bridges in war zones, the Engineers used pontoons which, once the bridge was secured, were later constructed into permanent bridges.

Working with the Signal Corps, they restrung communication lines and established permanent facilities to house the communications staff. They had built a total of 89 ship berths in French ports by the time the Armistice was signed.

The many American wounded soldiers, and the thousands sickened by the influenza outbreak, required the addition of more than 145,000 new hospital beds to existing ones. Often hotels were remodeled to make wards for the patients. These wards, if laid side by side, would extend 146 miles. At the same time other engineers constructed over 15,000 new barracks to handle the quartering of the 300,000 troops per month that kept pouring into France.

Providing safe drinking water for troops and civilians was often a problem. The main sources of water for Americans were village wells which often the French claimed had been poisoned by departing German troops. True or not, the local water often contained bacteria foreign to the American digestive system. To avoid an outbreak of dysentery, the Engineers chlorinated water sources wherever possible, and otherwise provided huge tanks of potable water on trucks. In the Bordeaux region of southwestern France, the Engineers provided four million gallons of safe drinking water per day for soldiers and civilians by drilling artesian wells in the region's soft limestone.

In addition to providing safe drinking water, there was also the problem of proper disposal of sewage from battle fronts and hospitals. One hospital alone required 39 miles of sewer pipe to be laid with an equal amount of pipe for water lines. The Engineers and Pioneers also built seven plants to produce the concrete needed for the project. Refrigeration plants were necessary to preserve the 5,200 tons of meat on hand and to produce 375 tons of ice daily. Construction of smaller bakeries in three other cities was brought to an end by the signing of the Armistice.

To provide power sources for all the newly constructed buildings, Engineers expanded existing power plants. They built new ones especially in war zones where they had been blown up by enemy artillery bombardment. Power plants were a vital target because it was important to cut the enemy's lines of communication and source of electrical power. (http://www.90thdivisionassoc.org/90thdiv – Chief Engineer Report)

A topic seldom discussed in World War I literature concerns the distribution of oil and gasoline from western coastal ports to the front lines. For the Allies, the oil originated in Persia, (today's Iran); Mesopotamia (modern day Iraq) and Azerbaijan, just north of Persia. The oil was then usually transported to the coasts of France and England in huge oil carrying tankers. Oil for Russia and the Central Powers was carried overland by specially built train cars from the same sources to various depots in Russia, Germany, and Austria. It was distributed in the same fashion as the Allies.

At the coastal sea ports, the AEF Engineers and Pioneers built 17 complete storage stations with pumps. Thousands of barrels of gasoline were pumped each day into smaller tanks. From these containers the gasoline was carried in small tin cans by truck or train to airports, lorry (truck) depots, and dozens of other places where gasoline was needed.

Raw lumber, fortunately for the Allies, was in plentiful supply for construction purposes from the heavily forested areas of France. Although the Germans used many of the woods to hide their machine guns, there were enough safe areas of forests to provide wood for fuel, that if corded, (see below*) would extend 375 miles. By October, 1918, there were 81 mills in operation. The Engineers worked together as usual with the Pioneers during the occupation of Germany which ended in July, 1919. (*A cord of wood is a stack that is 4 x 4x 8 feet or 128 cubic feet.)

Not to be overlooked were the Remount Stations and Veterinary Hospitals constructed by the Engineers, which together cared for 62,000 animals. While the Engineers were performing these jobs for the AEF, at the same time they left a legacy for the French. Engineers helped the French people with the daunting and costly task of rebuilding their country, which was reeling from the drastic effects of four years of fighting and destruction.

The French had a total population of 39.6 million people but they suffered a devastating number of casualties. (http://www.90thdivisionassoc.org/90thdiv – Chief Engineer Report)

The total French casualties both dead and wounded had reached nearly 6,000,000 military and civilian casualties. This was the second highest percentage of their total population of any Allied nation. Only Serbia's percentage of casualties for their population was higher.

American soldiers, by serving in combat with the French, not only saved the lives of Frenchmen, but the rebuilding accomplished by AEF Engineers provided the jump start a shattered people needed. The French had to rebuild their homes, businesses, churches, villages, and towns. In the years to come, France would strive to become a proud and prosperous nation again. A large credit for starting that process goes to the manpower, energy, and skills of 174,000 American Engineers, Pioneers and others, including 34,500 troops from other sources, 34,000 French civilians and 15,000 prisoners of war.

France, like Rome, was not "built in a day," but an impressive start had been made by 1919. That was when the last American troops were pulled out and sent home. Some historians would say the United States had at last repaid its debt to the French who helped the colonists win the War of Independence, or Revolutionary War, against Britain in 1783.

AN ARMY PIONEER

Corporal Russell Wise, 54thPioneer Company
(Courtesy of William Wise)

One day Russell J. Wise was building his own log house in the Minnesota woods. A few months later he was in France building army hospitals, repairing roads, and installing barbed wire defenses as a soldier in Company C, 54th Pioneer Infantry, Third Army. His previous experiences and skills helped him to achieve quickly the rank of corporal. The company had just recently been created, and good corporals were needed.

On January 4, 1918, the company was activated to provide shelters and road repairs for some of the 300,000 soldiers that sailed monthly from the United States shores to France. This story is told by his son, William " Willie" Wise, Belton, Missouri. Russell was notified of his 1-A draft status on August 26, 1918.

An official record, "Dates of Interest," shows the men had very little time for training stateside because the 3300 other men drafted brought the regiment to full strength. This new regiment was to construct new barracks, and repair roads and bridges in France. They began their journey overseas by train to Camp Wadsworth, South Carolina. Next stop was Newport News, Virginia, where they boarded ships for Brest, France. The trip took about two weeks.

Once they landed in Brest, they headed to eastern France to the sectors of Argonne and the River Meuse. Russell climbed into the 40 & 8 box car, arriving at Fleury, where a fierce battle was soon to begin. An all night hike found them in Clermont Woods, where they began engagement in the famous Meuse-Argonne offensive. An official Army record shows the men spent the night in the woods under shell fire.

One of the scariest incidents Russell experienced, his son recalls, was when German bombers dropped bombs over the mess kitchen where they had been eating. At that time, the pilots dropped the bombs by hand over the side of the plane, so their accuracy was poor. No one on the ground was injured and the building was safe, thanks to the primitive method of bombing. But everyone was a bit shaken up.

After the war ended, the pioneers were assigned to occupation duties in Germany. General Pershing had orders for 250,000 American troops to patrol the American sector including the German cities of Koblenz and Wittlich. Willie recalls a story his father told about policing civilians. One night on patrol, Russell spotted a German citizen carrying a lighted lantern. That was breaking a rule of curfew. Russell realized his German vocabulary was limited and did not include German words for "Put out that light." A skilled marksman, however, Russell simply shot out the light in the lantern. It scared the German man but he was unharmed. Willie said that German probably remembered the rule the rest of his life, thanks to his father's quick thinking and good shooting.

Russell liked to travel during when he had leave, and he brought home a collection of post cards depicting places he visited. He also collected commercial photographs of war scenes, bombed buildings, destroyed forests, and torn up fields. The folks back home had no idea of the great amount of damage to the French homes, farms, and buildings, Willie says. Some cards depict churches with only the outside walls standing.

Other photos show a cemetery with wooden crosses, no stone crosses yet; a mine crater 75 feet deep by 150 feet wide; and German prisoners repairing roads. Willie has kept these photos and other items including a list Russell made of items in his kit: "shelter (tent) half, 1 coom (comb), tooth brush, gas mask, 2 blankets, 1 O.D. shirt, tent pole & pins, soap and powder…" (Note. This is his spelling.) This list was made during the night of fighting in Clermont Woods. Perhaps Russell feared the worst, so he made a list of his belongings.

When he was discharged, Russell returned to Kansas City, Missouri, where his brother lived. There he met and married Mary Leona Alliett. They raised four children. Russell gave up his log house in Minnesota and worked for the Kansas City gas company, then got laid off. During the Depression they had a little house which they lost because of financial difficulties. "It almost ruined Mom," Willie reflects. "Times were hard, but Dad was real tough, so we managed." However, his father died tragically in a car accident on June 1, 1951.

He had survived a war, raised a family, bought and later lost his house, while managing to provide for his family to live through the Depression. Willie adds, "It didn't seem right, the way he died, but it happened. Dad was a tough man, but he couldn't survive that terrible car crash." Willie honors his father every Memorial Day by planting a small pennant with a Third Army star symbol embroidered by his sister. Willie dons his father's overseas cap with the pioneer insignia pinned on the cap. Then he stands at attention for a brief moment of silence.

"He was a good man, an honest and hard worker," he says over and over, as he thinks about his pioneer father. The father who exchanged his wood cutting ax for a rifle to help defend his country.

MEET ONE OF THOSE 315TH ENGINEERS

This is the only information about Gordon D. Jester that the Army officially has. He enlisted April 28, 1918, in Illinois, and went on to basic training, live in tents, and work with Company A of the 315th Engineers, 90th Division of the AEF in France from 1918-1919. He returned home and was discharged June 24, 1919. He suffered the effects of being gassed by the Germans. His granddaughter, Patricia Ruddy from Illinois, knows only the barest details of her grandfather's service. The rest was obtained from official sources.

He applied for a bonus for his overseas service, but there the official records end. A copy of a file card dated November 17, 1923, has the amount to be paid for 423 days of overseas service at $211.50. That probably was the amount he received. Any other records or cancelled checks or receipts are missing. They were most likely burned in the disastrous fire of 1973 at the United States Archives in St. Louis. Missouri.

He would be a "man without a past" except for records kept elsewhere of the 315th and its service in France. One source says that the 90th Division received honors at the Meuse-Argonne battle. In a booklet published by company officers, the deaths of ten men are listed and their places of burial are recorded. All died in action, mostly from shelling, although two were killed by rifle fire. There was no witness to one man's death, so the officers knew it must have been an instant death. This was determined by the fact that the soldier was holding a bundle of letters he had just received. Most of the dead were buried in the 315th Engineer Cemetery near Fay-en-Hay. The 315th also fought at Romange and Montigny.

There is a group photograph of Private Jester with the Second Platoon of Company A. His company began fighting September 13 and continued until November 5, according to the date of when he was wounded. Total casualties for the 90th were 1,387 dead and 6,623 wounded. (Ellis)

Gordon Jester was born July 18, 1885, and died March 20, 1954, at age 69. He is buried at Memorial Park Cemetery in Illinois. The engineers were a vital backup for the infantry and could shoulder a rifle as readily as pick up a shovel. Without their hard work, no troops would have been able to march down the worn out, almost non-existent roads. No wagons would have crossed a river where the bridge had been blown up, nor could any wounded have been sent to a hospital for treatment if the railroads had not been repaired and made safe by the engineers.

So to men like Private Gordon D. Jester, those important, hard working men of the 315th Engineers, 90th Division, tell them, "Thanks, buddy."

SCHEDULE OF A PIONEER COMPANY - Company A, 54th Pioneer Infantry – 1918

Aug. 20, 1918 – Entrained at Camp Wadsworth at 10:00 A.M. enroute for port of Embarkation.
Aug. 29 – Embarked at Newport News, aboard transport Duca d'Aosta.
Aug. 30 – Sailed from Newport News, Va.
Sept. 12 – Arrived at Brest, France.
Sept. 17 – Entrained at Brest at 5 A.M.
Sept. 18-20-Arrived Port d'Atelier, Amance, France.
Sept. 22 – Fleury – encamped in woods.
Sept. 25 – Night march 15 kilo's (sic) to Clermont en Argonne, encamped in woods, under shell fire.
Sept. 26 & 27 – Auzeville quarry. (Meuse-Argonne offensive to Nov. 11).
Sept. 28 – Bourilles sur Aire.
Sept. 30-Oct. 9 – Working parties under direction of 23rd Engineers south of Varennes.
Oct.10-Nov. 4 – Cunel, road detail furnished under direction of 23rd Eng. On Nov. 8th and 9th camp raided by German bombing squadrons.
Nov. 16 & 17 – Dun-Sur-Meuse.
Nov. 19-Dec. 1st – Baalon, road work.

Dec. 2 – Virton.

Dec. 3-15 – Arlon, Belgium.

Dec. 15 – Dec. 21 – Longwy, France, Company billeted, usual camp duties.

Dec. 22 – Entrained at Longwy en route to Germany.

Dec. 23rd – Detrained at Salmrohr, Germany. Billeted in village of Dreis.

Dec, 24 & 25 – Usual camp duties, Christmas observed as holiday.

Dec. 26 – Marched from Dreis to Unter Bergweiler – 9 kilos.

Dec. 27 & 28 – Usual camp duties.

Dec. 29 – Entrained at Salmrohr, arrived Coblenz on Rhine at 11 P.M.

Dec. 30 – Company billeted in Coblenz-Neuendorf.

Jan. 1, 1919 – New Year Day observed as holiday.

Jan. 2 – to date – Usual camp duties, detail Quartermaster Department, Ordnance Department and Athletic field.

    ??? ORDERED HOME!

(Note: This is exactly how the page ends-with question marks)

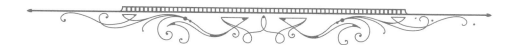

ARMY OF OCCUPATION OF GERMANY (AOG)

For 250,000 AEF troops, going home was postponed when they were selected to become part of the Army of the Occupation of Germany, along with soldiers from the Allied forces of England, France, and Britain each taking a sector beyond the Rhine River. The Allies determined it was necessary to police part of Germany to ensure the Germans followed the demands of the Armistice.

These demands included destroying certain weapons and delivering others to the Allies. In addition, all types of ammunition, trucks, airplanes, tanks, and other vehicles had to be in the possession of the Allies by a certain date. The Americans' assignment was to police a 2,500 square mile area in the southern part where almost one million Germans lived. The AOG had two weeks in which to pack up and begin their journey to their new duty site in Germany. This seemed to be an almost impossible task for the Quartermaster Corps. They had to issue new uniforms and boots, repair old ones, replace armaments, stockpile food, and make hundreds of other items available in the supply depots.

When the Americans crossed the Rhine River, this was the Americans' first sight of the German homeland. The fighting had not taken place beyond the Rhine, which created the border between France and Germany. The Americans started marching toward their assigned sector by divisions, each keeping as straight a line as possible. The divisions assigned to this duty included the First, Second, Third, Fourth, Thirty-second, and Forty-second* along with the Sixty-sixth Field Artillery Brigade. Added later were the Seventh Corps,* the Fifth, Eighty-ninth* and Ninetieth Divisions. (*The reader will recognize these units of the men whose stories are included in this book.)

When the orders came for the AOG to prepare to leave for their new posts, off came the dirty and torn uniforms. On went the clean uniforms and shiny though stiff boots. The

Americans were relieved to reach their posts where they were supplied with new blankets, tents, and personal items. The kitchen wagons had to be repaired and re-supplied; the medical tents needed new cots and bedding; and the machine shop had its own special needs. Each section or department had special requirements.

Marching up to 20 miles a day, proceeding in an orderly manner, the American troops encountered little or no problems with civilians. The Americans had strict orders not to fraternize with Germans, so the two groups of people remained apart. There were no complaints openly made from the townspeople and peasants, although they must have watched with conflicting emotions. Instead of their own German men marching toward them, they saw the strong, well fed, healthy, and victorious American soldiers passing through their villages, and passing their farms.

Some farms had been tended, but most were lying fallow or untended. The draft animals had long ago been taken by the military, and the plowing and reaping often were beyond the strength of the very old and very young civilians who were left behind.

What were the civilians thinking? Was it about their dead soldiers? Or those soldiers who survived that still were in Allied prison camps, and no one knew how soon they would be home? The German people also worried how they would survive the strict food blockade established by the British. The blockade continued for six long months or longer until the Versailles Peace Treaty was signed. Many civilians did not survive. They died of illness, malnutrition, and even outright starvation. Nearly 700,000 are believed to have to paid the final cost of peace with their lives.

Or perhaps the Germans were thinking that it should be their men instead, marching victoriously down the country roads to their village homes. No doubt, the peasants thought of the ones who would never return, who had been declared killed or listed as missing in action. The German military casualties were more than six million including the wounded, or 54% of the total men mobilized for fighting. (Sasse)

The German civilians must have also been reminded of the weeks and months of privations lying ahead with winter coming. They lacked food, clothing and heat, and felt a deep bitterness because their government had lied to them, had told them they would be victors-and that the war would take only a few months. It had been four years since the fighting had started. There were also other reasons the Germans felt bitterness and hopelessness. Their fields were not tilled or reaped unless old men and women and children did the work. The farmer/soldier had been away, killing men instead of raising food for his family.

Because of the food shortage for Germans, the AOG troops had to carry their own food and supplies with them. In one large warehouse city, huge supplies of blankets for the German troops had been stored. The 130,000 blankets found there were shipped to the Belgians, who had been greatly deprived of necessities by the Germans. Such other assistance as possible was also provided by the International Red Cross to the Belgians.

Ammunition depots yielded an unexpected treasure of 22 million rounds of small arms shells; 36,000 naval shells; and 2,000 tons of gunpowder. German uniform material was sent to France to clothe the Germans imprisoned there. Huge laundries were repaired and operated day and night to wash the clothing of Americans as they reached their destinations. (http://www.almc. army.mil/alog/issues/SepOct10/Coblenz_excellence.html)

In turn, the American marching along German country roads may have remembered the death or wounding of a buddy. He may have thought with resentment, even anger, about his weeks and months spent in the wet, muddy and cold trenches while under constant shelling, and some shells might contain gas. One never knew what type of projectile was flying at them. Maybe he or his friend were gassed before they could don their masks.

But miraculously, there were no serious outbreaks of disputes or breaches of the strict behavior rules imposed upon the troops. The AEF, too, may have harbored in their minds the same harsh and bitter thoughts as did the minds of the conquered. But finally, civility was returning to this part of Europe, and the AOG records brought commendation to those 250,000 soldiers when General Pershing praised their behavior.

Some soldiers may even have pitied the conquered people, once they saw their poverty and degradation. The earlier feelings of hatred and revenge may have vanished by now. Hostile feelings that had arisen naturally during the long, tense days of marching, seeing the earth scarred where a trench once stood, as they passed through France and Belgium on their way to northern Germany. They revisited ground that was once littered with pieces of bodies of friends they had known.

Each side exhibited the sternest of discipline during the long marches. The marches were made over a period of 25 days, with a few days' interval for rest. For some units, the march covered 300 miles to reach their destination.

Though the majority of troops were on the way home by summer, 1919, about 1000 soldiers stayed on until 1923. In the years that preceded 1923, and then later, the German people took to the streets with strikes and protests. Fights over elections for a new government erupted from pent up fury at leaders who had lied to them, who said, "The Germans would win the war in six weeks, they would rule the world." Now the world was ruling them, and they were suffering.

Army hospitals established in Germany served wounded soldiers from all armies. Prisoners of war, half dead from lack of food and harsh treatment, received medical care and good food. One division encountered about 4,000 Russians during its march, several hundred French, and a few Italians, and American former prisoners of war. The Russians, Italians, and French were treated until they were well enough to leave for home. Even some German deserters sought American medical aid. Many of the prisoners expressed a "dull relief" at their rescue and only wanted to start on their way home. (U.S. Army Medical Department)

Every day the Americans received large quantities of German war materiel as the Armistice terms required. Most of it was in good condition and had not been vandalized or purposefully destroyed. The Allies still harbored fears that the farther east the Americans marched into the German homeland, the greater the opportunity for hostilities to begin. So, as they marched, officers went ahead to prepare defensive areas for their troops.

Fortunately for soldier and civilian alike, no incidents took place that called for retaliation or punitive action. The Occupation, as a result of cooperation and strict discipline, and perhaps tempered with humanity, could qualify in history as a "successful operation." The hopes of people all over the world rose. Perhaps it would be the "War That Ended All War," as some people prayerfully thought.

Yet can such a hope be realized when a soldier, once your enemy, stands in your market place, or on your country road, holding a gun ready to shoot. Is conquering a nation ever a win-win solution? Or does it just plant vile seeds that will spring forth in an even worse war?

We all know the answer.

DON'T EXPECT ME HOME FOR 6 MORE MONTHS

Sylvan Gray on leave in Grenoble, France, talking with French policeman after the war ended.
(Courtesy of Tom Gray)

Sergeant Sylvan W. Gray, Quartermaster Corps, in a seven page letter to his family back in North Canton, Ohio, could at last write more freely about his many problems. The Armistice had been signed and fighting was over. His story is shared by his son, Thomas Gray, Overland Park, Kansas.

1st problem – His job was to supply everything from socks to bread, tires to bullets, and puttees to tons of beef for the two million AEF soldiers still in France waiting to be sent home. He wrote, "I'll be here at least six more months because of my job, supplying soldiers in France, as well as those in the Army of Occupation of Germany." (AOG) Folks at home couldn't possibly comprehend the tremendous task of demobilizing that many men immediately. Instead, they were anxious to get their loved ones home soon as possible.

Homesick, working at a detailed job involving a lot of hand writing, he used this letter to air his feelings. His resentment at having to be one of the last soldiers to leave Europe was made worse by the wet French winter weather.

2nd – "Continual rain" – "I suppose you are tired of hearing me say that," he admitted. Also, he patiently explained again that his address was not to a company. "You don't have to be in a company to be in the army," he added. His proper address was "American Regulating Station B."

This type of address was easy for him to understand, but perhaps not for his family. He didn't like to say the same thing repeatedly to his many relatives, who expected frequent letters. He did write his former employer, "Boss Hoover," founder of the Hoover (vacuum cleaner) Company. Mr. Hoover felt a strong obligation to write often to "his boys." Sergeant

Gray appreciated his boss's attitude and responded to Mr. Hoover's letters of encouragement and the reassurance that this job was waiting for him. In addition, Mr. Hoover sent him a check for $10.00 which at that time would have been valued from $175.00 to $200.00 now. (Measuring Worth)

3 – Another complaint was that his family, albeit a small one including only one sister, Laviroa, expected him to write each of them regularly. "I've got too many other letters to write…" referring to the letter writing also required by his duty assignment. But as her Big Brother, it was his duty to write to her with advice about which boys made suitable dates. Also which ones she should avoid.

4 – Next, he was upset that his family thought he had succumbed to the lure of the cigarette. The family may have concluded he was smoking, because "they think all soldiers smoke. My lieutenant has been in the Army for 20 years and he doesn't smoke. I have some will power yet," he boasted.

5 – He courteously asked his mother to write on the lines so her letters would be more legible. "Don't crowd it, I can read it easier then."

6 –He was peeved with the guys at home who thought "we are getting an excursion from Uncle Sam…We came over to work." In between his complaints, he inserted family talk about not getting to see the Christmas tree and presents; the time he encountered seeing an old friend in Koblenz, Germany (where Sylvan was probably stationed as it was a large centrally located city)and other chitchat. Perhaps the home fellows had heard about the long leaves most of the men were finally being granted, and their trips to parts of Germany, France and Italy. Few soldiers received any leave time at all during the war. They fought, marched, trained, or worked at some task for six to seven days a week. They were now taking their leave time at last.

7 – Lack of Protestant churches to attend was another irritant, as nearly all French were Catholics. Sylvan did not understand French proficiently and the services were in French or more likely, Latin; there were rampant rumors of him being sent to Russia (they were just rumors); and finally, the scarcity of photographic film A-116 autographic for his camera. He took many photographs while overseas and was proud of many of them, according to his letters.

The last three pages of this letter are now dated Feb. 21, 1919. This delay occurred because he had finally been given a relaxing and badly needed 20-day leave. He detailed the timetable of trains he rode to different places; the time they departed; where he slept each night; and what he saw. He usually bedded down at a YMCA or the Jewish Welfare Board facilities set up for American soldiers to use. "The scenery was superb," he wrote, describing place after place he visited.

He told his family, he was aware of the sacrifices and suffering the AEF men took at the battle for Verdun also. He had empathy for those soldiers and expressed his gratitude for their actions, actions he could not have physically been able to perform as he wore glasses and could not sight a rifle. His letter ended with the reminder he "has lots of letters to answer, "and "I promise not to write such a long letter again." He signs it, "Lovingly, Sylvan W. Gray, APO #921, AEF, France.

Sergeant Gray was promoted several times due to his efficient and diligent work habits. He eventually was discharged and returned to North Canton, Ohio, where he was active in the American Legion post there. On occasion, he spoke of his other experiences in the war, especially Verdun, where the fighting was "awful." Because of his glasses, his responsibilities in that battle were most likely clerical.

He spoke of seeing on his leave the devastation near Reims and the very severe damage to its famous ancient cathedral. All were a part of the Marne River sector where American troops and Marines had battled in June and July, 1918. More fighting took place on Armistice Day at Stenay, when a large number of Americans needlessly lost their lives because the high command did not observe the cease fire and ordered an attack. More than 300 Americans made the final sacrifice there. Sylvan was especially distressed by the shelled ruins of forests and village houses he saw at Chateau-Thierry.

Tom Gray says his father kept diaries until his death on September 12, 1968, age 76 years. He proudly owned a Harley Davidson motorcycle. When he went to war, he was even more proud of the Model T Ford car. For some reason, his parents sold it while he was in France. He was very upset about this, and wrote "they are selling for $550 now, probably much more than when I had bought the car." He continued with the urgent request to "be sure there is one in the garage when I get home."

Mr. Hoover was good with his word, and Sylvan had a job waiting for him. He returned the Boss's loyalty by working there a total of 40 years, including the time before and after his wartime service. The Gray family was well known in their home town and respected. Sylvan's father, Henry Gray, and uncle, U.S. Gray, for years owned a company making hand rolled cigars. They were the subjects of a newspaper article which Tom has in his possession.

President Wilson had voiced concern about discrimination against new Americans of German or Austrian descent in his early speeches. But prejudicial actions and words started circulating much earlier than the year 1917 when the United States declared war against Germany. This behavior made lives of German Americans intolerable sometimes. However, to prove their patriotism to America, the North Canton boys of German descent joined the army and risked their lives for all United States citizens, regardless of background.

The Gray family had a proud history in North Canton. So, in times like "The Great War," its citizens stood behind their "boys." That's what small towns were supposed to do. And, Syvlan Gray, despite his well founded complaints about his job in the army, was one of those patriotic boys.

CONGRESSIONAL MEDAL OF HONOR RECIPIENTS:

119 Medals of Honor were awarded during World War I, with 5 Marines as recipients. The 89th Division alone had 9 soldiers receiving this award. In the history of the medal starting in the Civil War a total of 3,491 men earned this award.
(moh/history/history_statistics.html)

A SOLDIER AND HIS COLLECTIONS

Roy Cardinell, right, with friends and a dog.
(Loaned by Virginia Wiszneauckas)

Two sons of an impoverished Canadian buggy maker and blacksmith were among the first American soldiers to set foot on French soil on April 25, 1918. The brothers were Roy G. Cardinell and his older brother, John. They served together in many of the most dangerous combat zones in France. While not much is known about John's service, records exist that show Roy enlisted in Mound City, Missouri, on May 29, 1917.

He and John were assigned to Company L of the 4th Infantry of the Missouri National Guard. As with other Missouri Guard units, it later became part of the 139th Infantry of the famed 35th Division. The brothers' early life had been difficult. Their father moved the family to Missouri but could not find work. For unexplained reasons, the father then left his wife and six children. The mother and children moved to Mound City, where Roy was born and grew up.

After they reached adulthood, Roy and John decided the army seemed like a good opportunity for them to do something useful with their lives. So they were among the earliest volunteers. The brothers had basic training at Camp Doniphan, Oklahoma, where most Missouri soldiers trained.

Their niece, Virginia Wiszneauckas, Raymore, Missouri, has many photographs of her uncles in nearby Oklahoma as well as far as off France. One photograph shows a partially destroyed village at St. Mihiel, scene of brutal fighting for the 35th Division. Roy made a notation about having lived in one of the bombed houses.

Other photos show pleasant times in Oklahoma with the brothers holding the camp mascot dog. Only two post cards from Roy's large collection bear messages from Roy. The rest of the cards are blank. One was addressed to his mother in Mound City. The other was mailed to a Miss Kathryn Cook in Topeka, Kansas. Virginia is unable to identify this recipient. Instead of a stamp, Roy has written "Soldiers Mail," words which served as postage for the overseas serviceman. Virginia recently donated a box containing Roy's souvenirs to the National World War I Museum in Kansas City, Missouri. Among them are two medals. One is the beautiful "The Great War of Civilization Medal," which lists major battles the AEF (American Expeditionary Force) fought in. The other medal was awarded to former National Guard members as recognition of their previous service in a guard unit.

Roy evidently was a practical man, considering the items he saved. They included two strop razors; unused razor blades wrapped in paper; two sewing kits in excellent condition; tissue thin paper for rolling cigarettes; a pay book; eating utensils; and a red service stripe that was sewn on the left uniform sleeve. This stripe indicates honorable discharge. His collection also contains a book of popular songs the soldiers sang as they marched along dirt roads, many of which were muddy most of the time. The troops also sang when sitting around a camp fire in front of their tent at night.

There was a "Rule Book for the Dauphine (France) Leave Area." Dauphin is in southeastern France and was a popular tourist site. The book detailed what a soldier was permitted to do and what was not allowed while on leave in the Dauphine. It was important to the army how the soldiers behaved among the French civilians. Only the best of behavior was allowed. Last item in the box is a book of English phrases translated into French.

How helpful these phrases were when Roy was among French civilians or troops is a matter of guesswork. Probably the French civilians had several good laughs at Roy's Missouri accent. The book is in good condition and does not look as if it were frequently consulted.

Virginia says she is pleased that the box the family has guarded so carefully for years now has a permanent home. Safe also is Roy's large collection of photos and cards. Virginia and her brother, Bob Cook (Roy and John's nephew), rescued their uncles' irreplaceable possessions when the two men died. Neither uncle had married, so Virginia and Bob were their closest relatives. When their uncles passed away, they carefully packed up the World War I treasures their uncles had accumulated and preserved them for many years. Finally they had the opportunity to give them to the National World War I Museum. *Through this donation many other people can see and learn from the items and have a better idea of what it was like to be a soldier in The Great War.*

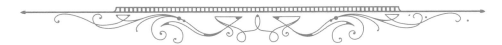

ODA FULLER — WE SALUTE YOU!

Oda Fuller's military record of where he served, could be a list of all the major American battles in France in 1918. Oda fought first in the Gerardmer sector near Alsace – Lorraine, then marched south to St. Mihiel, and from there to the Meuse-Argonne sector. Just as the war was coming to an end, he saw action in the final battles at Verdun. He participated in all of America's three biggest battles of World War I.

Oda was a member of Co. F, 140th Infantry Brigade, 35th Division, made up mostly of men from Missouri and Kansas. When he enlisted at age 21, his assignment was in the 356th Infantry, 89th Division of the National Guard. This was only a few months after the United States declared war on Germany. Later the Army integrated National Guard units into regular army units. That's why Oda's address started changing as he was transferred to different units and bases.

Oda's meticulous records and post card collections are in the possession of a great niece, Linda Noland-Criqui, of Topeka, Kansas, who provided this information. Oda was a native of Rea, Missouri, a small town north of St. Joseph, Missouri. He was among nearly 10,000 men who made up the famous 356th Infantry National Guard. He trained at Camp Funston, Kansas, which was near the present Fort Riley, Kansas.

He was one of several brothers. A family story tells that a younger brother had enlisted but died in 1919 at Camp Funston of the influenza that is believed to have started there. The lad was in training there. The brother was only 17 at the time and too young to enlist, but recruiters often ignored birth dates if the volunteer looked young and healthy.

Oda himself had enlisted October 3, 1917, at age 21 and rapidly rose to the rank of corporal. He kept a post card from a friend at Camp Sheridan, Illinois, who wanted to share stories about his own training. Their stories probably would be the same – a strict sergeant, a stricter lieutenant, maybe good food occasionally, and time for a softball game on a long summer night. Barrack lights out early, reveille early, and in winter, reveille before dawn.

After about seven months of the typical training, Oda was assigned to the 89th Division. His address continued to change. He was transferred one last time to the 140th Infantry, 35th Division, where he stayed until his discharge. In the meantime, National Guard units were being integrated into Regular Army service units, further confusing family and friends trying to find an address for their soldier.

Constant change of addresses and transfers to different units were not unusual early in the war. The Army was trying to enlarge its units until they reached battlefield size with the desired numbers of divisions and armies. American divisions were two and one-half times as large as British and French or about 25,000 to 27,000 men.(Ellis) Because the "Yanks" (a nickname they quickly acquired overseas) were needed as soon as possible in France, their training in the U.S. was shortened.

In France, Oda received additional instruction from the British and French in the use of the bayonet, hand grenades, and how to put on the ever important gas mask within seconds. This training was in addition to learning how to attack the enemy and how to defend oneself. For his actions in some battles, he received citations. The extra training had been valuable. Maj. Gen. Leonard Wood, who supervised their basic training, called them "second to none." There were nine Medals of Honor awarded to the 89th Division, evidence of their heroic actions in various campaigns. They were afterwards referred to as "Wood's Men." A military post in central Missouri was named after the outstanding general and is known as Ft. Leonard Wood.

As with all soldiers stationed in France, there was a delay in discharge. This was due principally to two reasons. One, it was important to ensure that Germany began dismantling her war production and started destroying her weapons. The other reason was to maintain peace in certain sectors of Germany. Immediately after the Armistice, several different political factions in Germany wanted control of the government. The Kaiser had resigned and left for exile in Holland. The famous German General von Hindenburg became part of the government.

There were food riots and strikes by civilians protesting economic conditions. The Allies feared that the Germans might even start the war again. Oda served several months as a member of the 140th Infantry in the Army of Occupation of Germany along with more than 250,000 other American soldiers.

Linda has no address for her uncle during these months, so being a member of the AOG may explain where Oda had been stationed until his discharge on April 8, 1919, at Camp Grant, Illinois.

His discharge paper said he was in good health, despite having been gassed, and it is known that he suffered symptoms of lung problems the rest of his life, probably from being exposed to gas. Unfortunately, the Army and health officials lacked the knowledge of the after effects of being gassed. Therefore, being gassed led many veterans to suffer in later years and possibly shortened their lives. This appears to have been true for Oda.

Other gaps continue in his story. He was given a travel allowance to Maysville, Missouri, although had no family there. Perhaps he had a girl friend or buddies there. The family says this is one of the mysteries their great uncle kept to himself. One of the family photos shows Oda standing at attention with his rifle at his right side, the family Ford and a big barn in the background. He looks proud, proud to be a Missourian, and proud to be a soldier in his nation's army. His family of great nieces and nephews are proud also of their Great-Uncle Oda, who fought in some of the war's most dangerous battles.

The stories of his experiences he kept to himself, as he told no stories to family members. He left physical evidence of his bravery in the letters, honorary medals, and certificates he received, each attesting to his courage and valor. Oda's relatives ask each other, were these symbols of his service worth the physical and possible mental suffering their great-uncle may have experienced? They can't agree.

Fellow townspeople also recognized his patriotism. One of the certificates reads: "gratefully awarded by the people of Andrew County, Missouri…" "for services rendered… in the Great World War…"

Oda married twice. There were no children from either marriage. This is one reason Linda feels so close to her uncle. He lived the last part of his life in St. Joseph, Missouri, near his devoted sister, Carrie Noland. Oda B. Fuller died at age 80 in Ft. Leavenworth, Kansas, on Feb. 1, 1977. An ordinary man, yet an extraordinary soldier, Oda B. Fuller was a veteran with an illustrious military record. He was a man with many addresses, many mysteries, and many unanswered questions, but a soldier second to none.

We salute you, Oda B. Fuller!

Oda Fuller stands in his backyard with Ford Model T and barn in background.
(Courtesy of Linda Noland-Criqui)

A MATTER OF DUTY AND CONSCIENCE

In every war, especially when there is conscription, the issue arises about what each individual perceives to be his duty and obligation. Most citizens will probably agree that service to country comes first, before individual conscience or perception, particularly if the war is portrayed as a matter of urgent national self-defense. By 1917, American lives were being lost on the high seas and democracy in Europe and elsewhere was being threatened by what was called "Prussian autocracy." For most Americans, such reasoning was sufficient to go to war.

Yet, there will be individuals who believe strongly that they have a duty to conscience that precludes them from engaging in combat and killing other human beings. These were the conscientious objectors who generally had the option of serving in war without using weapons, which meant they could, and did, serve as medics, stretcher bearers, and laborers outside the combat zones. If they refused any military duty, they were subject to incarceration in prison.

Still, local draft boards had considerable authority to decide on who could be exempted from combat duty and choose alternate service. That appears to be the case of an individual in this section who agreed to use his expertise in agricultural science to move to Canada and teach these skills to Canadians who were returning from military service. He remained there for most of the rest of his career. Undoubtedly, this was a very unusual case. Maybe it was an example of what later was called our "good neighbor policy" in the western hemisphere. One can only speculate about the discussion that went into this decision of a local draft board.

Other persons in this section display various responses as well, to the challenges posed by war. Their thinking and experiences also exemplify differing reactions to war during and after the conflict. One may decide for himself how he would probably have reacted under similar circumstances.

Commentary by
Niel Johnson, PhD., Guest Contributor

MEDAL OF HONOR

Private First Class John Lewis Barkley

Pvt. First Class
John Lewis Barkley
(Courtesy NWWIM Archives)

In this undated letter from France to his brother, Barkley describes the events of 7 October, 1918 which led him to receiving the Medal of Honor:

"How would you like to have been in the battle of the Argonne. There was not one second of this time but what there was a barrage from both sides of shrapnel and the strongest of gasses and the biggest of guns. The Germans shot some of the damnedest shells at us you ever heard of, bigger than nail kegs and four times as long and when one hit, you better look out.

"How would you like to have saw (sic) five thousand dead men to every thousand yards. Just think of looking from our house to our west line and then place this many men in the space. Across on the German side they was (sic) twice as bad. Don't ever let anybody with dutch (i.e. German) blood in their veins ever say anything to you or about me or anyone else.

"Don't think I am going to tell you anything about that tank deal, it is too bad to tell a civilized man. I played them dirty every chance I got and this is not the first time I ever did this. I fired my last round of ammunition (but) kept my automatic pistol for hand to hand fighting, plunged out of the tank with a sudden dash. I had three bullet marks in my clothes and a burnt legging string. I run (sic) for a ditch about fifty yards from me and went down it to our Major who was wondering what was taking place…"

The War Department's official description of Barkley's deeds which led him to receiving the Medal of Honor related that:

"For conspicuous gallantry and intrepidity above and beyond the call of duty in action with the enemy near Cunel, France, October 7, 1918. Pvt. Barkley, who was stationed in an observation post half a kilometer from the German line, on his own initiative, repaired a captured enemy machine gun and mounted it in a disabled French tank near his post.

"Shortly afterwards, when the enemy launched a counterattack against our forces, Pvt. Barkley got into the tank, waited under the hostile barrage until the enemy line was abreast of him, and then opened fire, completely breaking up the counterattack and killing or wounding a large number of the enemy.

"Five minutes later an enemy 77 millimeter gun opened fire on the tank point-blank. One shell struck the driver wheel of the tank, but this soldier nevertheless remained in the tank, and after the barrage ceased, broke up a second enemy counterattack, thereby enabling our forces to gain and hold Hill 253."

(This true account of Private Barkley's actions on that date was released to the author courtesy of the National World War I Museum Archives. A book describing this action by Private Barkley is listed in the Bibliography as "Fields of Scarlet.")

A SOLDIER WHO CHANGED HIS MIND

Freda Lathrop, Jesse's sweetheart
(Courtesy their daughter, Denise Omstead)

Jesse Albert Dennis

Jesse Albert Dennis was one of eight boys in his family and the only one to sign up for the Army. He was enthusiastic and believed he was doing his patriotic duty when he enlisted in Kansas City, Missouri, at age 21. The other brothers were too young or else working with their father in his various business enterprises. Jesse was assigned to Ambulance 139th Company, 35th Division and served in the areas of fiercest fighting, including St. Mihiel, Verdun, and the Argonne sector.

As a stretcher bearer, he would have carried many bodies of dead and wounded. AEF casualties were unusually high, due to the inexperience of the soldiers and lack of training. His daughter, Denise Omstead, Raymore, Missouri, tells her father's story.

Stretcher bearers were unarmed. Their job of retrieving wounded soldiers from the battle field, often in No Man's Land, was one of the most hazardous. This was because they made an excellent target for a waiting German marksman. In order to carry a man on a stretcher they had to walk upright to minimize the jolting as they toured around ruts, shell holes or even craters. Often barbed wire and destroyed weapons littering the field make their journey more difficult.

The bearers, usually four, walked at a steady pace, not hurriedly, because any movement to the stretcher often caused severe pain to the wounded soldier. Some men died of shock from pain and the long exposure they endured before being found. (Note: AEF troops were taught while advancing toward the enemy to run singly bending low to lessen their visibility. The bearers, obviously could not do this and thus provided an easy target for a sniper.)If the ground was muddy, one trip alone could take up to four to six hours to bring back one man.

His daughter related one of his experiences that helped him later to change his mind about war. He had carried several wounded from the battlefield to a nearby barn serving as a temporary first aide station and barracks. He and some buddies heard planes overhead but could not see them because of the dense forest. They were not expecting Allied planes in their sector of the Argonne Forest, so they decided they must be German airplanes. They quickly ran into the barn seeking shelter.

Despite the thick overhead shield of trees, the pilot spotted the barn and threw some bombs. It destroyed the barn, killing one of the soldiers lying next to Dennis. This was October, 1918, one month before the Armistice took effect. Dennis was gassed during the attack. Some bombs contained poison gas, while others were shrapnel, which consists of small metal balls. When the shell explodes, it sprays the hot pieces of metal. The sharp edges can seriously wound a soldier, cut off limbs, or even decapitate him. If the shell contains mustard gas in large enough doses, it can kill immediately. A small dosage can cause lifelong illnesses.

Denise says her father suffered from asthma later in life. At the time of discharge, he was labeled "No injury," so he was unable to file later for disability. He may also have been too proud to do so, she says. He was hospitalized from the effects of the gas attack and not shipped home until spring of 1919, probably because of needing to recuperate.

There was also a shortage of ships. It had been difficult during the war to commandeer enough ships to transport 300,000 soldiers each month to France. The Army used passenger ships, cargo ships, and any vessel into which they could double the number of usual passengers. Some ships had three or four levels of bunks, and the soldiers slept in rotation. Each bunk was occupied 24 hours a day. The same shortage existed after the war ended, but the army tried to make the voyage home less arduous, meaning a longer wait.

Before the war, Jesse worked on the family farm near Ottawa, Kansas, along with two sisters.. Two older brothers participated in the different enterprises, some war related, their father started. Five brothers were too young to enlist, so Jesse was the only one to join the service. His father, John Adams Dennis, bought a stallion from the United States government at the beginning of the war in 1914. Using good business sense, he bred his mares to produce horses for the U.S. Cavalry, as did some of his neighbors.

He proved to be a successful business man, by also raising sheep and owning a car dealership. "John Dennis introduced sheep into our section of Kansas," wrote Archie, one of the sons. Western sheep were not infected with stomach worms like the local sheep, so John Dennis bought sheep in New Mexico, or even the country of Mexico. He would buy as many as 3,000 at a time and have them shipped by train to his farm. The sons unloaded the sheep from railroad cars and drove them as a flock to the farm. The herd of sheep on a narrow country road stretched out in a line that was a mile long. Their father sold some sheep to neighbors but kept a flock of 400 or 500 animals for himself.

There was a high demand for wool for military uniforms. Their father probably did well financially by raising sheep and selling the wool to the government. Wool cloth was rationed to civilians and otherwise unavailable. Eventually the Army enlisted four million soldiers, and each had to have four wool uniforms and blankets. That called for a lot of sheep shearing.

When Jesse returned home in 1919, he labored on the farm to earn enough money to get married. He wanted a wife and family so he could settle down after his war experiences. Anticipating a good crop that year, and that his share would be ample, Jesse started looking for a bride.

He had been told there was a pretty girl at the Lathrop's house. Armed with a bouquet of flowers in one hand and a box of candy in the other, the young shy Jesse, arrived at the Lathrop's without notifying the family ahead of time. He knocked on the front door. The family was seated at the dinner table. Denise's Aunt Ilo, the older sister, was newly married. She said "I'll answer the door, I'm the closest."

There stood Jesse, ready to start his courting. He extended the gifts to Aunt Ilo and said, "These are for you." Aunt Ilo exclaimed, "Oh no, I'm married. You must have intended them for my sister, Freda." Embarrassed, but hopeful, Jesse accepted their invitation to join the family for dinner. Then he started the serious business of "courting" the beautiful 16 year – old Freda. But marriage had to wait until Freda graduated later that year from high school.

About once a week, Jesse would borrow a car from his father and his father's "Dennis Auto Company." Jesse would drive the car, an expensive sleek roadster, called "Templer,"to the school when the school day ended. There would be Freda in her stylish "hobbled skirt." She had to be lifted up into the car because the tight skirt restrained her from climbing in. She was the envy of all her friends. Jesse had to wait until the crop was sold before he could get paid, so it was not until July, 1920, the young couple, now madly in love, could be married. Freda was 17 at the time and had graduated. Denise was born a year later. Her mother and aunt were known as fashionable ladies, and "bobbed" their long blonde hair. They later traded hobble skirts for long narrow ones, but by now, cars had side doors which made entering the car more convenient.

After he married, Jesse had several other jobs before he felt the "call" to the ministry. He was working a mail route in Edinburg, Texas, when he asked the pastor of nearby Edinburg Christian Church if the pastor would mentor him. Because men training to be ministers often were married and had a family to support, they could not afford to attend ministerial school. So having a qualified pastor as a mentor was an acceptable way to be trained.

Time passed and World War II approached. By then Jesse had become a conscientious objector. He wrote and edited the *"Texas Herald,"* a monthly Christian Church magazine. His denomination had been objectors in World War I, and Jesse knew that his own position on war now coincided with his church's belief. Finally, he was at peace with himself.

He died in 1988 and was buried in San Antonio, Texas, at Fort Sam Houston Military Cemetery. In his older years he had strongly objected to war, but as a young man, he had done his patriotic duty. He had survived bombardments, suffered from poisonous gas attacks, and helped retrieve the dead and wounded. He had come home when many of his buddies had been killed in the fighting of the Argonne and other sectors.

Perhaps he was meant to survive to fulfill two more roles in his life. Those roles were that of a Conscientious Objector and a pastor in the Christian Church.

CONSCIENTIOUS OBJECTOR — A DIFFICULT DECISION

Evan Allen Hardy
(Photo from bio written by R. Bruce Shepherd and printed in University of Saskatchewan Archives)

For Evan Allen Hardy, once the United States declared war on Germany and instituted the draft, he had only one choice. It was a difficult one that could result in public disfavor, ostracism, and harassment. But registering for the draft was against every principle he had ever stood for. His story is told by his proud grandson, Michael H. Day, PhD., St. Louis Park, Minnesota.

Hardy declared himself a "Conscientious Objector" and prepared to face the consequences. Would it be imprisonment, serving as a noncombatant in the army? Or perhaps, worst consequence of all, being executed. In England, Conscientious Objectors were vilified with thousands of white feathers thrown at them, or placed in their hands. This signified they were considered cowards. The English "C.O." faced one of these three consequences above, plus the stigma of lacking the courage to defend their country in uniform. Their names and reputations were forever blackened.

Evan was not one to despair or to give up easily. He had just completed a degree in agricultural engineering at the University of Iowa at Ames, and planned a lifetime of helping farmers in the Midwest to raise better and more plentiful crops. Now the war would delay or end that ambition. Still he had one more option to explore and it involved Canada. Since Canada's entry into the war in 1914 as a dominion of Great Britain, massive recruiting efforts were made in the United States by Canadian army recruiters. The results paid off in the enlistment of about 5,000 Americans to join either Canadian or British armies, depending upon their background. Some, eager to be pilots, enlisted in either the French or British air corps.

When Evan received his draft notice, he formulated a proposal based upon the cooperation among the populations of Canada and the United States. He took the proposal to his local draft board and discussed it. He would accept an offer he had already received to teach at the University of Saskatchewan, and meanwhile, obtain his master's degree. Already known through the Midwest farming community for his good agricultural ideas, he would spend his career teaching the returning Canadian WWI veterans the principles of agricultural engineering. The wide, almost limitless wheat fields of Canada would flourish, and the veteran-farmer would prosper. His draft board decided to grant him a deferment, allowing him to fulfill his proposal.

Early in life, Evan had shown a keen interest in the engineering of tractors. Also he knew how to work with metal, for in his high school days he had helped his father in the family blacksmith shop. As a student, he became interested in the English sport of rugby and in his spare time, Evan reveled in playing rugby. He became an outstanding player, in both rugby and football.

His work on improving tractors would help the Allies forces who used the tractor in France to haul the huge artillery field guns. These guns were too heavy to be pulled, especially in mud, by the usual teams of 6 to 12 horses. So the Ford Motor Company improved and manufactured tractors to be shipped to France. They also had manufactured 47,018 motor trucks by the end of the war.

In his teaching, he and six helpers gave 150 demonstrations showing the most productive way to plow and care for the land. The old plowing method was called, "Plow Down, Costs Up." The farmers, following the newly learned techniques, would get into their tractors while Evan Hardy walked behind them. He noted the pulling power and gas consumption, and made sure the farmers had their tractors adjusted to the proper height.

He also taught how rubber tires on the tractor were less costly, and stressed the proper alignment of the wheels. He repeated over and over, "It's not the top four inches you're interested in..." He had determined to show that decreasing the tillage depth from four inches to three inches was much more economical.

His techniques helped save the prairies from being pulverized and kept the soil from drifting. He emphasized that tractor speed should not be more than five and one-half miles per hour. Using the old moldboard plow cost the farmer 33-50 % more than the one-way disc. Hardy helped save both the farmer's pocketbook and the land he plowed.

After fulfilling a lifetime career of teaching in Canada, Hardy "answered the call from the United Nations to conduct a program of dry land development in Ceylon in 1951." (Biography) This also was in line with his religious and humanitarian beliefs. His program included principles of irrigation, transportation, and harbors. He continued his programs until 1961.

Hardy died in 1963 and was cremated in his adopted homeland, Ceylon. More than 5,000 people attended his state funeral out of respect for his life as a "great teacher, scientist, and public benefactor." (Biography for Saskatchewan Agricultural Hall of Fame.)

A quote from the American author, Nathaniel Hawthorne, might well have been written with Evan Hardy in mind. It reads:

"Every individual has a place to fill in the world, and is important in some respect – whether he chooses to be so or not."

Perhaps Evan's place was to teach hundreds of farmers better agricultural methods in two very different parts of the world. Who are we to say?

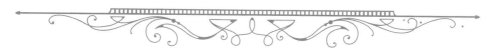

JOB WAS TO SAVE LIVES, NOT TAKE THEM

Herman B. Engel was another doughboy who signed up for the Army despite the displeasure of his parents of German ancestry. Their particular religious background caused them to feel strongly against the carrying of firearms, so partially to appease them, Herman joined the Sanitary Corps. His story is told by his two sons, Crosby Engel of Kansas City, Missouri, and Stewart Engel, Fredericksburg, Virginia.

In the days of World War I, the Sanitary Corps was a branch of the Medical Corps whose job was not what the word "sanitary" implies today. At that time, the job included driving ambulances, serving as field medics, and working in other ways to help the wounded or dead. The Corps personnel were not armed and may have worn the Red Cross arm band, indicating they were non-combatants. Herman himself held other hesitations at becoming a rifleman. His family came from the Palatinate area of Germany and had family and friends there. He was afraid he might at some time face them in battle. In the Sanitary Department he would not be allowed to carry or fire a rifle, and this satisfied his fears.

One story Herman told, when he returned home, illustrated the wisdom of his decision. He was young and patriotic but had still another reason to stay out of the infantry. His family consisted of three boys, three girls and their parents. Herman's father, born and raised in a sod hut near Lawrence, Kansas, in 1866, had received a college education. He wanted a similar education for his children.

Herman's father earned bachelor and master degrees at the University of Kansas in Lawrence, and later was awarded a Ph.D. degree in German from Harvard University. He was a member of the highly regarded Phi Beta Kappa scholastic honorary and remained at Harvard teaching German. He eventually became head of the department. In 1912 the family had the opportunity to travel to Marburg, Germany, in a teacher exchange program. The trip to Marburg was too much for the family to resist. So Herman and siblings spent an unforgettable year at Marburg, saturated with German culture and language. They also made friends with their German neighbors.

The story Herman told after the war was about when his loyalty as a AEF soldier was tested in a unique way during the fighting. His officers, knowing his background and German language skills, called him one day to help with the interrogation of captured Germans. To Herman's great surprise, one of the prisoners was a boyhood friend from Marburg. Fortunately, the friend was not considered a valuable prisoner and had little information to share with the Americans. The two boyhood friends quickly overcame the awkwardness of the situation and exchanged anecdotes and memories.

Another family story concerning Herman tells about when the Sanitary Detachment was advancing with the troops of the 137th infantry. The Detachment's supply wagons were far behind the troops because of their size and heavy loads. One task the Sanitary Department was responsible for was to test the water supply from the farm wells.

Stories had been widely spread of how the Germans poisoned the wells when they abandoned a site. So before the American soldiers were allowed to replenish their thirst and fill their canteens, water safety tests had to be performed. This was part of Herman's job as a sanitary engineer. There must have been some very thirsty soldiers anxiously awaiting the outcome of the tests.

Herman related a tale about the time the troops came under "enfilade fire," a dangerous situation where troops are vulnerable to gunfire from both enemy flanks. The enemy could shoot in a straight line along a trench or column against troops that had no protection or way to take shelter. American casualties were high, and everyone was on alert. Herman squatted down next to a soldier who was shot in the femoral artery (the main artery of the thigh) and had begun to bleed profusely. Quickly Herman staunched the flow of blood and probably saved the man's life.

The 35th Division troops and several other divisions were fortunately spared participation in the next massive offensive which would move through Metz, France, on into Germany. It was to begin November 12. However, with the signing of the Armistice the day before the massive offensive was scheduled, the campaign was cancelled. Doubtless, hundreds of thousands of American and German lives were spared.

Herman's army career had begun in 1916 when he served with General Pershing on the expedition to capture the Mexican bandit, Pancho Villa. The bandit had harassed and killed some American citizens who lived near the Mexican border. With the declaration of war against Germany on April 6, 1917, America and General Pershing turned their attention from Mexico to Europe. Meanwhile, the wily bandit escaped into the hills of the region. Herman became one of the first American soldiers to step onto French soil. An experienced soldier, he accompanied Pershing and formed part of the AEF's First Army. They were to become involved in some of the toughest fighting of the war.

In 1919 Herman arrived home and was discharged at Camp Funston, Kansas. His army career was finally over. He was true to his word and never fired a shot at the enemy. His job had been to save lives, not to take them.

THE END OF THE WAR "TO END ALL WARS"

The Versailles Treaty that was signed June 28, 1919, was denounced a decade or so later by a petty German agitator who had been a corporal in the Great War (WWI). He formed his own party by which, after leading his party into power in 1933, he became the dictator of the Third Reich, the so-called new Germany. His name was Adolph Hitler.

Meanwhile, four great empires that had existed when the war started in 1914, disintegrated and were no longer on the map. Twenty or more new nation states were carved out by the two leading powers, France and Great Britain, with little regard to the desires of their populace. Democracy was not saved. It was not even wanted by many peoples or nations.

In the wake of the war, the Communist system took root in Russia and threatened to spread to neighboring countries. It attracted millions of peoples in Europe and the Far East. In America this movement damaged the lives of some notable citizens. Once the label of being (or suspected) Communist was attached to their names, these unfortunate ones lived the rest of their lives in disrepute. Thus was the advent of the "Red Scare" in America, inspired by the Bolshevik Revolution in Russia.

Another great war, epidemic in its number of victims, lasted longer than the first Great War. It came to be known as World War II. The war ended when an unheard of technology consumed 100,000 or more victims with just two bombs. The bombs were built based on the recent discovery of how to split the atom.

Is there another catastrophe – a World War III – in the future? What will it take to prevent it? We need leaders wise and skillful enough to avoid an event of such apocalyptic proportions.

As citizens, we must have the wisdom and the moral strength to prevent such a crisis. These questions were first formulated after World War I in the minds of poets and artists, some politicians, and some intellectuals. But no one believed them. Now we have proof that such an occurrence is possible. It is also preventable. We have to make the choice.

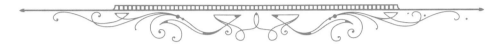

SAM BENJAMIN — EARLY JACKSON COUNTY SETTLER

Sam Benjamin
(Courtesy of Betty Axtel)

A young man, only 18 and one-half years old, Sam Benjamin, joined the American Expeditionary Forces (AEF), thinking he might have a glorious and exciting career ahead of him just like his two older brothers. They were fighting in the Argonne Forest sector of the Meuse-Argonne campaign, and he was anxious to join them.

But time was against him. He enlisted in October, 1918, just a month before the Armistice was signed and was sent to Camp McArthur, Texas, for training. He stayed there, his new uniform scarcely wrinkled when he was discharged a few months later.

His brothers, like most men from Missouri and Kansas, had been assigned to the 35thDivision and were engaged in ferocious battles. Also serving nearby in the 35th Division was a future president of the United States, Captain Harry S. Truman. Captain Truman commanded four field artillery batteries of the 129th Regiment.

Betty Axtel, of Raymore, Missouri, is Sam's only child. She points with pride to documents that show family members have been involved in every war in which the United States has fought. She tells about one of her uncles, Maurice, who suffered a head wound in World War I and had to have a metal plate inserted to heal the wound. The other uncles came out of the war without a major injury. A family story tells that the uncles were shipped overseas in "cattle cars." Probably the more accurate story is that after they arrived in France by ship, they were sent to their new unit in the famed 40 and 8 French railroad cars. The cars were called the 40 & 8 because they could accommodate either 40 soldiers or eight horses and keepers.

Meanwhile, Sam, who had no middle name, soon was on his way back to civilian life. His brothers, thousands of miles away with the rest of the two million Americans in France, had to wait impatiently for many months before their discharges came through. Obtaining enough ships to return that many soldiers to the United States just was not possible in a short time span.

After his discharge, Sam later moved to central Jackson County, Missouri, near Kansas City, where he purchased 1200 acres. A cemetery is located there now. At the southern edge of the property, the family established the popular Benjamin Stables. It included a riding school and small restaurant. Every July 4th weekend, hundreds of people attended the popular rodeos held there. Betty had a horse and rode every day, but at only 4 feet, 10 inches in height, she didn't qualify for rodeos.

Once Sam returned to civilian life, he met his future wife, Cleta Donovan, at a barn dance. It was love at first sight. They married and Sam started a small store located on a dirt road. During the Depression, Sam helped many neighbors with food and necessities from the store. At the day's end, Cleta gave away unsold food that was still edible.

The store was the local meeting place with neighbors gathered nightly to listen to Sam's radio. Listening to the news and popular comedy programs brightened their days. Radios, like money, were scarce too. The companionship of friends helped them bear the trials and disappointments of the Depression years. Despite making a livelihood from the store and owning large pieces of land, Betty says her father was a "worrier," especially when property taxes were due. With 1200 acres, the taxes were significant when cash was scarce.

But Betty, in later years, did not have those worries. The property increased in value as Kansas City quickly began to expand south toward their land. It became prime land for real estate sales, and suburban developments sprang up as a new interstate highway was built. Life for her father wasn't all worries. He had an early model Chevrolet in which he drove on his car taking Betty and other children to a Kansas City school. The city schools were much better than the rural school, and Sam enjoyed the fun the children had riding in his car. Betty could attend the city school because her father also owned some land there.

They attended the big stone church built in 1905, located in the nearby village of Hickman Mills. Betty proudly announces she was the first baby to be baptized in the church. By his choice of school and church, Sam dedicated himself to provide the best of both city and rural life for his family, as well as helping others. He did this by serving in his country's army, even if for a brief time; and by operating a general store, which helped his less fortunate, needy neighbors. His greatest pleasure, though, was in raising horses and having the Stables where others could ride. Little Betty treasured having her own horse to ride any time she wanted to.

Betty claims she "had the best possible life any child could have." Thanks go to her father, Sam Benjamin, an early Jackson County settler. He lived up to his proud family heritage by his actions and his deeds.

DO YOU RECOGNIZE THESE WORDS FIRST USED
IN WORLD WAR ONE?

Over the top • Buddy • Trench coat • Red tape • ticked off • rookie • Pushing up daisies • sniper • washout • kootie • zero hour • zoom • pipe down • mess up • kick the bucket • chow down • cushy • missed the bus • humdinger • basket case • Hit the Deck

They were first used in the Great War and are still in use today.

(World War I Facts)

SOPHIE SELLS POPPIES ON A SCHOOL DAY

Sophie Shelley, 85 years old.
(Personal photo)

"Will you please buy one of my poppies?" Twelve year—old Sophie Shelley, Kansas City, Missouri, shyly asked shoppers and merchants in downtown Kansas City. It was in 1940 or 1941 when she and six or seven girls her age were excused from classes at the old Henry Clay School. They boarded a city bus to go to nearby downtown and sell the poppies. They also carried small boxes into which they deposited the coins they collected. Asked if her feet became tired, Sophie smiled and said, "Probably, but we wouldn't admit it."

The poppies were small and usually made by disabled veterans. Cut from orange-red tissue paper about 1 ½ inches square, they had a stem of thin wire wrapped in green. The girls were thrilled at the honor of being chosen. It was an exciting day, one she has always remembered. At first she was shy asking people to buy. Then, as more people donated money and took a poppy from her hand, she grew bolder. She and the girls happily walked up and down the street, poppies in one hand and boxes in the other. It was just a few days before Memorial Day in May, and the streets were crowded with people.

It was exciting especially when some business men gave the largest amount, a quarter, although most coins were nickels or dimes. When Sophie grew brave enough to ask, the donor would usually smile at the timid little girl and take money from pocket or purse. Sophie is 85 years old now, but these memories are as vivid as yesterday.

She still proudly wears a poppy on Memorial Day, May 30. This day was designed in 1868 as a day to honor Civil War veterans of both the South and the Union. It was first named "Decoration Day," because by that time of year, fresh flowers were available to decorate the graves. The first formal ceremony was at Arlington Cemetery, and General James Garfield, later President Garfield, spoke.

What we now know as "Veterans Day," November 11, was originally called "Armistice Day" in the United States, because it was on that date the World War I ended. The name was changed to "Veterans Day "in 1956 with an act of Congress to honor American veterans of all wars. President Dwight D. Eisenhower, who had been Supreme Commander of the Allies in World War II, signed the act with pleasure. As for Sophie, at age 85, she now proudly wears a poppy on both Memorial Day and Veterans Day.

THE FIRST AND LAST SHOTS OF THE WAR

A sergeant in the Sixth Field Artillery is credited with firing the first shot by an AEF soldier in the war. The last shot was probably fired by thousands of AEF at about 10:50 A.M. on November 11, 1918.

CAPTAIN HARRY AND HIS MEN or
"YES SIR, CAPTAIN HARRY — uh, PRESIDENT TRUMAN!"

Captain Harry Truman, commander of
Battery D, 129th Field Artillery,
35th Division
(Courtesy of the Harry S. Truman Presidential Library)

Of the dozen or so famous men who served in World War I, two names stand out prominently in our nation's history. These two became the 33rd and 34th presidents of the United States. One was Lt. Col. Dwight D. Eisenhower, commander of the tank corps at Gettysburg, Pennsylvania, and the other was a lower ranking officer, Captain Harry S. Truman, commander of Battery D, 129th Regiment, 35th Division.

In his handwritten autobiographical writings later, President Truman tells how he rose from the rank of lieutenant in Battery F to the captaincy of Battery D. He joined the National Guard in 1905 and served with the battery for about six years. Later, when war was declared against Germany, he rejoined the Guard and made arrangements with his sister and a "good man" to take over the family farm. When he told his sweetheart, Bess Wallace, that he was joining up, "My love cried on my shoulder," he wrote, and added, "That was worth a lifetime on this earth." (Ferrell, Autobiography)

The French versatile 75 mm artillery gun used by Captain Truman's four batteries.
It was the most favored gun used by either side in the war.
(Public domain)

From May to August 5, 1917, he drilled in Kansas City, Missouri, with what was then designated as the 2nd Missouri Field Artillery. He helped expand Batteries B and C into a regiment and was elected a first lieutenant in Battery F when it was organized. On August 5, the batteries were federalized and incorporated into the Regular Army and became the 129th Field Artillery Regiment of the 60th Brigade, 3rd Division. In late September the regiment of 1100 men was transferred to Camp Doniphan, Oklahoma for further training. Nearly two hundred men were assigned to each battery.

Thousands of men from Missouri and Kansas would be trained at Camp Doniphan during the war. Lieutenant Truman's training was learning how to be proficient in the firing of artillery projectiles. He recalled in his autobiography, that "It seemed to be the policy of all high ranking officers to make a deep, dark, mystery out of the firing of a battery. They taught us logarithms, square root, trigonometry, navigation, and logistics but never did tell us all they wanted to do was to make the projectile hit the target." Later, as a trainer in France, he adopted a more direct approach to aiming and firing.

While at Camp Doniphan, he also was assigned the job of the regimental canteen officer. Having had no experience in the commercial world, he was able to get his superior officer to transfer his friend, Sergeant Edward Jacobsen, who had the "know how," to actually operate the canteen. If canteen officers charged prices that were too high, they could be accused of "gouging" and sometimes investigated by the army. If prices were too low, the canteen risked bankruptcy. With proper management and monthly audits, the canteen under the two men flourished with few if any complaints while they were at Camp Doniphan.

Another issue of concern was the matter of promotions. Lieutenant Truman and two others of similar rank were summoned for interviews and had to wait outside the building on a cold wintry Oklahoma day in February, 1918. Lieutenant Truman saw his nemesis at the table in the form of General Lucien G. Berry, and his heart pounded. They "took me over the jumps for about an hour," he wrote, confident he had failed the interview.

Soon after, in March, 1918, Harry Truman was ordered overseas "with the special school detail of the division." Arriving in Kansas City, the train made a stop which allowed Harry time to call Bess, his fiancée; his mother, Martha Truman; and his sister, Mary Jane Truman. He noted, "It was the last time I talked to either for a year and two months." On March 30 he boarded the ship *George Washington* and arrived in Brest, France, on April 13, 1918, after an uneventful crossing. He would be schooled in the firing of the well respected French artillery piece, the 75mm artillery gun. He would be knowledgeable enough to teach others. He rejoined his regiment on June 8 at Angers, France, and a month later, as a captain, he would become a battery commander.

One of the Most Frightening Days
It was not until April, 1918, when they were in France that the word came confirming that all three men were promoted. They had the rank and authority of captain. However they were not paid the extra money the rank entailed until October, 1918, when the promotions became "official." Truman had a few words to say about that, as might be expected from him, but it was of no use to protest.

Soon the new captain would experience one of the most frightening days of his life, the day he assumed command of Battery D on July 11, 1918. He now was in charge of about two hundred men who already had been through three commanders. In short, they had been an unruly outfit. Many of them were Irish and German Catholics from the mostly Catholic Rockhurst neighborhood in Kansas City. Here was a new commander who was short in stature, a Baptist and a Mason, and to make matters worse, he wore glasses. Overall, he looked more like someone who belonged behind a desk, rather than a battle field commander of four artillery guns. Scared as he was at this first meeting, he calmly looked each man over carefully, and finally announced, "Dismissed."

Later that day, the men staged a show by stampeding the horses. A few engaged in a roughhouse brawl that damaged some barracks furniture and caused four of the men to visit the infirmary. Captain Truman reacted the next morning by demoting several sergeants and corporals and warned the others, "I didn't come over here to get along with you. You've got to get along with me. And if there are any of you who can't, speak up now and I'll bust you right back now." (Daniels)

He made it clear that he would be firm but fair, and his message got through. In a letter to Bess, a week or so later he confided, "The men are as fine a bunch as were ever gotten together but they have been lax in discipline…I started things in rough-cookie fashion. The very first man that was up before me for a lack of discipline got everything I was capable of giving. I took the Battery out to fire the next day and they were so anxious to please me and fire good…"

He shortly afterward could report that his battery had "outfired" the others in the battalion, making himself "rather swelled up." He also admitted to Bess his doubts about his own bravery; "when heavy-explosive shells and gas attacks begin, I am like a fellow uncle Harry (Harrison Young) used to tell about. I have the bravest kind of head and body but my legs won't stand."

A First Taste of Combat, and the "Battle of Who Run"

In August after his first exposure to combat and shelling by the enemy, he proudly wrote to Bess that his greatest satisfaction "is that my legs didn't succeed in carrying me away although they were anxious to do it." He also noted that a German shell had exploded about fifteen feet away from him and he did not get a scratch, leading him to remark in a jocular mood, that "no German shell is made that can hit me." Other shells fell all around the battery without killing or wounding any of the men, inspiring Truman to comment that "the Lord was and is with me."

Still, the shelling in this first experience of combat could cause panic among the men and it did. Truman noted that in this instance the first sergeant did not get the horses up in time to pull the guns out of the way of a German shelling. He told Bess that "the sergeant ran away and I had one high old time getting out of that place…" He added, "The boys called that engagement the Battle of Who Run, because some of them ran when the first sergeant did and some of them didn't. I made some corporals and first-class privates out of those who stayed with me and busted the sergeant." This episode occurred in the Vosges Mountains, the first of several engagements in the Battle of the Meuse-Argonne and in the Verdun sector. (Ferrell, *Dear Bess*)

More Challenges for Captain Truman

Other anecdotes related by President Truman in his autobiography shows his spunk and fiery spirit. It was the night of September 26, 1918, when he made his sleeping spot near the woods by a battery position. He awoke at 4 A.M., got up and walked on, coming back to find the Germans had fired on the place where he had been sleeping. Later, he commented he would have died if he had not gotten up and walked away like he did. Later in the day, while he was marching on a road under an embankment, a French battery fired its big gun, the 155mm, over his head. "To this day," he wrote years later, "I still have trouble hearing what goes on when there is a noise. I went back and told the French captain what I thought of him, but he couldn't understand me—so it made no difference."

Another time he told the operations manager of the regiment, Major Paterson, who had asked him to arrange a barrage in 10 minutes, "to go to hell, that I couldn't figure in ten minutes, but I'd try." Another time when he almost met trouble face to face, was on September 28 when he fired on three enemy batteries that were out of the 35th Division's sector. Each battery was assigned a geographic sector within which they are to fire. Truman had a clearer view of the artillery emplacements than did the officer of the 28th Division's sector next to Truman's and saw the threat they made.

His actions destroyed one enemy battery and "put the other two out of business." When admonished with the threat of a court martial for not keeping within his sector, he thought of the men of the nearby 28th Division whose lives he had saved. He later added, "They were grateful in 1948," (when he was elected President of the United States. He had been elected Vice President in 1944 with Roosevelt winning the presidency).

Life in the Battery: Memoirs of Sergeant Verne Chaney
One of his sergeants, Verne Chaney, wrote his memoirs as Chief of Section #3 in Battery D. He told of waiting hours for the French trains which would take them further inland. Each battery required about 30 cars. They broke a record time in loading guns, caissons, horses, other items and the men. Their new record time was 48 minutes.

Two days later they arrived at their destination in the Vosges Mountains, unloaded, and moved to the front in a night long hike. They were required to take 105 horses, four guns, and five American caissons. The men carried a full pack weighing 70-80 pounds. Everyone was exhausted, including horses. The stallions fought each other, so a guard had to be posted. The sergeant took the position and let his men sleep, which they did, even though it rained. Serving in the army required physical stamina and muscle power. Calm nerves also were a highly prized asset.

Next the battery was assigned to Kruth, France, a part of the Alsace-Lorraine region Germany had captured from France in the Franco-Prussian War of 1870. Most marching had to be done at night under cover of darkness. While darkness provided better protection for the troops from German guns, night had its own hazards, especially with animals and artillery guns. The foot of one of the cannoneer's slipped while pushing a piece of the limber, and the limber ran over his legs and arms. Luckily, no bones were broken, and the man suffered only a few bruises.

Food on the march left much to be desired. For example, breakfast, laboriously carried up the mountain side, consisted of cold canned salmon, jokingly known as "goldfish;" coffee (probably lukewarm), and three pieces of hard tack. No time for any cooking. Caution was taken for the batteries to stay out of the sight of the ever constant German airplanes patrolling overhead tracking their path and passing the location back to the German artillery.

After arriving at the designated position, the troops got their shovels out and began digging. This was often in great discomfort since they had to wear gas masks, even when there was no detectible gas. The glass eye pieces fogged up quickly, the mouth piece was uncomfortable, and the mask itself weighed several pounds. If they were ordered to load for a gas attack, they would begin unloading and stacking artillery shells, which when filled with chlorine gas, weighed about 19 pounds each. Chlorine gas vaporized quickly and was not as deadly as mustard gas. It was used mostly to stall the enemy's progress and disrupt plans for advancing.

It was dark when the firing began. When it did, Chaney wrote, it was as if "hell broke loose not only where we were, but in the woods all around us (it) spit out a flame that said 'we are with you.' It was good to look upon." Sometimes the rate of fire reached 40 rounds per three minutes. "The men had to load and fire in the dark with settings (on the fuses) checked by flashlight."

An experienced crew could fire up to 25 rounds per minute for a short period. Then the gun barrel would become overheated and could rupture. The batteries took turns firing three guns at a time, with one gun being cooled down with water and sometimes even wet blankets.

At times the German artillery zeroed in on the Americans and shelled the gun emplacements. Men sought shelter where they could, sometimes untying the horses from their rope line. Sergeant Chaney wrote about seeing horses race past him, pulling their harness and traces. With shells pounding and whizzing overhead, and the sound of the air powered klaxon horn announcing the approach of gas, the night was one of terror. The noise frightened the horses as well as men.

Accidents occurred occasionally with resulting losses of horses and equipment. One night while returning to bivouac, one of Battery A's guns accidentally overturned, killing one horse and injuring one man. Traveling at night on narrow mountain roads that were scarred with deep ruts, often meeting up with a group of infantrymen, or truck or ambulance convoys, the battery had to practice the utmost alertness. Danger was not just from German shelling, but from the roads, terrain, and other troops also.

In another incident described in Chaney's memoir, he told of arriving near the Argonne Forest after "traveling 500 kilos (sic) overland thru (sic) mud, rain, light feed for both horses and men, irregular feeding, and long hours carrying packs." They arrived just a few miles from the front line.

Here they were ordered to be allowed five days of rest. But the army changed its mind, and orders changed, when at 4:30 that afternoon word came that the order for five days of rest was cancelled. The batteries were needed at the front. This was the beginning of the Meuse-Argonne conflict, which became the last big offensive of the war.

Congestion on French roads with fleeing civilians competing with the military for road space
(Courtesy VFW Magazine, 2004)

Progress was slow while they were traveling. They encountered truck convoys, roads jammed with other artillery units, autos, ambulances, motorcycles, field kitchens, and hundreds of recalcitrant horses and their handlers. The passage of several hundred tanks had made big holes into which unlucky caissons fell, and horses and even men slipped into the cold waters. Often teams had to unhitch to haul out struggling horses or men from these death traps. Chaney said, "You can imagine what an ungodly, tangled mess it was." This was an understatement of the situation.

Somehow they arrived at their assigned place and began firing at 4:30 A.M. When they came to the limit of the distance that their guns could reach, (about 7500 yards), "they limbered up (hitched) in a hell of a hurry" and moved on in a state of sheer exhaustion. The engineers had been repairing huge holes in the roads made by shelling with whatever scraps they could find. It might be logs, rocks, animal carcasses, or even disabled vehicles. Anything to keep the roads passable. One lieutenant commented, "it took two and a half hours to travel the last mile," while they waited for the road to be repaired.

The Final Stage
This next episode occurred during the march of six American divisions to the Meuse-Argonne area for a full scale attack days later. Many of the 90,000 horses and mules used in the march died in their harnesses from exhaustion and lack of food. The men had traveled 500 "kilos" (probably kilometers or about 310 miles) in 27 days from Kruth. They ended up only about one mile from the front. This time they did have a five day rest before moving on.

They were to participate in the battle for Verdun, which has the unenviable reputation of being the longest continual battle in recorded history. The battle between the French and Germans started in 1916, and at the end of that year the total estimate of casualties was 1.5 million men. (Chaney) The battle in 1918 resulted in American casualties of 117,000 or 40% of their total casualties in the war. This figure includes dead and wounded. (Rickard) The 35th Division had not been active during the St. Mihiel campaign because it was marching to the Meuse-Argonne sector.

The Division began to prepare in early November for the advance to Metz as artillery support for the 81st (Wild Cat) Division. However, early on the morning of November 11, Captain Truman was notified of a cease-fire to begin at 11 A.M. Therefore, he kept his batteries firing as ordered until 10:45 A.M. at the small village of Hermeville, northeast of Verdun. At the designated time, 11 A.M., the guns ceased firing, and the men relaxed. The rest of the day "was so quiet it made your head ache," wrote Truman. Loyal soldiers until the last, Captain Harry's men "stayed in our positions all day and then crawled into our pup tents that evening."(Ferrell)

Captain Truman would get a letter of commendation from Maj. Gen. P.E. Traub, commanding general of the 35th Division, when the war ended. By that time in November, Captain Truman calculated his battery had fired over 10,000 rounds "at the Hun." He also mentioned that a battery of the French large 155 mm guns was firing nearby at the enemy until the Armistice was signed on November 11.

In his opinion, "For all their {Germans'} preparedness and swashbuckling talk they cannot stand adversity." He was especially sympathetic to the French for all the punishment they had taken on their own soil and yet did not give up. (Ferrell, *Dear Bess*.) Truman was grateful that there were no fatalities in his battery of 200 men. Those men would return the sentiment later on by presenting him with a silver cup and referring to him as "Captain Harry" in postwar meetings.

"Captain Harry's" war experiences helped prepare him for the toughness of politics in his future career, including making some of the most difficult decisions a President has ever had to face. But up to his death in 1972, he remained the humble, self assured, and smiling Man from Missouri.

HAIL TO THE CAPTAIN!
(Who, a generation later, became Commander-in-Chief)

NOTE: This story is co-authored by Niel Johnson, Ph.D., and retired archivist at the Truman Presidential Library in Independence, MO. He is the author of several books; the latest is *Power, Money, and Women: Words to the Wise from Harry S. Truman*. In the past 21 years he has been an impersonator of President Truman, and given over 600 appearances nationwide of the President he greatly admires.

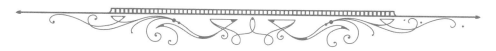

LOOK, THERE'S "THE LADY" — A YANK RETURNS HOME

Statue of Liberty, New York City.

The Statue of Liberty in New York City harbor welcomed AEF soldiers home.
(Public Domain)

One of the last sights of America the soldier saw when going overseas, and one of his first views, when he returned from France, was the Statue of Liberty in New York harbor. Shouts of cheers arose and caps were thrown in the air as America's Lady came into their view.

Crowds of loved ones and even strangers welcomed the men who were disembarking to joyful kisses and hugs. Weeks and months the troops had spent, dirty and wet in trenches, slogging muddy roads, and eating cold food, were behind them now. They went home to Mom's good cooking, the warm embraces of wife and perhaps children, and handshakes and back slapping of old friends and other relatives.

Then reality sank in. The old job was gone, perhaps. The house needed to have repairs, the farm required backbreaking labor to be productive again. And most of all, the veteran needed to be re-acquainted with wife and children. To his frustration, the bonus from the Army was delayed. To assist the veterans, some organizations were founded, such as the American Legion. Also to aid the veteran was the Veterans of Foreign Wars, which was started much earlier, in 1898, after the Spanish-American War. For those who had lost a son or daughter, the Gold Star Mothers Association was formed in 1928 to provide comfort to the grief stricken mothers.

The private's pay of $30.00 per month now looked better to the veteran when he had no other source of funds, and no job was within reach. The highest paid military enlisted men were a master signal electrician and aviation mechanic whose pay was $121.50. Still, the average American soldier's pay of $30.00 was the highest of all the armies. (Sasse)

Nevertheless, to his joy, he was home. The arriving soldier, soon to be a veteran, had adjusted to army life, performed admirably on the battlefield, and his final hurdle – adjusting to civilian life – was one that most veterans would achieve. Upon the departure of the AEF soldiers in early 1919, General Foch, Supreme Commander of the Allies, said of American soldiers lying in French graves, "Resting there, they are as a symbol of our indissoluble union."

The veteran could now say to himself: "I've learned to obey orders, to respect authority, work hard, endure hardships, and survive. I am proud to have worn the uniform of the American Expeditionary Force or the National Army. I can and I will adjust to my new life as best I can." (Sasse)

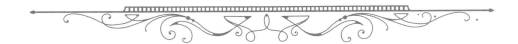

FAMILIAR SONGS THE AMERICAN SOLDIERS LIKED:

REVEILLE

I can't get 'em up, I can't get 'em up, I can't get 'em up in the morning;
I can't get 'em up, I can't get 'em up, I can't get 'em up at all;
Corp'rals worse than the privates;
Sergeants worse than the corporals;
Lieutenants worse than the sergeants;
And the captains the worst of all.

Chorus - I can't get 'em up, I can't get 'em up (repeat)

OVER THERE

Over There, Over There, Send the Word, send the word,
Over There that the Yanks are coming, The Yanks are coming,
The drums rum tumming everywhere. So prepare, say a Prayer,
Send the word, Send the word to beware,
We'll be over, we're coming over, and We won't be back
till it's over, over there!

KEEP THE HOME FIRES BURNING

(British)

Keep the Homefires burning While your hearts are yearning,
Tho' your lads are far away They dream of home,
There's a silver lining Thro' the dark cloud shining,
Turn the dark cloud inside out, Till the boys come home.

ACKNOWLEDGEMENTS

Few books, if any, can be written solely by the author. The help and advice of many friends and strangers were involved in the compilation of these stories and the textual passages that help to explain the motivations and actions of the chief characters – the veterans themselves.

I want to thank my readers of the drafts. These readers had to deal not only with issues of grammar and clarity, but also evaluating matters of fact and fiction. They included Carol Moore, Tracy Moore, Twyla Dell, Roger James, Ray Nixon, Betty Waite, Rosemarie Goos, Linda Brosnic, and Dorothy Morse, who proofread almost the full manuscript.

For archival assistance I received valuable help from Jonathan Casey, archivist of the National World War I Museum, Kansas City, who supplied me with copies of rare photographs; and Doran Cart, senior curator of the museum, whose voluminous knowledge about artillery was invaluable. Also helpful were the professional staffs of the Harry S. Truman Library; and the Kansas City Public Library and Missouri Valley Room. The VFW organization allowed me to use public archival photos from its 2004 magazine.

Much knowledge and inspiration came from two tours I made of Belgian and French Battlefields in 2012 and 2013 led by Clive Harris, owner of Battle Honours Tours, London, England; and his esteemed colleague, Michael Sheil.

In addition to information provided by the families of these veterans, I was able in many cases to obtain copies of official records provided by the state historical societies of Oklahoma, Iowa, Kansas, Illinois, Nebraska, Texas and Louisiana. The United States Marines Museum, the United States Navy Museum and several other military museums provided necessary military information about battles and strategies.

I thank Barbara Peden, library volunteer, for rescuing from the discard pile, the two books with early copyrights (Ellis and Becker). These authors provided "hot off the press" information about current status of World War I from their time period, 1918-1919.

I am grateful to Niel Johnson for his help in editing these stories, and especially co-authoring the story of Harry S. Truman. He is an acknowledged authority on the life of the President, having served for 21 years as an impersonator of President Truman in appearances throughout the United States. Niel's knowledge of military terms was essential to the accuracy and setting of atmosphere of some stories, while his continued encouragement kept me focused.

Also, many thanks to my computer technician, Roger Hunt, who through my days of despair when the printer or computer, or both, were inoperable, kept them repaired or replaced.

Last of all, to the many, more than 95 persons and family members interviewed for this volume and the next book, my utmost gratitude is extended. Their delight in learning more about their military relative far exceeded my expectations. It repaid me many times for my numerous hours of frustration with the difficulties of research and writing. Thanks to each and every one of you! Your pleasure is my reward.

GLOSSARY

AEF – Initials for American Expeditionary Force which designated the United States Army forces

Allies – Consisted at first of the British, French and Russian armies. Later countries joined, including the United States to make a total of 23 nations.

Armistice – A written agreement that stops fighting and calls a truce between two or more armies. It is not the same as a peace treaty.

Barrage – Artillery fire by large number of guns directed to fire into an extended line of enemy infantry.

Battery – Consists of usually four, but maybe six, artillery pieces, along with ammunition caissons, water tank, kitchen and other support. A section chief directs the activity.

Blitz – The nine-month bombing campaign in World War II by German planes mostly on London. Occurring almost nightly, it killed thousands of civilians and destroyed or damaged much of London and surrounding areas. The English developed swift fighter planes and other means of defense which brought the raids to an end.

Blighty – Nickname for England where a soldier, if badly wounded, would be sent for medical care and rehabilitation.

Boche – Derogatory or negative name for a German soldier.

Caisson – A chest holding the ammunition on a two wheeled vehicle to service an artillery weapon.

Casualties – This designation applies to the number of dead, wounded, captured, or soldiers missing in action.

Central Powers – At first consisted of Germany and Austria-Hungary Empire. Later the Ottoman Empire and Bulgaria joined.

Command Post (C.P.) – Where commanding officers made their headquarters. It could be located in a chateau, village house or as primitive a site as a dugout.

Creeping or Protective barrage – Firing is directly in front of one's troops to guard against the enemy's advancing troops. A certain timed pace is essential for troops to be behind the firing.

Curtain barrage – Firing is continuous on one line of fire without changing direction.

Doughboys – Nickname given American troops. Origin is not certain.

Draft – A law and procedure requiring eligible men to register for military service.

Dugout – A shelter dug into the ground or a hillside, with sand bags and perhaps timbers to reinforce it.

Fritz – A slang word meaning a German soldier. Also slang words used were "Boche"and "Hun."

40 & 8 – Train box cars that could carry 40 men or 8 horses, the typical French railroad car.

Gas Canisters – Shells containing gas that were fired especially into woods and areas with ravines, low lying spots, or marshes where the gas would remain for days. Not blown away by wind.

Grenade – Designed in various shapes and sizes, it is a small bomb to be thrown by hand or from a special rifle attachment. The early ones were called "potato mashers" because of their shape; the later smaller ones were called "pineapples" or "apples."It could contain poisonous gas.

Helmet – Made usually of steel for wear in combat zones and held by strap under chin. The American and British ones weighed 2.5 lbs. each and had webbing inside to be more comfortable. It provided minimal protection from gun fire and shelling. The German helmet provided the best protection because it covered the ears and was made of 16 layers of laminated steel.

H-Hour – The hour a proposed movement or action takes place.

Horses – Six horses were required to pull an artillery weapon. Other horses were needed to pull water cart, kitchen and caissons, so a minimum of 35 horses was necessary for each gun.

Landwehr – The Territorial Army in Germany, comprised of well trained men, usually from ages 28-38.

Landsturm – The German Home Guard, made up of mostly the oldest soldiers, up to 45 years or older. Used in a reserve role.

Limber – A vehicle with two front wheels on which the ammunition chest (caisson) was carried. A pole is attached to which the horses are harnessed.

Outpost (or O.P.) – An observation post usually found up high in a tree, often is camouflaged to conceal its presence. Also can be a fake hollow tree.

Protective barrage – Firing is directly in front of one's troops to guard against an enemy's advancing troops.

Puttees – Long wraps for legs and ankles to keep water out of the boots. If not wrapped properly or too tightly, it could allow "trench foot" or even gangrene to develop. They were worn by American and British soldiers. The word came from India.

Range – the maximum distance at which an artillery gun can reach when firing.

RAF – Royal Air Force of Great Britain began as Royal Flying Corps.

Remount station – Veterinary station or place where animals were inspected or treated. It lacked the facilities of veterinary hospital.

Rolling barrage – The range is gradually increased in short periods of time in front of one's own advancing infantry. (Also can be called "creeping.")

Rookie – A new recruit or replacement in the line.

Salient – A U-shaped piece of land extending outward that could be defended on all three sides and was difficult to attack and seize. St. Mihiel is good example of a famous salient in WWI.

Shell or round – The shell or round for the 75 mm gun weighs 16 lbs. and has a maximum range of 5.3 miles. Rounds could be fired up to 20 rounds (times) a minute with an experienced crew before the barrel became so hot it could rupture.

Shrapnel – A special artillery shell containing metal balls or pieces which explode upon impact. Small pieces are hot and sharp and can cause serious injury, decapitation, severing of limbs or instant death.

Sniper – A rifleman with excellent aim who shoots from a concealed place.

Stand to – At dawn or dusk soldiers were alerted to be prepared. This usually was time for an attack. They had to be fully armed and wearing a gas mask.

Strafing – An action in which a low flying plane fires its machine gun at ground troops or wagons, ambulances and trucks.

Trench – An excavation of earth, usually in a strip, for protection of soldiers from enemy fire. They were usually six feet or more in depth, sometimes with wooden planks as flooring. If no planks were added, then when it rained or snowed, ground would be extremely muddy. The sides were reinforced when possible with branches, boards, sand bags or other materials. Built in a zigzag pattern to discourage enfilade firing. Usually three rows of parallel trenches at a minimum.

Trench foot – A painful condition of the feet caused by frostbite or prolonged exposure to water, moisture and pressure from tight fitting boots. It can result in gangrene, possibly requiring amputation of the toes or entire foot.

Treaty Protection of the Neutrality of Belgium – A treaty signed by all major nations in April, 1839, when the nation of Belgium was formed. Germany violated its signature when its troops crossed Belgium's borders in August, 1914, in World War I.

U-boats or submarines or Unterseeboot – After the Battle of Jutland in 1916 against England, Germany concentrated on building fleets of U-boats to attack and sink all ships carrying supplies and armaments headed in the direction of Britain and France. They were quite successful at first, sinking more ships than could be built. When the U.S. entered the war and set up the convoy system, sinking rates dropped to a low of 5 % of the previous amount. Sometimes passenger or even hospital ships were torpedoed.

IMPORTANT UNITS FROM THE U. S. FIGHTING IN FRANCE THAT ARE MENTIONED IN THIS BOOK:

First Division – (Big Red) – Regular Army
2nd Division – and 4th Marine Brigade (Fifth and Sixth Regiments)
26th Division – National Guard
33rd Division – National Guard
35th Division – National Guard
42nd Division (Rainbow) National Guard
69th Division
78th Division – National Army
87th Division – National Army
89th Division – National Army
369th Regiment – under French command
315th Engineers
354th Infantry
5th and 6th Marine Regiments
92nd and 93rd Regiments
164th Depot

Place names where important fighting took place involving large numbers of American troops mentioned in this book and number of AEF troops involved:

Aisne-Marne – 270,000 troops
Belleau Woods – 2 Marine regiments (6500) & 2nd Division
Chateau – Thierry – Not available
Cantigny – first action by AEF forces of 4,000
Champagne – Marne – 85,000
Gondrecourt – on Meuse River-1st air base
Second Battle of Marne – 250,000
The Somme – 54,000
St.Mihiel – 550,000
Meuse-Argonne – 1,200,000
Montfaucon – included in above
Verdun – at least 375,000 – 700,000

NOTE: This selection is made by the author. Many other writers and historians may disagree. Selection is partially based on interviews in this book.

BIBLIOGRAPHY

Army Trade Tests. The Personnel Manual Developed by the Committee on Classification of Personnel in the Army. U.S. Adjutant-General Department. Washington, D.C., 1919.

Asprey, Robert B. At *Belleau Wood.* Denton, TX. : University of North Texas Press. 1996.

Banks, Arthur. *A Military Atlas of the First World War.* South Yorkshire: Heinemann Educational Books, Ltd. 2003.

Becker, Carl. *Modern History.* New York: Silver, Burdett & Co. 1931.

Billington, Mary Frances. T*he Red Cross in War.* London: Hodder and Stoughton. 1914.

Blatt, Heiman. *Sons of Men. Evansville War Record.* Madison, WI: Abe P. Madison, 1920. New York: New York University, 2013.

Brooks, Max. *Harlem Hellfighters.* New York: Broadway Books. 2014.

Cart, Doran. Senior Curator: World War I National Museum. Kansas City, MO. Oral interview, January, 2015.

Chaney, Sgt. Verne. *Memoirs of a Sergeant in the 129th F.A.* Personal papers at Truman Presidential Library, Independence, MO.

Conner, Owen. USMC, Oral interview. December, 2014.

Cosic, Dobrica. *South to Destiny.* San Diego, CA: A Harvest/Book.1981. Translated by Muriel Heppell.

Drinker, Frederick E. *Our War for Human Rights.* Washington, D.C. Austin Jenkins Co. 1917.

Easley, Ian. *The Road to Verdun.* London: Pimlico. 2002.

Eisenhower, John S.D., *Yanks. The Epic Story of the American Army in World War I.* New York: The Free Press. 2001.

Ellis, Edward S., ed. Library of American History. *America's Part in The World War.* Cincinnati Ohio: The Jones Brothers Publishing Co., 1918.

Ferrell, Robert H. *Collapse at Meuse-Argonne.* Columbia, MO. University of Missouri Press. 2004. Ed. The *Autobiography of Harry S. Truman.* Boulder, CO: Colorado Associated University Press. 1980. Ed. *Dear Bess. The Letters of Harry to Bess Truman,* 1910-1959. New York: W.W. Norton & Co. 1983.

Fremantle, Michael. "Gas, Gas, Quick, Boys!" The History Press reprint Feb. 1, 2014. Stroud, Freidel, Gloucestershire GL522G: The Mill, Brinscombe Port.

Freidel, Frank. *Over There. The American Experience in World War I.* Short Hills, N.J.: Burford Books. 1964.

Gilbert, Martin. *The First World War: A Complete History* New York: Henry Holt and Company. 1994.

Gray, Randall and Argyle, Christopher. *Chronicles of First World War, Vol. 1, 1914-1916.* Oxford: Facts on File, Ltd. 1990. *Chronicle of First World War, Vol. 2, 1917-1921.* Oxford: Facts on File, Ltd. 1991.

Hallas, James H, Ed. *Doughboy War. The American Expeditionary Force in World War.* Boulder, CO. Lynne Rienner Publ. 2001.

Hanson, Neil. *Unknown Soldiers.* New York: Vintage Books, 2007.

Heiman, James. *Voices in Bronze and Stone.* Kansas City, MO: Kansas City Star Books, 2013.

Holmes, Frederick, M.D. Professor, University of Kansas Medical Center. Kansas City, KS. Oral interview, September 2013.

Holmes, Grace E., M.D. Emerita, *Preventive Medicine,* University of Kansas Medical Center, Kansas Oral interviews, September and December, 2013.

Jones, Will K., Lt. Gen.(Retired). *A Brief History of the Sixth Marines.* Washinton, D. C.: U.S. Marine Corps. 1987.

Kansas City Star. Article. Sept. 5, 1918. Kansas City, MO.

Lee, Jay McIvaine. *The Artilleryman: The Experiences and Impressions of An American Artillery Regiment in the World War. 129th F.A. 1917-1919.* Kansas City, MO: Press of Spencer Printing Company, 1920.

McCullough, David. *Truman.* New York: Simon and Schuster. 1992.

Mead, Gary. *The Doughboys. America and the First World War.* Woodstock, N.Y.: Peter Mayer Press, Inc. 2000.

Meyer, Duane. *The Heritage of Missouri.*

Meyer, G.J. *A World Undone. A Story of the Great War. 1914-1918.* New York: Bantam Dell. 2007.

Miller, M.G. Dr. Ed. *Trench Foot. History of the Great War, Based on Official Documents, Medical Services. Surgery of the War, Vol. 1*; Ed. by Maj. Gen. Sir W.G. MacPherson, KCMGA,L.L.D. 1922.

National World War I Museum, *Chronology Wall-East Gallery.* Kansas City, MO.

Persico, Joseph E. *Eleventh Month, Eleventh Day, Eleventh Hour. Armistice Day, 1918.* New York: Random House, 2005.

Pipe, Jim. *World War One, A Very Peculiar History.* Britton, BN: Book House, 2012.

Sanford, William R. and Green, Carl R. *The World War I Soldier at Chateau Thierry.* Mankato, MN: Captstone Press. 2005.

Sasse, Fred A. *Rookie Days of a Soldier.* St. Paul, MN: W.G. Greene. 1924.

Strachan, Hew. *The First World War, Vol. 1.* Cambridge: Oxford Press, 2001.

Sullivan, Mark. *Our Times, The United States 1900-1925 , Vol. V, 1914-1918.* New York: Charles Scribner's Sons. 1933.

Willmott, H.P. *World War I.* New York: DK Publishing. 2009.

Wright, William. *Meuse-Argonne Diary. A Division Commander in World War I.* Columbia, MO: The University of Missouri Press. 1994.

INTERNET BIBLIOGRAPHY

American Battle Monuments Commission.
www.abmc.gov

Army Sustainment.Coblenz.1919.
htttp://www.au.army.milalogissues/SetOct10.Coblenz_excellent.html

Base Hospital No. 5 History
http://www.ourstory.info/library/2-ww1/hospitals/bh5a.html

CAC:
http://www.wwvets.com/CoastalArtilleryCorps.html

Caroline Hampton Halstad: the first nurse to use rubber gloves in the operating room.
http://www.mcbi.nlm.nih.gov

Cemeteries:
https://www.abmc.gov/about-us/history

Deccan Indian Calvary: Calvary and WorldWarOne:
www.historylearningsite.co/ul/calvaryworld_war_one.htm

ENGINEERS;"A FEW FACTS AND FIGURES ON ENGINEER ACCOMPLISHMENT IN FRANCE." OFFICE OF THE CHIEF ENGINEER, HISTORICAL-TECHNICAL SECTION, AMERICAN EXPEDITIONARY FORCES. ENGINEERS AND PIONEERS:
www.history-war.org/articles/battles-st-mihiel.html

325TH Infantry.
www.327infantry.org/regiment_history/htl/

"82nd Division orders. Center of Military History."
http://www.history.army.mil/documents/wwi/82ndiv/82div.htm

HORSES:
http://www.historylearningsite.co.uk/horses_in_world_war_one.htm.

MARINES:
Marine War 1 Vets.co.

hqmc.marines.mil

World War 1 Vets.Com. "The Marine Corps in WW I" www I

http://www.wwvets.com/marines.html

MEDICINE:
"History of the Great war, Based on Official Documents, Medical Services, Surgery of the War,"
Volume 1. Edited by Maj. Gen. W.G. MacPherson, KCMG. CB. LL.D.1922.

http://www.vlib.us/medical/trenchfoot1.htm

Fitzsimons Medical Center:

en.wikikipedia.org/wiki/Fitzsimons_Army_Medical_Corps

MESSENGERS:
Getting the Message Through – Chapter 5.

www.history.army.mil

MONEY EQUIVALENTS:
"Measuring Worth."

http://www.measuringworth.com/uscompare/relativevalue.php

POISON GAS:
http://science.howstuffworks.com/mustard-gas2.htm

SWEENEY SCHOOL:
http://en.wikipedia.org/wiki/Sweeney_School

TROOPSHIPS:
http://en.wikipedia.org/wiki/Amer-Exped_Forces

http://www.gwpda/org/naval/lcastl.11.htm (those are the letter "l" as in leaf)

http://www.globalsecurity.org/military/systems/ship/sealift-ww1.htm

http://www.spartacus.schoolnet/co.wk/FWWtroopships.htm

http://militaryheritage.org/Subchaser.html

http://www.splinterfleet.org/sfww1.php

WORLD WAR I. TROUBLE IN THE AIR:
http://www.history.army.mil/books/30-17S_5.htm

http://firstaerosquadron.com/articles/first-aviators/

YMCA:
The Service of the YMCA and Red Cross in WWI

http://www.wwvet.comYMCA.html

RECOMMENDED READINGS:
(In addition to Bibliography)

Duffy, Christopher – *Through German Eyes: The British and The Somme*
Eksteins, Modris – *Rites of Spring*
Farwell, Bryon – *The Great War in Africa 1914-1918*
Ferguson, Niall – *The Pity of War* – (A must read)
Fromkin, David – *A Peace to End All Peace* – (Another important read)
Graves, Robert. *Good-bye to All That* – (Disillusioned soldier/writer tries to accept the price of war)
Hanson, Neil – *Unknown Soldiers* – (Story of three soldiers whose bodies were never found)
Horne, Alistair – T*he Price of Glory* – (Another classic)
Groom, Winston – *A Storm in Flanders, Ypres Salient 1914-1918*
Johnson, Niel, Ph.D. – *George Sylvester Vereck: German-American Propagandist* (Includes his role as apologist for Germany before America's entry into the war)
Junger, Ernst – *Storm of Steel* – (A powerful book by German officer & storm trooper)
Massie, Robert K. *Castles of Steel* – *The Navies of both Armies* – *Dreadnought* – *The Arms Race*
Nicolson, Juliet – *The Great Silence* – (How the 1919 Armistice Day was remembered)
O'Shea, Stephen – *Back to the Front, An Accidental Historian Walks the Trenches of World War I*
Ousley, Ian – *The Road to Verdun*, (Epic story of 9 month fight for Verdun in 1916)
Remarque, Erich Maria – *All Quiet on the Western Front* –(The earliest "classic" of World War I)
Slotkin, Richard – *Lost Battalions* – (Stories about fascinating yet frightful episodes)
Strachan, Hew – *The First World War* – (Authoritative book on the War)
Thompson, Mark –*The White War* – The Italian Front 1915-1919
Tuchman, Barbara – *The Guns of August* – (Another early acclaimed "classic")
The Proud Tower – *1890-1914* – (The world before the war)

FICTION:
Barker, Pat – *Regeneration* – Part of excellent trilogy
Vera Brittain – *Testament of Youth* – One of several books she wrote about the war
Dos Passo, John – *Three Soldiers* – Story of the French "poilu"(infantryman)
Fauks, Sebastian – *Birdsong* – A love story; one of several he wrote about war
Helprin, Mark – *A Soldier of the Great War* – Excellent story about Italian soldiers
Manning, Frederick, *The Middle Parts of Fortune* – Well written thoughtful story of a soldier examining himself (The title is a phrase from Shakespeare)

POETRY:
The poetry of World War I set the standards for the next decades. Poets who are "must reads" are Ivor Gurney, Wilfred Owen, Siegfried Sassoon, Ford Madox Ford, Issac Rosenberg, Rupert Brooke, Rudyard Kipling, Edmund Blunden, Thomas Hardy, Frederick Manning, and Charles Hamilton Sorley. Look for Canadian poets also, as the above are all English. NOTE: The hazard of recommending books is NOT including ALL the good books and poetry of the period. Please know there are many other outstanding authors to be enjoyed and learn from. This is only a starting place for you.

ABOUT THE AUTHOR of
"UNHEARD VOICES, UNTOLD STORIES"

Nancy Cramer has been a teacher, counselor, small business owner, and now an author. Writing was her first love, but family and fate interrupted an early newspaper reporter's career. Then upon retirement nearly four years ago, she began to volunteer at the National World War I Museum, and wrote curriculum for the Education Department. This led to more writing and research, resulting in three books about World War I. Nancy has plans for at least two more. Her biggest challenge will be writing a book about the historic retreat of the Serbian army in 1915. This is a tale of exceptional courage, unimagined hardships, and determination by the Serbian people to preserve their nation. This they did.

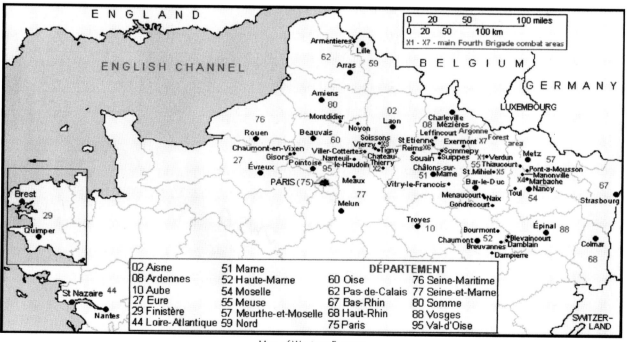

Map of Western Europe
(Courtesy of United States Marine Corps)